MW01487996

C J Carroll

Taos

Angels in Forever
In Search of My Self

Claudia Carroll

Angels in Forever
In Search of My Self
ISBN: 978-0-557-70667-9
© Claudia Carroll 2010

CJ Carroll
The Creative Entrepreneur
cjcarroll.taos@yahoo.com

For my Sister, Rosalie,
earth-angel, listener and encourager

Introduction

The story that follows is a collage of excerpts from an inner and creative journal spanning some fifteen years. It is a journey through parallel worlds, that of the "real" and the necessary, and that, which often seems more "real" to me: my conversations with my "angels," in the inner and creative world. I have decided to leave most personal relationships for another time, and perhaps another write, and though I may refer briefly to family members or someone as an "other," this is a very personal quest. Even as I have formatted this "collage," I am surprised that I could have come from where I was when I started this journal, to where I am now.

Actually, though, my quest did not begin twenty-two years ago, but is one that I feel I embarked on when I was born, perhaps even before I was born. The journaling of both my angst and achievements, and my time spent "in the presence of angels," some sensed, some imagined, some real people, some in nature, and even God's critters, has been of infinite personal value, especially as a road-map charting the paths I have traveled, from then to now, to there and back again.

I publish now, not just for myself, but for you, to encourage you that no matter the circumstances of your life at the moment there is a wisdom, a love, something beyond and above your circumstances that wishes to guide you toward a fulfilling life. I urge you to keep your own journal as you read mine. I hope, that in the process, you will access your own personal wisdom, and let it guide you toward love and the re-discovery of your own true Self.

1.

How do I know this is true?
By looking inside myself.
~Tao Te Ching, Lau-tzu

Daughter, receive now the healing balm of forgiveness and release from projecting the wounds of the past onto the body of the present.

The communication started sometime in the early 1990's. I was living in Mexico, dissolving yet one more relationship that had become difficult and distant and I found myself once again, now past fifty, wondering what I was going to be and do when I grew up.

This was not the first time I would write down the impressions of my inner world. I was, after all, a writer from childhood, an art-maker, a dabbler in theater, an avid reader and wishful dreamer. But these uninvited, loving and gentle "impressions" seemed to come from a different place than that I had always known as "imagination."

From my earliest years, I had explored a variety of religious and philosophical teachings, read of "other worlds," whether on the planet, past and present, or in the imaginary future-reaches of science fiction. It wasn't escape, but rather an attempt, a deep need, to make some sense of my life and of the world, and my place in it. Finally, I had found peace only in nature.

1

One day, living only a block from the run-down beachfront in Tijuana, Mexico, I walked down to the small café I frequented, sipped my strong, cinnamon flavored coffee and stared out at the gray, flat ocean. A feeling of depression had wrapped itself around me like a heavy shawl.

Suddenly, a ray of light broke through the clouds and spread its halo across a small patch of dull sea, sprinkling it with sparkles of gold. At the same time, astonishingly, I seem to hear an inner voice urging me to forgive myself. I picked up my pen to continue writing in an ever present journal. I seemed to sense a feminine presence, a "something other" than myself. An Angel? Feminine aspect of the Holy Spirit? My higher self?

I don't know. I still don't know, but I do know the communication that followed has been instructive, encouraging, and wise beyond my ordinary self, and that the feminine presence came to be known to me by her name.

I finished my *huevos rancheros* and looked around the now empty café. Hardly anyone came down to the beachfront in the late afternoon, which was the way I liked it.

There were times I enjoyed the downtown Tijuana, Mexico area, but here, just a block from my little rented house in a residential area near the beach, I could be alone on my days off from waitressing in San Ysidro, experience some peace from one more, falling apart relationship, and not, for a day or two, have to cross the busy, crowded border to the U.S., and work.

I was out of answers for my life. It wasn't just a matter of finding a different job. I was so incompetent at most things required in the workplace. I had always been a dreamer, a creator of things with words and paints and found stuff, but woefully without ways and means to pursue these on a consistent basis.

What if I forgive *me*, I thought suddenly. Oh darn! Which book did that come from? I'd read through whole library sections it seemed, trying to understand myself, my place in life. I'd investigated religion, psychology, philosophy. I'd attended

2

motivational, goal setting, inspirational and writing seminars. I'd attended churches, Alanon, practiced Buddhism, meditation, had a born-again charismatic experience.

I'd worked for not-for-profits, waitressed, and tried, from time to time to market my writing or art with some success and only a little money. But everything I did seemed to be a one-shot thing; the roads always led to dead-ends.

I'd married, more than once, and had two precious children whom I love, but had been emotionally and economically incompetent to raise. In between it all, I had lovers, hoping one of them would turn out to be a husband-father type, then cried all the way home. Nothing satisfied me, got inside me, to where it mattered, to where, if there was such a place, some energy igniting transformation might be birthed into the world in which I lived, where I could make a difference in my life that mattered.

I sighed and looked out at the ocean again. Why did it all have to be so complicated? When was this dead-endedness of my life going to change? I had to move myself out of this dark place and forward. I didn't know how. I had no money, no dreams, no love left in my life.

Sitting in that funky little café, I scarcely knew I was on the verge of having an on-going spiritual experience that would within the next few years, completely, change my life. Inexplicably, I "heard," or said to myself, *"Just forgive yourself."*

I felt like cry-laughing. But what did I have to lose? Not much. *"Mas café, señora,"* I asked the restaurant owner. She smiled, and indicated she would make fresh coffee for me. Mostly, she sold beer and coca cola. *"Gracias, señora,"* I smiled back.

Then I picked up my pen. O.K., I shrugged, answering myself. Let's see if this works. I started to write, addressing the journal entry to myself with some amusement, mentally donning my priestess robes in preparation for the grand pardon I was about to bestow on myself.

"I forgive you for all past actions in which you hurt,

3

neglected, rejected, and disappointed yourself or others." I wrote the words self-consciously, but suddenly, I felt intensely sober. Somehow, my pen did not want to stop writing. But something had shifted. The words did *not* seem to be coming from me.

Daughter, receive now the healing balm of forgiveness and release from projecting the wounds of the past onto the body of the present. In this process, which is now, this moment, yours, you are healed in body, mind, spirit. Receive this knowingness with clarity.

I continued to write as fast as I could, taking down what seemed to be some kind of internal dictation.

You are free to be alone if you wish, or with another, knowing now, deeply, that you are not alone, but we are with you always. Free others of their sense of obligation to you, of promises to care about you.

You are O.K. now! You are safe. You are eternal spirit, which cannot experience rejection or abuse. These are of the physical realm.

Dis-invest yourself of the desires for love, for physical manifestations of love, and know yourself as full in Spirit. As you already know, when you are full, you are not hungry. Thus, when you become aware of the spiritual you as being whole, complete, eternal, and without hunger, you will no longer experience lack in your life.

You are eternal now. You are whole, full, complete now.

You have chosen this life period to learn, experience, and contribute to raising the consciousness of the earth. Recognizing the spiritual bonding of those with whom you have contact, even

4

minimal contact, you will be looking beyond the physical, raising the physical to the spiritual world.

While the physical vibrates at the spiritual level on the life-force plane, at the level of life-energizers, it slows down in frequency at the physical plane, much as steam, or vapor results from water, or water becomes ice.

In such a way, you can "see" the spiritual, mental and physical aspects of life represented as merely different vibratory levels of the life-force. It is through the mental realm that we can communicate with you, because, at the level of spiritual frequencies, language and imagery such as you are familiar with do not exist.

You might say the mind, with its capacity, and each cell's capacity for memory, and imaging, along with the electrical capabilities of sending, receiving, and making sense of such signals serves as a bridge or transformation, or translation, center.

You are perplexed because this is not a new, nor breakthrough idea you are receiving, and that there is nothing here which can guide you, practically, as it were, into the place where you can say, "I'm doing what I am supposed to do in my life, and I hunger not." Yes, we know this.

We want you to experience our love for you and for you to release dependence of the love of others, on the physical plane. We want you to come into the fullness of your life in this incarnation. But you must become de-attached to the physical, in the sense that you are always looking for, or seem to need, something others can give, or with-hold, from you.

5

Know yourself as spirit. Soon, we will call you by your spirit name so that you will know who you are. For now, know that you are a "Giver of Light."

This announcement astonished me. While I've always been concerned for the downtrodden of life, I was more often than not one of them. As to forgiveness, my children, for sure, had not experienced much light giving from me. How could I ever forgive that?

A week later, I again walked down to the tiny cafe on the Tijuana beach front, and ordered French toast and boiled coffee. I put the toast aside after finding odd-looking little black critters in it, but figured the coffee, boiled, to be fairly safe. I was not at all in a spiritual mood. I picked up my pen to complain to my journal, and instead, seem to access the sweet voice which had "spoken" to me before.

So it is that you chose difficulties and frustrations of those who, like birds with broken wings, have known great struggle in life just to survive. Bring them the light.

We have guided you in your search, waiting patiently for you to return to us, knowing you have chosen to give a time of this life to another in the physical plane. But it is accomplished.

You must move on to a place in the physical realm where you can stay more consciously in contact with us.

You are lonely for others. We will bring them, other light givers, together with you. Look to the light.

Go now into your mental transformation center: image yourself writing, teaching, guiding, revealing, inspiring.

6

When the temptation comes from the physical plane, the learning plane, to say how, where, when, choose peace and know that your clues have been correct ones.

You are now, in whole time, holo time, in spirit, a teacher, inspirer, light-giver. Remember that others, those whom you've encountered chose also to encounter you. You will come to understand this in the days ahead. Peace child, we are here.

Just as abruptly as the message began, it stopped. I drank my hot coffee, folded my notebook, and left the café.

That evening I would have to work in San Ysidro. A half hour to dress. An hour to cross the border, then the bus to the restaurant on the San Diego side. Eight hours of serving burgers and chicken fried steak to the seniors and truckers and street people who frequented the coffee shop.

I turned to look back towards the sea. I longed to go home. Not to my little house. Not to the U.S., but home, to the place where Leytha lived, where I was known, and knew myself to "be."

Some days later, again at the beach-side café, I took out my pen and wrote, "Dear Friend in the Light." I still felt self-conscious about beginning these writings. Still, the process already seemed to be giving me some hope, even if only anger at my situation. But that emotion was better than the dreary, depressed state I had fallen into.

"I'm beginning to feel a rage at myself," I continued, "for not being able to change my life and move on from a place where I clearly do not want to be." I'm ashamed to ask for help, I thought. And who is there to ask? Why can't I do this for myself?

The shift occurred. Where did I feel it? In my mind somehow, as if there is a transmitter with "pin-drop" sound clarity between my ears. In the back of my neck. In my heart-space. I sensed my light-giver's presence and began to write:

Dear one: You are projecting your fears of rejection and abandonment onto others. You cannot be separated from your self, nor from the allness of others. They are you. You are "them."

Image the response you desire, while projecting love, fulfillment, joy, to and around, all concerned. You are, by experiencing pain, still acting out of the past when you simply did not remember, or did not yet know. Release yourself. The past is vapor. All is now.

You know that this is a time of completion for many. You are being given these clues, these signs, in your studies. We are lovingly urging you into completion. You must rigorously discipline your body and your mind to operate in the light.

You cannot allow yourself the indulgence of operating in linear time, or past, present and future time; nor in the emotional realm in which you experience hate, anger, irritation, depression, fear, regret or lack of forgiveness.

These emotions are as destructive to you, in the sense that they diminish the light and prevent it even from functioning, and are as antiquated to those walking in the light, as a cave is to a modern city-dweller.

Realize that the realm of negative emotions is a dark cavern into which you ran before, out of ignorance, and from which the light instantly frees you. Why enter the cavern again? Why live in darkness when now, you not only have the light, but are coming into remembrance that you are the light.

On another day, at the Tijuana beach cafe again. I smiled then, and now, thinking of what an unlikely spot to receive spiritual guidance. Perhaps I thought, amused, I'd stumbled into a

8

yet to be discovered "new age" vortex! I put my pen to paper and asked how I could change, how I could come into a greater sense of light, and of fulfillment.

You want to know how it "works". Well, at this point, you will understand it best in terms of your positive emotions: love, givingness, gratitude, a sense of peace and joy. You can enter your transformation center and image light, image your Self and others surrounded by, and one with the light, and give them all that you would give yourself: health, wholeness, joy, peace, abundance.

This is not a new idea to you, but consider: if you wish to dance, and are given a dance pattern to practice, you would not progress unless you practiced. Having followed through and risen to a higher level of competency, you would have greater skill, and develop the ability to dance in a more complex, professional, graceful manner.

So it is with studies in the light. Practice what you know, what has been revealed to you, and in the process, in the results, more will be revealed to you.

It is as if, as you are now, you were the seed, the plant, the leaves, the roots, flower, fruit, sun, earth, rain, all at the same time. In nourishing your growth, you grow to nourish. You are the light, and this realization can be instantaneous. But because you function mostly in the physical realm, you will often retreat back to the cave again.

Just be gentle to the body and mind, and remind them they are of the light, and release yourself into now by consciously, again and again, choosing peace, projecting love, acting in givingness."

9

Choose peace.

Project love.

Act in givingness.

I wonder *who* is writing. Am I? Is my communicator real? I sense the peace. The gentle presence. The guidance beyond, so far beyond where I walk on a daily basis. But I must ask:

"Dear Friend. How do I know who you are? Are you me? How do I trust what I write here?" Once again I easily access the inner presence.

If you could permit yourself to experience the total love of the light, now you would know. I am here because you've asked to commune with me. If I were to call the sea by another name, would it change the sea? I am you, and you are me, and are one with the light. Go in peace. Be kind to yourself child. There is no need to suffer. Forgive yourself.

I sensed the conversation was over. I started to put down my pen but felt impressed to write something else....*Leytha.* That was all. Her name was, is, *Leytha.*

Some weeks later. It is a Sunday. A few families are just leaving the beachfront cafe, probably there after Mass. A trio of street musicians is playing some *ranchero* songs for an amorous couple, he, in cowboy hat, paying for the songs, she in tight sweater flirtatiously revealing her ample charms to the band. The waitress brings my coffee, without milk, knowing me by now. I bravely order *huevos rancheros.* I am imagining fresh *tortillas*, freshly chopped *salsa*, fresh eggs, refried beans no more than a day old.

Remembering former meals I dismiss any hope of that, but thus far, I've survived these once a week meals. It is ten a.m. The musicians pop open foaming cans of *Tecate*. I sip my hot coffee. It is too strong. I ask for milk.

How in the world, in this environment, in any environment, to stay merged with my inner voice? I begin to write, immediately sensing Leytha's presence.

You are merged, inseparable from Self. If you drive, you must watch the road. If you cook, you must watch the stove! If you wash your face you must give attention to your face, the movement of your hands, the choices you make.

So it is if you work with others, you give attention not only to them but to your whole environment, and your sensory reaction and interaction with all this. This requires an expenditure of physical energy.

So in paying attention to the physical world, you can simply lose sight of, or consciousness of, the parallel world which is within, or beyond, what you ordinarily perceive.

While you are inhabiting the physical world, you will also have to "go away" to find the inner, and the beyond. If this does not seem particularly profound to you, it is because you have a tendency to want to see the spectacular, rather than the obvious.

Body knows, mind knows, spirit knows. As you stop fighting life, each aspect of this trinity blossoms into fullness of power, a living, pulsating power, always at your service.

It is equally as important to feel oneness with ugliness as with beauty, with poverty as with wealth, with pain as with fitness, with aloneness as with oneness. This frees you to flow with life, not

11

be bumped and buffeted by it like an unwilling object being transported down a raging stream.

Give up fighting life. Accepting your oneness with ugliness, you can transform it into beauty, poverty into abundance, pain into fitness, aloneness into allness. Being one with life, with any object, any state of being, transforms your separateness into "isness." Being the ugly, the pain, the lack, you no longer fear it.

Weeks later. At the beach-side café, the waitress smiles a "*Hola*," and brings coffee to my little table on the balcony, without asking. I take out my tablet and pencil.

"Oh Leytha!" I felt I was writing a letter of desperation to a dear but distant friend. "The days, the work, the loneliness. There's not a single place in my body that doesn't hurt. I'm fading away. Wearing out. How far I am from being who you say I am. If I am in transition when will I arrive at the place where you are?"

Looking out at the water, I find it hard to understand why I experience this rich inner life, at least when writing in this journal, and yet my outer life is such a mess. More than a mess. I still have made no progress to change anything. Could it be that just this writing process *is* a kind of change?"

I order some chicken soup with corn tortillas and extra limes, then pick up my pen. I immediately sense Leytha's presence.

It is time to watch the power, the peace, that comes into your life as you merge, not only as you have done with the self you see as the whirling inner light, but as you merge with the life you know as reality, your the outer life. In reality, there is no inner life, nor outer life, no higher self, no lesser self, no opposites.

There are perceptions, some taught, some learned: death is an ending, birth a beginning, peace is the inner life, fitness the outer life, and so forth. Consider instead birth as the ending of a cycle and dying the beginning; peace as a state of knowing; fitness as energy in process.

Do not fight life. Embrace ideas, hunches, intuitions as good messengers long awaited. Swim in the mind-space with child-like joyfulness. Trust!

Reality is not created from nothingness, but rather from somethingness. Your reality is an unconsciousness that is manifesting itself irregularly and is fragmented. Call to your Self, call from your Self, a deeply calm wholeness. From wholeness, you will create wholeness. Create your life and let others be drawn to your light and power and joy.

Transition is like a re-birth. In the space of a few seconds or a few hours you move from one environment to another, governed by laws somewhat foreign to you. There is an urge to retreat to a safe, familiar zone. It is only criticism of yourself that pains you.

Beginnings are only concrete manifestations of desires long-held, seeds planted and nurtured in the ground of mind. Seeing the first signs of growth, you must move from faith to acceptance, from patience to care-giving, from hope to expectancy.

All is process, nothing is static, moving not towards, but out from the core of beingness that is God, that is life, that is you. Image your Self as that core of radiant beingness.

The warmth of your radiance heals. The light of your radiance guides. Be the radiance. It is. You are.

At the beach cafe. Another day. Some fried shrimp, with

13

beans and fresh tortillas, lots of limes. It is my day off. No crossing the border to waitress in the cafe with the dreadful manager who yells at me because the salt shakers are not filled to his precise instructions. My work life has been a nightmare thanks to supervisors who were surely former military drill sergeants.

In San Ysidro, many of my customers, retirees, low-incomers, at the restaurant where I work, do not leave tips for me. I remember a different day and age when I could actually make a decent living waitressing.

Today, here by the water, I ignore the broken rocks of the waterfront, and make a conscious effort to pretend I am just a writer living "the life" in Mexico. I order a *Tecate*. The waitress, unasked, brings me a glass. The musicians come to the table. Do I wish to hear a song? Why not, I think, pushing two dollars towards them. They play *Blue Spanish Eyes*. I *am* blue. I want to cry.

"Leytha!" I am soon writing. "How far I am from being who you say I am. If I am in transition when will I arrive at the place where you are?"

This time, I did not sense Leytha's presence. Instead, I pulled out a bit of writing done years before when I'd attended a religious training school. Very much a fish out of water, I didn't believe half of what was being taught. But I was there out of the generosity of a dear couple, Christian fundamentalists, who felt the school experience would open doors for me to find that "place" in life, one of service and love, that I so longed for.

Quite bored with a dry lecture one day, I drifted into a day-dreaming state, my pen still held aloft, mid-note taking. I was jolted into a kind of reality, realizing I was writing, and it had nothing whatsoever to do with what the lecturer was saying.

Child...sister... I am that of which you seek. But I am like a

14

prism. Most see an aspect of me as the face of their own being reflected back to them in a mirror. But I invite you to abide in me, not viewing one plane of the prism, but to come inside to dwell in the very Heart, in the very Core, in the very Cause, of Life.

I recall feeling astonishment. Where was this coming from? I felt urged to continue writing. The "voice" seemed masculine, but kind, knowing, gentle, wise. It sounded mystical in content, and I wondered at the time, if I was just making this up. Still, as I continued to write, a sense of peace came over me, that I was tapping into something other than, or beyond my "self."

Some are deluded by the sparkle of the prism. But I would not lead you into this temptation. Say not, "I know God" when you have seen only the plane of the prism. Enter in. Abide in Me. Become, not a reflection of the plane, not the prism even, but merge with Cause, with Spirit.

You will enter, retreat, enter. You will examine the prism from afar. Or approaching, you will even polish its crystalline planes, satisfied for a time that you have "found" God.

I will call, continue to call you, until My Life in you can no longer bear the sense of separation, illusion though that separation is, from Me. You will enter in one more time and I will be in you and you will abide in Me.

You will come to know that you are cause itself choosing to manifest as one plane of the prism, but that plane is a chosen one and not separate from the whole.

Radiating from the center of the prism is my Life. Whoever drinks from the depths of the springs of Life shall never thirst. You have heard this, read this. Drink now and be filled. The spring is,

15

was, always shall be. Pause. Be still. Drink, and be refreshed.

Having drunk deeply, remember then your choice in the beginning of time. Remember, you chose this manifestation. Remember you chose to live at this time and place.

Child! You are near! You have sensed my presence. You have sought me. You have yielded and I have spread my Grace before you like a carpet of new fallen snow.

I have wrapped my Grace around you.

I have been the Grace through which others perceive you.

How can it be otherwise? I am that which you are.

Grace I gave you in the beginning. Grace has never left you nor forsaken you. Grace bathes you like a soft summer rain. Grace cleanses you as a mother her cherished child.

Grace brings you face to face with others who sense, even vaguely, but persistently that Grace calls to Grace, Spirit to Spirit. We are One.

Those of the Choice who gave all, sacrificing even memory of Life with me , and having given all, chose to walk the pathways of faith I have charted before time.

If you would be guided by me, stop frequently in your journey through the forest of time and space. I will guide you unerringly. See, I have gone before you to prepare the way. If I do this, then tell you that you shall do greater things than you do now.

Your spirit is already free. See, know the body as Spirit and

16

your body shall also experience freedom. If you would walk with
me in the garden, know the body as Spirit and Spirit as Body,
Breath of my Life, Life of my Life, Light of my Light. Eternal. The
Love of Spirit is manifest in you as You.

I was amazed to re-read these words. "Yet tears of aloneness are welling up," I wrote feverishly in my journal. "I long to walk with you, to hear the soft healingness of your voice."

What lone-walkers we of the stars, I thought. Forever winding our way homeward, only here and again encountering, too briefly, one another.

"There are moments," I continued writing, "when I see you in the eyes of those to whom I give love, and in the eyes of those to whom I allow myself to be open to love. During these moments I see only spirit-lights, not earthbound beings at all." I looked up as the waitress brought my food. I glanced at the entwined lovers and the musicians playing songs for dollars, and the mother feeding bits of tortillas and beans to the baby on her lap. All too often, I thought, I see myself, and everyone else as flawed and imperfect."

Still, I envied those around me in the cafe, knowing they'd probably gone to Mass that morning or the evening before. In believing, not questioning, perhaps they had a peace I did not. As true-believers, they could in saying yes to dogma, shut out the injustice of the rest of the world.

Days later. It was cloudy afternoon when I climbed some steps to get back to the cafe. I had walked along the beachfront a bit, staring at the fence that separates the U.S. and Mexico. Anyone could walk into the ocean there and go around the fence. Many did, sometimes just for the day, families picnicking in what was called the "international friendship park" or on blankets down on the beach.

The purpose of the park, I'd understood, was to give families on both sides of the border a place to meet with one another, when some members were legal on the US side and others

17

were denied entry. I wondered vaguely if this was not way of understanding my writings to and from "Leytha." A friendship park, a place where two parallel worlds came together, finding oneness for a short while.

The beach-front had never been reconstructed or even cleaned up much, after the devastating floods that ravaged the coastline from Alaska to the tip of Baja. Buildings were toppled on their sides, concrete broken into chunks. Sipping a beer, I sat next to the open windows so I could see the ocean. Below me, a young couple sat on one of the broken blocks, arms entwined, unaware of anything likely, but their feelings. I ordered a fish special; with beans and French fries, and a second beer, then picked up my pen.

"Teach me," I asked, thinking of Leytha, "to be 'in the world but not of it' in the midst of the doing. How much I long to be home with you! The world makes no sense to me! What am I to do with my life?" The message was simple and direct.

You are looking at your life as if it were an instrument to be manipulated, but life simply is.

"Let there be light," can best be understood this way: let the clarity manifest, let creative dream manifest. Out of this light and word comes the manifestation, the conceptualization of light. So it is with you for you are that same light stuff.

Write your world. Create your world. Let it come forth. Image it. Speak it. Let it be. Do not struggle so. You are loved. The way will appear.

My meal arrived and I put down my pen. The couple below me were still entwined. I felt sad. As wonderful as the words were that I had received, I still had only words as a companion.

2.

The path into the light seems dark,
the forward seems to go back.
~Tao Te Ching, Lau-Tzu

Meanwhile, struggling to make sense of a life that seemed to be crumbling around me, I determined to continue my inner journeying via writing.

Looking back, I think the changes were beginning to occur, but I could not yet see them. There was, it seemed, an unbridgeable chasm between what I sensed in my bright, light-giving "parallel" world, and the dreary reality in which I lived.

The one constant was writing. I'd begun, I think, as way of communicating back to those I'd always admired the most, writers of books, plays, songs, musicals, poetry. I'd written my first play at age thirteen, producing and directing it for my school, a version of the Christmas scene in Louisa Mae Alcott's "Little Women." I'd played Meg, but it was Jo I wanted to be when I grew up.

During my late teens, it was theater that called to me, then, finding myself with two babies, and dashed dreams of Broadway, I turned to the piano, and studied daily at the local library, trying to absorb the art and craft of writing stage musicals.

I published a first magazine article when I was nineteen or twenty, something called "Approach to Learning," and can still experience the emotion of that acceptance letter, the $5 check and the two copies as payment. I still have that magazine, now fifty-two years old.

I'd written other things over the years, particularly during the sixties, living on Venice Beach, and later in Malibu, married to a writer. Though he too never made the "big time," he supported us, his two children and my two, with his published pieces and quick-write, on-assignment books, and opened editorial doors for me to write articles and poetry for small magazines.

During that period too, I d wrote (and threw away) lots of sketches and one-act plays, starts at novels and completed some stories for children.

Finally, in two week fit of writing inspiration, I created a musical version of Dickens' "A Christmas Carol," and produced it on a penny budget and lots of good will, with a talented cast, at a beach community, cabaret, dinner theater.

In the late 80'ies, living in San Diego and waitressing, I'd written another play, *Clinton and the Treehouse* (about a boy named Clinton, not the presidential family). The play was published by Kids for Saving Earth, an organization created in honor of the real Clinton, a 12 year old, who, before his untimely death, had cared deeply about the environment.

I was thrilled about the acceptance of the play, but in all these years, neither KSE nor I have been able to push the play forward beyond a few school productions.

I use the word "push," because I had *never* seemed to be able to push through a seeming barrier wall with any of my creative projects, to achieve the kind of success that *led to something* more stable, financially. It was always back to another café, and waitress shoes.

During that period, living partly in San Diego and partly in Tijuana, I knew I needed something outside of myself, a helping hand, perhaps, to put me in touch with ...what? My authentic self? God? My soul? Something, or someone who could give me a nudge in a life-affirming direction.

I had read several of Shirley MacLaine's books. In a dream, still waitressing, I found myself serving her, lovely in a pink angora sweater, at a banquet. I wanted so much to tell her we were sisters in spirit, and how lonely I felt when I had to leave the covers of her books, but I could not. Recalling her experience with past life regressions, I finally surrendered to the impulse to visit a trained hypnotist.

"I feel silly doing this, Mary," I said, still sitting, uncommitted, on the edge of the practitioner's couch. "I'm a writer (though a far cry from a financially successfully one) I apologized silently, and have a good imagination. How do I know I won't just be making this stuff up?"

"Oh you won't make it up!" the motherly, buxom lady laughed, sitting calming on the chair opposite me in her small apartment. "You'll just be able to see things more clearly, and possibly express what you see better than some, but you won't be making it up."

"Some people," she continued by way of explanation, "don't 'see' anything at all. Rather they may sense where they are, or even hear or smell where they are. This depends somewhat on your own sensory orientation and how you 'receive,'" she concluded.

I wanted to ask her if I could "write" my experiences, just as I did in receiving the Leytha communications. But I was here to experience something other than that, and so, lay back on the couch, uncomfortable in this vulnerable "patient" position. Mary asked quietly what I'd like to get out of the session.

"In other words," Mary said, summing up my explanation, "you'd like to know what your own life purpose is here in this incarnation."

Trying to formulate the words had brought tears to my eyes. Now the tears overflowed and flooded my face.

"That's O.K.." Mary said, reaching across the short distance between us with a box of Kleenex. "Tears are just an indication that you are receptive to the inner life. If you are ready?"

I wiped at the tears and nodded, keeping the tissue box handy. I was sure I'd need it again.

Mary began to lead me in a simple countdown of deep breathing. I felt my body becoming quite numb. I seemed to floating just a few inches above the sofa. I heard her ask me to move my arm. I could not.

Then, she suggested that I was going down a winding staircase. While my body felt numb, I was able to talk, quietly, in a monotone it seemed to me.

I didn't like the staircase. Going down any kind of stairs, had always meant death to me, conjuring up a vision of my mother trapped in her coffin underground. I explained this to Mary, but had to struggle to form words.

She suggested that instead I see a very beautiful staircase, a movie staircase. I scrunched my eyes and tried to see myself floating gracefully down the steps like a glamor queen.

"I keep shifting scenes, Mary," I complained, perturbed. The scene at the end of the curved staircase was one of a beautiful white marble floor with Grecian columns and an azure sea beyond. An inviting pool lay off to the right. Then the scene would shift channels, and I'd be headed down a rock-like staircase descending into caves.

"That's natural in a first experience," Mary assured me. "You've been in both situations. Where do you prefer to be?"

I   chose the more elegant scene. "Do you see anyone there?" Mary asked.

I looked around. I was alone. "Mary," I said, my eyes closed, watching. "I feel as if I want to go *between* the two shifting scenes. There seems to be an opening. A way through to some other place."

"Then go there," Mary said softly.

I saw, or was rather aware of looking through the eyes of my body, which now stood on a grand, green hillside, a *Sound of Music* meadow. It seemed to stretch forever and beyond, the bluest of skies before me. Behind me, further up the hill, a wooded, Alpine-like area.

I waited for Mary's guidance but when she said nothing, I asked if I should describe the scene to her.

"As you wish." she said, listening, but I could not answer. "Alright," she guided "Look down at your feet. What kind of shoes are you wearing?"

"Umm, something like high-topped moccasins with ties around the ankles and calves. I was surprised to see my feet!

"What else are you wearing?" she asked.

"Feels funny. Something like soft leather, bulky, long sleeves and leggings. Like a kid would wear in snow country. But it isn't cold."

"Are you a boy or girl?" she asked abruptly.

"Umm. Dunno.?"

"Nine!" I said quickly. "Nine and I'm a girl."

"Look around you," she directed. "Do you see anyone?"

"No, I'm alone. I think I've run off by myself, but I'm not lost."

"Go back to the wooded area. Is there a house there?"

"Yes, a kind of cabin. I'm standing in the doorway. There is a blue table. A young man and woman are standing behind the table. They are laughing, talking with each other; seem to enjoy one another; are ignoring me, not in a mean way, but just because they are enjoying each other.

"Is there anyone else in the room?"

"Yes, a baby in a cradle on the floor."

"Do you recognize anyone?"

"They are...my parents perhaps, or the people who care for me. The baby is theirs."

"Do you recognize the baby?"

"Umm. No."

Mary was quiet for a moment. "You are now a young woman of perhaps 18. What has become of you?"

"I've gone away," I said quickly. "To a city. It is something like London... no, like Austria. Vienna, maybe."

"What year is it?"

"I'm not sure. It seems like the 1700's. Late in the 1700's. I am in a very elegant town-home." I watch the scene unfold without Mary's guidance.

"I am there to...study. I care for the couple's children in exchange for my studies. I am studying music. It is a passion with me. The man is a composer, a professor of music. His wife is also a teacher. The house is filled with music, and accomplished friends. I am joyously happy."

"Do you recognize them as people in your current life?"

"No."

"And do you recognize these other people?"

"Umm. No."

"You are now an older woman. What is the most significant thing you remember about this lifetime?"

"I am quite old. 70 perhaps. Old for that time. I am being honored in a big hall. Something about being accomplished as a composer...for a piece I've composed."

"Funny. My parents...the young couple who cared for me, are in the back of the room by the door. They are smiling but don't come in. How can that be? They would be dead by then!"

"That is the why you see them as a young couple," Mary said. "And that is the reason they stand at the back and cannot join in. The departed often join us in spirit to celebrate with us."

Tears filled my eyes. "They want me to know they loved me even though they could not understand who I was."

"You are now going to look at your passing during this lifetime," Mary said quietly. "You will view this calmly and without fear. How did you die?"

Death has always conjured up unpleasant visions—a child's view of my own mother's death when I was six, and all the horror movie deaths a child is subjected to. So, to my amazement, I saw myself, unafraid, alone, a very old, very frail lady, but with a mind sharply aware.

"I'm lying on a narrow bed, in a darkened room. There are white linen curtains hanging from above my bed. A heavy dark curtain is pulled partially back from a window.

I know that I am dying but I am not afraid. I've lived a full life. Someone attends me...a woman, a dear young friend who is devoted to me."

"Is there anything else?" Mary asked.

"Yes. A tinge of regret only. I must not forget that the children are what's important."

"Now you have passed on," Mary said. "Where are you now?" No vision came to me.

"Would you like to explore another life?"

"Yes," I said. Oh yes! I could do this for hours, I thought.

"Let us move forward then, to a lifetime nearer the present one. Where are you now?"

I laughed. People had always criticized me for my "inability" to stay in one place. But I suffered from an incurable wanderlust, a near poverty budget, and my short attention span to a project or relationship had caused some, in derision, to call me a gypsy.

Now here I was...in a gypsy camp. A group of people were gathered around a night campfire. A fiddler played. Some sang. Some looked my way and laughed.

"I want to leave the camp...to go to the city. I want to learn things. I want to be someone. They are making fun of me for wanting to be something other than a gypsy. I think I threaten them. I don't care. I'll go anyway! There is a man across the campfire. He is older, heavyset. He seems to have a beard. He looks something like the professor. He is saying, "The only thing we are responsible for is our lives. Go live yours as you choose."

My belongings are already wrapped. The man walks with me to the edge of the camp and wishes me Godspeed."

"And what became of you in that lifetime, after you got to the city?"

I smile at the scene which unfolds. "I have a shop of my own. It is on a narrow street. Perhaps London, like London of the early 1800's. I'm selling fabrics. Brightly colored fabrics. That's right for a gypsy girl, isn't it? There is a man there, a younger version of the bearded one at the camp. He is kind, a teacher, I think. I learn from him. There are two dark-haired children playing in front of the counter. My children, I think, but not the man's. He is like a father to them though."

"And how do you feel about this lifetime?"

"Well, I wanted to learn things and I did. I have my own income. I am not beholden to anyone. It is not all that I wanted, but for a woman like me, for my station in life, I am content."

"Do you recognize the man or children as anyone in your present life?"

"No."

"Would you like to explore a more recent lifetime?"

Of course. But I was disappointed as the scene began to unfold. "Mary, I've seen this before. Once when I was just writing, this scene came out on paper. How do I know if I'm not making it up?"

"You were probably experiencing a spontaneous memory of this lifetime," Mary counseled. "These experiences happen to many people, but most of the time we just dismiss them. Go with it and see where it takes you."

The oddity, though now I was becoming accustomed to this, of being *in* the scene, and looking around, almost like stepping into a virtual reality world, only the world was mine, and I was not creating, or imagining it, but rather re-visiting it. And I *knew* that.

"I'm in the old west...the late 1800's, I think. I'm not sure where. Somewhere near a river. I'm a tutor. I'm Irish, red hair, a woman still. I'm teaching the son of someone of importance in an Indian tribe. He is just a bit older than me. We have fallen in love."

It is a forbidden, impossible love, of course. I know I must leave him, because we could never marry. He would leave the tribe for me. I cannot let that happen because his responsibilities are to his people.

"I tell him I must go and he is distraught. He informs an elder that he will leave with me. The elder comes to me and wisely, kindly, insists that I leave, and must do it soon and secretly, for the sake of all. My heart is broken, but it is a decision I've already made."

"And what became of you in that lifetime, after you left?" Mary asked.

"I am in the east. New York, I think. I teach. No, I am a headmistress at a girl's school. I am content. I never marry."

Mary suggests the time is up and that three lifetimes are quite enough to explore in an hours. She begins the count back suggesting I make the journey up the staircase to an alert state of relaxation and well-being.

"Mary," I say, reluctant to open my eyes, "Something has come to me. I had to leave people in these lifetimes (and in the current one) to become my own person. Did I ever leave happily, with their understanding?"

"You may go back now." she said softly, "and ask each of those you've been with today."

I was disappointed. It was like a movie in which the spirit tries to contact loved ones but no one responds. All seemed to go about their business as if I were not there.

"I guess I never did, Mary," I sighed, "leave anyone under happy circumstances. That's all." As the odd tingling and heaviness of my limbs faded away, I listened to Mary's summary.

"I can see a strong thread through your lives, which places you in cultural situations such as theater, music, teaching. Color is important to you. Yours has been a life lived very much alone even when with others, and I suspect it will continue thus. But it seems to be your choice rather than..."

I was fully awake. I felt energetic, restored. I'd met my Self and my Self was not wanting. There was continuance. Was this reincarnation? Imagination? Inner-visioning? Well, no matter, as Mary had explained, I'd experienced myself, communicating with *me* and saying all is well.

I continued to waitress across the border, hope for continuance of a relationship I knew had to end, but mostly I searched for ways out, of myself, mostly. I read books by people who were supposed to have gotten through to the inner self, and diligently practiced. There were no answers outside. I had to look inside.

One day, pen and pencil in hand, I decided to have a conference in my *Inner-visioning Room*, with some healers. The experience, another one of writing as fast as I could what I seemed to be experiencing in a parallel world, was tinged with humor, a good sign, I thought afterward, amused at parts of what I'd written.

My *Inner-visioning room*, is an imagined room in my mind designed years ago after reading *Silva Mind Control*. One side of the room is graced by Greek columns and opens onto a cliff overlooking a brilliantly blue, breeze-swept sea.

The interior resembles another favorite imaginary place, the bridge of the space ship Enterprise, complete with a conference table, a futuresque viewing screen, and an instant access door through which my guest guides enter.

Not knowing just who to call on for this first conference, I decided to just "stand" behind my conference table, ask about my physical distress, and see who showed up.

The consultations would be a lot less expensive than the array of doctors I'd been seeing. Hopefully, in contrast, my *imaged* consultants would provide me with clues to getting well. (I often use the word "image" rather than "imagine," as it seems to indicate greater substance).

Suddenly, the first *physician* appeared. Not surprisingly, it was Star Trek's feisty Dr. McCoy. He smiled, and came right to the point.

"It's plain to me!" he said. *"You just need some good old-fashioned R and R."*

Before I could question him as to the how, where, and when, he'd "beamed out." Standing in his place was none other than Edgar Casey. Perhaps it was only a hologram of the good doctor, because he did not look at me directly, but merely began his diagnosis much as he had done, long-distance, when he was alive on the planet.

"The patient," he said, referring to me, *"feels guilty for having over-reached herself. In other words, reaching beyond what those in her surroundings were accomplishing. Healing here will be progressive, and will come with water therapy, vitamins, minerals, and an acceptance of the calling of the spirit to which the patient is committed.*

"The patient," he continued, as I watched and listened in my mind, writing as fast as I could in real time, *"needs to accept herself and put herself into an environment which is more conducive and supportive of the work she is called to do and create."*

As suddenly as he had appeared, Dr. Casey was gone, leaving me with his powerful prescription. Then the most Beloved Physician appeared, smiling, quiet, assured, he called me by name.

"Claudia," He paused, as if waiting for my full attention, *"Your spirit has a withered arm. Take up your bed and walk, and in the process you will be healed as you go. Go into that inner place and commune, as I did with the Father, and you will leave that place knowing which path to take.*

All," he explained, *"who come to the Father are able to return to fulfill their mission on earth. Begin now to be healed. Fear not, I've gone before you to make a way."*

Perhaps the words *had* been said before. But never to me, personally, in the private sanctuary of my own mind and spirit. I felt my healing begin.

Later, typing my notes so that I could meditate on them with greater ease, I was prompted to summarize my physicians' advice. From that time on, each time I visited my *Inner-visioning Room*, the summary was presented to me as well.

1. Rest and recreation may be order.

2. Physical illness is often the final stage, the stage we are willing and able to recognize, in the progressive un-wellness of the job we are in, the relationship we are in, the stresses we are experiencing, the denial of talents, the guilt we are creating and repressing.

3. Healing may be progressive and consist of a combination of steps to take.

4. Self-acceptance is vital to health.

5. Find an environment which is conducive to your well-being and creativity. Inner guidance will help locate the source of illness. Inner communication will strengthen you and give you direction.

6. Proceed as if you were being healed.

7. Consider your own needs for friends, personal finances, education.

8. Love your Self.

9. Fear not. God, according to your understanding is always with you.

The next evening I returned to my *Inner-visioning Room*, this time with the intention of talking to some "successful people." Could they not shed some light on this business of living? The first person to appear startled me. Not a personal role model by any means, he was however, a business "successful people!"

"Take a risk!" Donald T. stated in no uncertain terms. *"You may have to stay in one place long enough to build a base, but don't be afraid. You've taken risks before, life changing risks,- so why be afraid now? It's just a game for a few years out of eternity anyway!*

"Why not have fun, for God's sake! Do what you enjoy doing. Otherwise, no effort is worth it!" He started to leave, then turned back. *"As for relationships,"* he advised, *"If they are toxic, get out. Believe in yourself. Make life happen."*

As before, my first adviser seemed to just 'beam out' to be replaced by another. Standing before me was my heroine, Shirley M., actress, dancer, writer, teacher, lover, seeker. She sat easily, elbows on the table, resting her head in her hands.

"Well," she began, *"I had an advantage because my relationship with my family gave me the emotional freedom to focus and concentrate. The belief in myself which came out of that, and the freedom of earning my own living, allowed me the freedom of ending relationships which didn't work.*

"So, I can't say 'do it my way' but you do need to take whatever steps you can to strengthen your position, inner and outer, so you can do all the wonderful risky things that you are so good at. "Hanging on is not for you," she continued. *"Ask to be shown. Demand to see."*

She was gone, and in her place, surprising me quite as much as my first guest, was movie star and strongman, Arnold S.

He paced the floor, thinking. *"You sometimes have to do what's there for you to do! I don't think anybody can be successful in the beginning by considering too much what others want or think. You just have to concentrate on your own path.*

"Of course, when you have financial freedom, that lets you think of others. The only key I can give you meanwhile is to surround yourself with health. A healthy body, mind, environment gives you the foundation. If food, people, situations, are toxic, avoid them. They are worse than a plague."

Of course, this is a bit amusing, as I format this book for publishing. I certainly had no idea this 'counselor,' a movie star at the time, would, one day for better or worse, become the governor of the state I would live in, struggling with statewide financial challenges. I wondered if in actuality, he was able to deal with toxic situations.

I had hoped for keys to financial success, but instead my famous advisers offered a different kind of advice. I had after all, asked them about the 'business' of living. I summarized what they had told me.

1. Take a risk.

2. Build a base.

3. Don't be afraid.

4. Have fun.

5. Get out of toxic relationships.

6. Believe in yourself.

7. Make life happen.

8. Strengthen your inner and outer self.

9. Ask to be shown.

10. Demand to see.

11. Do what's there for you to do.

12. Continue on your own path.

13. Surround yourself with health

14. Avoid toxic people, food, situations.

I'd begun to feel like a train on a track that had at last reached a switching place. The rails were creaking, groaning, resisting. But the switch would take place. It was beginning. I could feel it. Looking back I can see the time of pain and stress in my life as a blessed one. Not that it *was* in real time, but because, in not being able to come up with any solutions, not being able to resolve anything, not being able to make it better for myself or anyone else in my life, I *had* to turn within.

I did not communicate further with Leytha for a while. She had comforted me, guided me far beyond that which I deserved, but not being able to take action, I felt the way one feels sometimes about a dear friend. I just couldn't burden Leytha anymore with my 'woe is me' tale.

I was embarrassed too. I wasn't facing a battle with cancer or aids. I did not have small children to worry about. I was not the victim of war, nor suffering the kind of poverty I had seen during my travels through Guatemalan villages.

But much of the time, I *was* so depressed I could not think clearly, nor take any positive action for myself. I would never seek medical help for my depression, knowing in advance that medicine would destroy my health and well-being completely. I needed a friend. I needed a life. Very slowly, I was discovering that my friend was me.

Sometimes I'd find myself longing for an old-fashioned town, where you knew "Fanny" at the beauty shop, and "Nellie" at the cafe, and old Mr. Burroughs at the bank. I wished I could just drop into a nice old black and white movie and stay forever.

In fact, my daughter had joked that should I become senile, she planned to create a room with 40's furnishings and a projection machine that just played an endless version of Casablanca. The idea was not that unappealing to me.

But why wait to become senile? I was ready to go there now. No more traffic jams, no more fast food meals accompanied by loud, mindless music, no more meaningless jobs, no more 10 o'clock news horrors.

No more being the unwilling eavesdropper to dumb conversations in lines at the bank, supermarket, drug store, DMV, post office, where the common, very common topic had been gleaned from a T.V. talk show. No more toxic relationships. No more wondering what I was doing here, and which way was home.

But no such town or room existed for me in real time. Still, for some reason, I was beginning to feel that someday, one day, I could find the answer, change things, change myself, live life unafraid, perhaps even sip a cup of peaceful tea with a bit of joy to top my biscuit.

Maybe in the presence of angels, I was shedding false beliefs, and, if not changing, I was, rather, becoming.

One day, I took pen and paper in hand and went again to visit my inner world. I saw a little tiny me in a very big squirrel cage.

"How do I get out of this squirrel cage?" I ask anybody who might be listening.

A big person stops the cage from spinning. The big person does not respond but merely asks, as Mary had done, *"Where are you now?"*

I look around, no longer in the cage.

"I'm on a cruise ship headed towards Southern waters." Oh sure, I think. From squirrel cage to cruise ship! Wishful thinking! Likely story!

"Try another door." said big person, probably sensing my disbelief. I open a door on the other side of the room. *"Where are you now?"* big person asks. It seems to me, being the instigator of this little test, that big person should know without asking *me*!

"I'm in a television studio." Oh great, I think. Another likely. How would I get there from here? I ask about money.

I ask all my brain cells. They are dark. Asleep no doubt. But one area is very large, reddish orange, and undulates like an underwater flower. I look to my right, and see a library with books stacked clear to the ceiling. Finally, I summarized.

1. Ask a question.

2. Recognize what you are feeling and saying.

3. Stop spinning around in circles. Just say stop!

4. A little person feels trapped, in a cage. A big person has the power to stop the cage from spinning. The little person in you may need the big person in you to take over, calm things down, until the whole person can see there is a door, or more than one door, and options.

5. It is not necessary to analyze the inner-visioning. You may if you wish, but the activity that takes place here is sufficient

to begin the healing process, bring about change, guide, or open doors.

6. Try another door.

7. Don't give up. Try another door.

8. Learning can provide the map.

9. Imagine your way out of the cage.

10. You know. Your brain knows.

3.

When they think they know the answers
People are difficult to guide
When they know that they don't know
People can find their own way.
~Tao Te Ching, Lau-Tzu

One Sunday afternoon, I'd done some photography for a small wedding in the North County area of San Diego. Everyone had been late, and I'd come away with a blinding migraine headache. It was still difficult to drive, due to a work injury and my hand and arm were aching. I looked for a place to have a bite to eat, and rest and pulled into the parking lot of a country-style cafe hoping they'd have a jukebox and some country music blaring forth so I could pretend I was in Texas or New Mexico or anyplace where I be closer to the earth and growing things.

There was no jukebox, but the radio was tuned to a country station. I ordered, then picked up an L.A. Times newspaper by the counter. I'd given up looking at ads in the San Diego newspaper. I could recite the job classifications by memory, and week after week, none of them fit. Besides, I still couldn't lift anything with my right hand and arm, so falling back on waitressing wouldn't work. I ate my supper, scanned the ads in the Times, and circled one. By the end of the month, I'd packed up my car, and along with my daughter's parakeet, Kiwi, crossed the border from Mexico,

37

and was on my way to Angeles Forest to work in the intake office of a refuge for wild and exotic animals.

I was assigned to two bedroom trailer, which gratefully I didn't have to share. A couple of weeks later, another "caring misfit," (as I'd come to think of myself), arrived to share the trailer. When I came home for a lunch break and saw the mountain of furniture, and two dogs, I asked to be moved, and happily was soon ensconced in a cozy, tiny travel trailer. Kiwi seemed happier too.

In the mornings, peacocks walked on the roof, or came up to the door begging for a handout of seeds or bread. I'd then walked down the hill to the rustic shack that served as our office, and half way down, stop to say hello to a sad and lonely old chimpanzee who'd once been part of an animal act. During the day I answered hundreds of phone calls, and in between, helped admit injured sparrows, owls, foxes, an opossum mother and her babies, an exotic bird, a coyote, even pet, white mice; all rescued by some humans with hearts. Some could not be saved, but many were, the larger animals like wolves, lions, consigned to cages, but treated, within that context more humanely than they had been in their pasts. .

In the evening, with no television, no partner to be irritated with me, no sounds to distract me except the muffled roars of lions and howling of wolves, or the excited warnings of chimps suddenly disturbed by peacocks alighting on top of their cages, I read, and wrote, and while I had no further sense of direction, I began to feel calm.

One evening I explored a type of mythic journey. The guidance I received was to simply accept this journey as a real experience taking place in my inner space, and the only interpretation necessary was merely to acknowledge the guides I would encounter, as the experience would initiate a healing process, or be the cause in the physical, mental or spiritual realms where change or transformation was needed.

I curled up on the narrow settee in my tiny kitchen and picked up my journal and pencil. In my mind I see that I am standing before a wooden bridge which spans a stream. Beyond the far shore appears a misty woods.

"Who goes there?" a voice calls.

"It is I," I reply.

"We are glad you've come. Pass over the bridge unafraid."

I look but do not see the speaker.

"The path itself will direct you," the unseen guide encourages. *"The council awaits your arrival."*

I cross the bridge. The path is warm to my feet, the flowers fragrant. Birds and butterflies flit overhead. A mist, a presence, moves between birds and sky, obscuring the treetops. *"Go there,"* a huge tree says (perhaps the Tree from my children's play), pointing out the way with his branches. I go in the direction he indicates. I see a group of fairytale people and creatures sitting on a stone circle. There is a place in the stone circle for me. I know this, and take my place there.

"You have made our circle complete. What news of the outer world do you bring us?"

"I much prefer," I respond, accustoming myself to my surroundings, "to hear news of the inner world, Good One," sensing this is how he is called. "It is you and greater harmony that I seek." The others nod approval on hearing my words. "However," I continue, sensing I am expected to, "it is well with me in the outer world. I am once again living the life which combines simplicity and service, and though I work hard and labor long, it is pleasing to me to play a small role in bringing safety and comfort to a few of our Mother's creatures."

"*We are pleased too, Real One*," the elder says, addressing me, "*that you represent us in the outer world. We know how you have struggled to be freed from the tangled web in which the Queen of Fear has ensnared you. But you are not yet free. It is of this that we shall speak to you tonight. We shall give you weapons, and armor, to enable you to conquer the Queen. Listen well, Real One. Listen well*." Good One waves his arm towards the center of the circle. A blue-flamed fire flares up. The council members move closer to warm themselves.

"*The Queen of Fear,*" Good One says, looking into the fire, "*is created by your thoughts. Thoughts can be changed by speaking the mantra of the All-One.*"

"*Seeing all that passes before you,*" counsels Some-One, "*as a mirror world, will encourage kindness on your part. Know that criticism of others is Self criticism, and thus criticism of a member of the council, of the council itself.*"

"*Trying not,*" speaks None-One, "*is a powerful tool when used to try not to be important, superior, or better than. These are thought energies used by the Queen to trip you up.*"

One-by-One tells me that "*...harmony within the body could be achieved by giving the body permission to relax so that it might heal itself during sleep, and even as one goes about one's day.*"

And so it continues through a long, enchanted, misty eve. Each *One* shares a simple wisdom with me, giving me power to

40

disappear the *Queen of Fear*. At last, I bid them all *well-being* and they respond in kind. Moving into the fire they ascend to the sky and became the smoke and the mist. The path appears, the great tree once again extends his branches, and soon I stand before the bridge. I cross over into Real World.

This was my first meeting with the *Council of the Ancient Ones,* I wrote. I will return soon. I wish to know more about the mantra of the *All-One.* I was so intrigued by this journey, that I found myself reluctant to write down that 'real world' summary that seems to follow these inner-visionings. Still, a feeling of incompleteness plagued me for a day or so, and I finally surrendered.

1. Fear is produced by thought. Thought can be changed by prayer (mantra.) Fear is personified as a Queen who would ensnare us and do battle with us. The Queen can be overcome.

2. Seeing life as a mirror will encourage you to be kind.

3. Criticism of others is self-criticism and criticism of the inner self. Criticism of the self is criticism of the Creator.

4. We are always being encouraged to "try." But "trying not" may prevent the Queen of Fear from putting us on an   ego trip.

5. Give the body permission to relax so that it can heal itself during sleep or activity.

6. There is a bridge of willingness which connects us to the inner world and the ancient world. Seeking harmony, even the earth, trees, creatures, will guide our paths.

41

June passed quickly. I worked 10 hours a day, six days a week in the refuge station office. The humans there, mostly people who loved animals were not so suited to getting along with other humans, played out their daily lives in a kind of back country sitcom which too often pulled me into its web, if only as an annoyed observer.

After our long days ended, the younger workers headed down the hill to a boot-stomping country bar. The Latinos went up to their trailer plateau to sit on front steps with cold beers, or played ball with their kids and dogs. The California cowboys went out to the back forty to take a moonlight ride through the foothills on their horses or to roar down the narrow mountain road on their "bikes."

I tried the country bar one night, but left when a fight broke out. Another night, the Latinos invited me to a friendly, fun, family party to celebrate a baby's christening. But usually, now struggling with and likely addicted to loneliness and the safety of that, I just went back to my books and typewriter.

One evening, my inner-vision turned to the mountain woods where I had gone to camp when I was nine or ten years old. I approach a woodland bridge. To my surprise, no one is there to meet me. I cross over and find myself in a sun streaked mountain forest. It felt comforting to be there again. I was 11 again and sat down on a familiar old log. I'd loved this place. I could be alone here and feel the wind and sun on my face. I remember wanting to stay there forever.

A very friendly bear walks up and sits down beside me. I am not afraid. She is just looking around enjoying the scenery, as am I. "*Would you like to go for a walk?*" she asks.

"I would, but I shouldn't," I reply."I've been told not to leave the camp with strangers."

"*Very well then. We shall play right here,*" she says, folding her paws in her lap.

"Why have you come here?" I ask. "What is your name? Do I know you? Why do I not fear you?"

"*So many questions!*" she laughs. *I came here to play with you. You are such a serious little girl, and lonely too. You can call me Bear Hug and you can hug me any time you feel lonely.*"

"How very strange to be sitting here talking to a Bear."

"*Not so strange,*" she smiles. "*You talk with many others just as imaginary as I!*"

"I do?" I ask.

"*Of course! You are always talking to Gremlin Worry and Goblin Regret and a whole host of others. I'm much more friendly than they. And I won't ever hurt you,*" Bear Hug concludes. "*I am your friend.*"

"Yes, Bear Hug," I answer. "I think you are my friend. I do need someone to play with. I get too lonely sometimes and feel like crying. But I won't cry any more now that I know I can call on you."

"*I'll always be right here,*" Bear Hug says as I start to leave. "*But you must promise me that you'll come here often to play with me.*"

"Is that why you came here," I ask with sudden realization. "To teach me to play?"

43

"Yes," says Bear Hug. *"But it's enough for me to know that you'll play with me the next time. Now run along,"* Bear Hug saysd, giving me a big hug. *"It's time for you to sleep and time for me to snooze too."*

I wave goodbye and walk down the path towards camp. Who would believe I'd been talking to a bear! And as for play, how in the world would I play with a bear? Perhaps, I think, if I pretend she is just a teddy bear she will become one. Then she could go home with me when camp is over and we'd both be friends for evermore.

I laughed at this writing, knowing I'd probably done some healing for the six year old me whose mother had died. A day or so later a volunteer brought a car load of stuffed animal toys. The small ones were placed in the baby animal nursery as surrogate mothers for raccoons, and squirrels and foxes and 'possums. The larger stuffed toys found their way into the welcome arms of the children of several of the Latino workers. One stuffed animal, a very large, very fluffy, white teddy bear came home to live with the child in me. I still have her these many years later.

That evening, I curled up on the couch-bed in my trailer and my little parakeet, Kiwi, soon fell asleep on my shoulder. Wanting someone to talk to, I put a piece of paper in my typewriter. I sensed I would confer with the ancient ones, and prepared to follow the scene which would unfold.

I go to the bridge and wait.

"Who goes there?" a familiar voice calls out.

"It is I. I come seeking the council advice for another."

"This is a Holy Request," the Ancient One replies. *"Enter and become as we."*

I cross the bridge and become the mist. I am in all, as all, of all. I am the All-One, but yet am myself. The mist separates, swirls, forms. The circle appears. In the circle, not sitting as before, but standing together, are separate beings whom I sense are unified in mind, purpose and power.

"Join us," invites Good One, extending a robed arm. I take his hand and am drawn into the powerful oneness of the circle.

"As *it is with us,"* Good One explains. "so *it is with you of Real World. As we are separate beings, but unified mind, power of spirit-light, so are you. You are never separate from us in this place, nor from the one or ones for whom you seek a blessing, a healing, or guidance. "Therefore,"* Good One continues, *"ask as if for yourself. Receive knowingness for yourself. Then include the other or others for whom you are concerned, within your circle of power. The greater your ability to receive, the greater will be the blessing or healing or guidance for others."*

I reach out towards the bridge and draw the one for whom I've come, to me. The Ancient Ones open the circle and enfold him into their midst, closing inward like a flower. It is I now who stands apart.

"Speak the Words you desire for this one," Good One's voice booms, shaking the very ground upon which I stand. *"What you speak for yourself will be done for this one in our midst."*

It is difficult to begin. I try to focus, knowing however what he always wanted. "I," following Good One's guidance, spaking for my 'other,' "desire prosperity, great wealth," I stammer,

45

knowing this is what I want for him, because he wants this, but have never truly desired this for myself, preferring freedom above all things and people. "I also desire the love that respects, inspires, strengthens." I pause, feeling awkward. "This is very difficult Good One," I complain, "speaking the Word for another as for myself."

"*It is enough*," Good One says. "*Your intention is sufficient.*" The Ancient Ones' flower unfolds as petals opening to the morning sun, revealing my friend, who walks towards me radiant, joyful. Good One waves his hand, and he and the Ancient Ones disappear into the misty sea.

My "other," and I walk along the sand looking out to the sea, acknowledging our good fortune, our wonder-filled life. We arrive at a Japanese garden and step onto a narrow stone bridge, pausing to throw coins of gratitude into the brook below. I leave him there and walk to the other side, stepping onto a stone pathway and into Real World.

I felt that something happened in this realm for his benefit. I could not know what. But I had a sense that some healing was beginning to take place in his life as well. As for myself, I had not experienced any change. I was not released from the relationship though, not yet. However, as before, I felt urged to make notes of what I'd learned.

1. Praying, imaging, for another is held in high esteem by the inner world.

2. While you cannot physically bring another into the inner world, nor even yourself, as you go there mentally, requesting, receptive, you will merge with the inner life, and thus enabled, you will invite the presence of another for whom you are *concerned, to join you.*

46

3. Ask for another as if asking for yourself.

4. Include the other in the Inner Circle of power.

5. Your ability to receive will determine the blessing, healing, or guidance to be received by the other.

6. Realize the activity is taking place in the Inner world, and will manifest in the "outer" world. However the time-frame is not the same.

7. Take the presence of the other with you and make the transition into Real World.

8. Express gratitude.

Again, I had failed to say thank you. When would I learn this lesson!

The next day, I told Marcos, our magical bird caretaker, that I was thinking of leaving the refuge center and asked if he would keep my parakeet friend, Kiwi. Marcos had trained the tiny green fairy creature to sit on a branch on my desk in the ranch office. If I walked outside, Kiwi would fly as far as her clipped wings would allow her, straight to my shoulder. Even if I stood among a crowd of people, she would find me.

How was that possible? Why had we bonded? Did she realize I'd freed her from the cage she'd had to stay in for her own protection in my daughter's cat inhabited apartment? Did she know she was here in the wild, among others—exotic birds, foxes, coyotes, bears, bobcats, lions, cockatoos, crows, and tortoises angels all, perhaps, rescued by humans from the abuse of other humans? Was Kiwi a tiny green-winged angel?

I carefully considered my decision to leave. To do so, would mean once again getting involved in a relationship with

47

someone I loved, but with whom living, for me, was too difficult. My arm and hand were getting better, but with a sudden twist, like opening a door, I would be in pain again. Emotionally, I felt incapable of coping with the real work world. Here at the ranch, among the rest of my misfit co-workers who'd sought refuge here and found a peaceful haven among their abused and abandoned animal brothers, I too felt at home. I gave notice that I was leaving, but still doubted my decision. I wondered what I might encounter in the inner world, that mysterious realm where wisdom and beauty prevailed, transcending the mess I seemed to have made of my life.

I am at a crossroads, I typed, preparing myself for the inner journey which I can imagine freely through my writing. I see three roads. One road goes ahead continuing the life I am now leading. One goes to the left, back to where I was before. One road goes to the right and an unknown place. Which road am I to take? I see an Ancient One walking towards me on the road straight ahead. As he approaches, the road behind him simply fades away.
"It is I, Good One," I say, acknowledging the now familiar guide.

"You will follow the road to the left," he says without ceremony. *"It is a road of completion which shall be accomplished by the end of your Real World year. Do not fear the outer world you will encounter. Keep your inner ear tuned to the words of the council. They will guide you. Each of your concerns may be resolved at the circle of the Ancient Ones.*

"Do not hesitate to contact us. Doing the work of the inner world is our only reason for being. However, unlike other aspects of your physical, mental, spiritual being, we do not work or intervene autonomously. You must contact us and request our guidance for inner work."

"I understand Good One," I reply, a little overwhelmed by this offering. "Thank you," I said, at last remembering. "But I again do battle with the Queen of Fear, and also with self-doubt."

"You speak of intimidation. This occurs when your power is given to another."

"I understand this, Good One," I reply, sighing. "But how do I take this power back? I am most embarrassed at being so easily intimidated, made to feel shy and apologetic."

Good One takes my hand and bids me follow. We walk down the central path, the mist unfolding before us like a carpet of clouds. We stand above a wide expanse of beach. *"Look at the sands of the sea,"* he commands. I do so, a sense of wonder filling my soul. Good One waves his hand and the sky pales to blackest night and stars come forth in limitless abundance as if to dance for my benefit alone. In a blink, we stand atop a snow-shrouded mountain, the highest mountain, where I perceive all the glory of the earth. Then we are, in an instant, in space, the blue home planet floating softly against the blackness of infinity.

"Now perceive yourself," Good One speaks gently, and I am in space between Good One and earth, seeing, feeling my imperfections. *"Stop!"* Good One commands and the unpleasant emotions subside like a tide. *"You who have been created by that which is the creator of all you have seen, are no less wonderful."*

I am beside Good One now, still viewing the cloud-draped earth. *"Is there one,"* Good One asks somberly, *"on that planet who could create one grain of sand, one mountain, one star, one planet,"* Good One asked, *"...one you?"*

Without waiting for my reply we are once again at the crossroads. *"Who then,"* Good One says, waving his arms to the left and the right, dissolving the crossroads. *"Who then has the power to cause timidity in you?"* Good One does not smile, but I sense an overwhelming kindness. It lingers around me like a warm shawl, even as the mist enfolds him and he is gone. Still, his voice comes to me on a gentle wind.

"Consider the sands, the mountains, the stars. Consider the earth, the worlds beyond. Consider the Creator. Knowing then the glory of the creations, and you are no less than these, who then can take your power? Who among you is greater than the Creator or the created? Who?"

His voice disappears in the wind. I stand where the crossroads had been. There is no confusion, no fear. I walk towards a familiar bridge, crossing it into Real World. None whom I shall meet, he has promised, will be other than the created. But none greater than the Creator. None are there to whom I shall ever again pay more respect, nor less respect than to myself.

One morning, in the "real world," I packed up my stuff. Almost everything I owned now would fit into my car. I was going back to the city. My Kiwi-angel would stay. Marcos would carry her on his shoulder as he made the rounds to feed the other birds. Here, she would not have to live in a cage. I would miss her terribly.

4.

I stay my haste, I make delays
What avails this eager pace
I stand amid the eternal ways
And what is mine shall know my face.
~Waiting, John Burroughs

Back in Mexico, still nursing the pain and weakness in my hand and arm, I diligently read San Diego help wanted ads that I could not fill. Finally, I set up my typewriter in the upstairs bedroom which had a view of the ocean across the roof-tops, and made the room my own.

One day, looking over some of the inner-visioning notes I'd made while I was at the ranch in Angeles Forest, I came across a writing in which I'd envisioned myself in another time period in the past. At the time, I'd wondered if the scene, so clearly recalled, was one of the spontaneous reincarnation experiences Mary had mentioned to me, especially since the *me* I saw there was so very unlike me.

I saw myself riding a horse. I seemed to be in a hurry to get to a house, a ranch or estate of some sort. When I arrived there, I jumped off my horse and ran into the house. Someone from England or the Continent had arrived. A handsome man, a good friend. I was so glad to see him. He told me that my love, his best friend, had been at last set free, and would be there within the

51

week. I was ecstatic. Suddenly, I excused myself and left the house to go through the gardens, up a hill, to a place where a small shrine had been set up. I placed a flower, a rose plucked from the garden, on the altar, and knelt in gratitude for the news I've just received, and ask protection for my love. Rushing down the hill I stumbled and fell but was not harmed. My friend was there to help me up and together we returned to the house to discuss the news with the family over tea and biscuits in the large hearth-warmed kitchen. Retiring to my room for the night, I took pen and paper and write again to my love, letters not mailed these four years but faithfully written and saved for the time of his return. It was an odd vision, perhaps another of the spontaneous life remembrances Mary had mentioned during my reincarnation session.

Later that week I went time traveling at the library in San Diego. Mexican American history which had always interested me, and I checked out several books. Back in Tijuana, I curled up on a pallet in "my" room to read. In a few days the outline for a novel was bumping around in my mind. The scene in my inner-vision was to become the opening scene of the novel manuscript, written on a typewriter in those "BC" (before computer) days. I have the manuscript still, not yet converted to Microsoft Word. At the time, the writing calmed my mind, satisfied my heart, and made me consider again, that were I to find a way to provide for myself, without using me up in the commercial world where I did not fit, I might write and publish.

One day, my partner and I made our decision to separate for good and it had come about painfully and quickly. In two days time, he was gone, while I stayed on for a month in the little house in Tijuana, with my two cats. Everyday, the three of us would hurry to the window at the sound of every passing car, but he did not return. I read the classifieds again, but fell into despair over the lack of any prospects I could fit into. I could type, but only for short periods on my own writes, and even then my hand and arm would ache for days. Most of the work I'd done in the past, work

52

not restaurant related had been with non-profit organizations, like the wildlife ranch, or the seasonal tour in the mid-west with the children's theatrical company. Exciting, low-paying and temporary at best.

I'd wracked up some free-lance writing credits over the years, but knew I couldn't compete with those with degrees in English or journalism. Having a play published, two produced, a role in a film, some time spent writing for bi-lingual newspapers, a six week community television program, three months with missionaries in Guatemala was all very interesting for a gypsy, but how was I ever to fill out a job application? But my real despair grew out of a lack of self-esteem. So, once again, I took a waitress job across the border in San Diego. That night, I cried about everything, unable even to sleep because of the pain in my hand and arm, and wracking cough of what would likely become an unwelcome bout with bronchitis. My daughter's cat, Sushi, and my little kitten, Chickiada were my comfort. Each night they would wait patiently for me. Arriving home I would see them, perched on top of the T.V., their heads poked through the venetian blinds.

The next day, I crossed the border early, and re-enrolled at Southwestern College in Chula Vista. I only needed another semester to accomplish an AA, and then, if only I could finally get a degree...but to do what? The next week, I slipped at the curve of the narrow staircase in my apartment and fell to the bottom. The cats ran to my side. I sat on the stairs and cried until the pain left, grateful nothing was broken.

A few days later, I sat with one of my co-workers, eating a prime rib sandwich, and talking with our tall, football player busboy. Suddenly a piece of meat stuck in my throat and I could not breath. I tried to wash it down with coffee, but the liquid stayed in my mouth. I jumped up and gestured to the busboy to do the Heimlich maneuver on me. Over six feet tall, he grabbed me, just five feet tall, from behind, his hands on my ribs, and squeezed, lifting me off the floor. I thought he'd broken my ribs. "Oh God," I thought, "he's not doing it right....I can't breathe...I'm going to die...So much unfinished....Please Jesus!"

Somehow I pushed his hands below my ribs and into the middle of my diaphragm. The piece of meat popped out. I left the restaurant, stopped to get some ice cream to soothe my throat and my nerves, and drove home. I had not died. But nobody was around to care if I were living. Something was radically wrong with living life this way. The next morning I could barely move. My ribs hurt so badly that I gasped in agony with each breath. I had the next day off. I could not afford to see a doctor.

I struggled to get into my car and drove to see a pharmacist friend in Tijuana. He gave me an injection for the pain and wrapped my ribs. It would be more than six weeks before I could move or breathe without pain. Less than a week later someone backed into my car. The headlights were broken and the front end smashed in. I'd just received a cancellation notice on my overdue insurance. I managed to drive the car to work, but when I parked, an ominous stream of green water poured out from under the car. I called my daughter living in downtown San Diego, to pick me up after work, and the next day I took three buses to get back to the restaurant where I had left the car and drove it a mile to a repair shop. I needed a new radiator. There was no money for one. I called the leasing company and surrendered the car.

I asked to get off work early so I could get back home before dark, and considering my need of a miracle of any size, they scheduled me to come in earlier, and leave at eight P.M. So I began the long trek back and forth the border to get to work and then, home again. A bus, then the trolley to the border, then a bus downtown Tijuana, and a neighborhood taxi to *Playas*. Then a half mile walk uphill in the dark to my house.

Graffiti scrawls now covered every flat surface like some wall eating bacteria. My block had been spared, except for the corner houses, Apparently those two houses had secured the territory, but it would only be a matter of time until the gangs, from the U.S. Side of the border, resident neighbors said, would be back. One evening, exhausted, I got to my own tree shaded postage stamp front yard, I saw that someone had marked "my" rock wall.

For a few months, I'd been able to stand in my doorway, and look past the wall, across the toll road leading to *Rosarito*, and up the hillside and still see a green and brown vista not yet destroyed by poor wooden shacks, or hastily constructed earthquake nightmare condos. It was my little bit of nature amongst the ugliness here, and sustained me. Now, my view of the sea from my second story bedroom window in the back of the house was being destroyed. Three of four houses just below and across the street had built on second stories. The completion of the fourth building project would pull down the curtain. The sea view would be gone.

I stared at the graffiti with growing anger. How dare some young punks ruin my wall, I thought, going over to examine it. But the graffiti was just a copycat effort from a neighbor child. It was done in chalk. I could salvage my wall, for a little while anyway. I went into the house, threw my things down, and filled a bucket with soapy water, and with all the neighbor kids watching in silence, I scrubbed my wall. A few days before, a pipe in the pila, the well, under my driveway had broken. A plumber had repaired it, but replaced the metal rimmed, concrete slab cover at an angle so that an edge of it jutted above the surface of the driveway. A wide shallow hole, with some sort of gauges in it, was positioned just in front of the concrete well cover.

Before, I had parked my car in such a way that the hole was under the car. Now, I was preoccupied with cleaning the wall, thinking sadly that it was only a matter of time until the next graffiti would be etched in spray paint, emptied the bucket into the street, and headed back to the house. Suddenly, I stepped into the hole, fell forward and landed on one knee on the jutting metal edged concrete slab. I nearly fainted with the pain. A neighbor ran up, followed by his wife, and thinking I spoke no Spanish, they tried to explain they did not speak English, but could they help me.

The pain was so intense I could not speak or move. At last I whispered, "*Ayudame*," help me, and tried to guide them to lift me up. I was sure I'd broken my knee. I asked them to help me into the house and put me into a chair, then insisted I'd be O.K. Some children ran to get their mothers, and they came, offering iodine and bandages, but though my knee was cut it was scarcely bleeding. The pain had given way to total numbness.

It was nearly dark, but I'd have to sleep in the chair. There was no way I could get up the stairs to go to bed. Sushi and Chickiada hovered around me, and I pulled a small pillow out from behind me and laid it over my knee, worried that Chicki, still young and rambunctious would jump on me. She did.

I felt cold inside. "I am not supposed to be here," I thought. "It's time for me to let go and move on." I reached for the phone and dialed my sister, across the bay from San Francisco. Yes of course I could stay with them. They were coming to San Diego for the wedding of a friend's daughter in two weeks. They'd rent a van and take me back with them.

I called my daughter. Yes, she sighed, long accustomed to my gypsyesque moves. She would take the cats. What were two more cats. Sushi had been her cat originally anyway. She was sorry I was having troubles, again! She was glad, and relieved, I knew, that I could stay with my sister. She'd come over and help me on moving day.

That night, I watched PBS, and Star-trek, ate ice cream, and put off going to sleep as long as possible. In the mornings, awakened by the kids or dogs outside, or the garbage, gas, or water trucks, or the cats insistent meowing to be fed, I sat on the edge of my bed wrapped in despair and wondered what had become of me. Something bright and wonderful had died inside me, and I didn't know how to get it back.

5.

If you open yourself to insight
you are at one with insight
and you can use it completely.
~Tao Te Ching, Lau-Tzu

September. A while since I left Tijuana. My sister and brother-in-law seemed glad to have me stay with them, and I was happy, grateful to accept this refuge until I could put my life into focus. Sitting in a wooded area in back of the apartment complex one day, I talked with Leytha again, longing to connect again with that life which makes me feel whole.

"Leytha," I write, immediately sensing her presence. "So very long since I've talked with you. How do I put the past behind me and begin a new life here - fulfilling my potential as a creative, loving person?"

I had, at last discovered some angel books, read of inner guides, and come to realize that I was not alone, nor crazy, in being receptive to these communications. Yet, I still felt as though I was "bothering" Leytha when I wrote her name, thus establishing our contact. Have I asked too much, I wonder? Will the page stay blank this time?

57

Dearest One, the words flow gently across the paper. *I have never been far from you. But I could not intrude into your life or into the life force which held you bondage and had to, as did you, let it dissolve.*

The past is as a leaf fallen from a tree. It is disconnected from the life force and becomes part of a new life line, or other life line.

It is no longer part of the "tree" which is you. The memories you hold are selective ones fueled by emotional energy.

To turn off this energy merely bless the "leaf", thank it for having grown from your "tree", and let it fall from your branches, to join with the earth.

In letting go, and blessing, these leaves of the past you release your "tree" energy to produce new growth.

Release the idea, bless it, let it fall away, of "fulfilling potential". Walk among the familiar where you are as a healer. Teach, share what we reveal to you.

Later that week, feeling more peaceful, but with little insight into how to move from my today into my tomorrow, I again, pencil in hand, I ask, then "listen" for Leytha.

"Why do I have so little self-esteem that the only job I can do is waitressing when my soul cries out to create beauty with words and art and be a healer?"

Your karma has followed you doggedly to confront and diffuse pride. You remember at times, a life-time in which you had, and misused power. You died in regret, unforgiving of yourself.

58

Born again quickly, you wished to make up for these errors by punishing, denying, yourself in this life-time.

If you so choose, you can make amends now, by forgiving yourself. In truth, forgiveness is unnecessary as the progress of human life is to go through fear, doubt, striving, comfort, pride, and regret to consciousness and self-awareness

Her voice is like the whispering of wind; of a many dimensioned stringed instrument echoing in the empty halls of space. It is rainbow colored. It springs forth from pure light.

You have come into this life to deal with regret. It may seem odd to you that this is so, but even in the angelic realm we experience these lessons. Again we urge you to know your Self as not separate from the light, but a vibrant being in through whom beauty and healing may be expressed.

Even now you are reluctant to think you are worthy of this. Focus on the light and let it heal your wounds of regrets. Emotional flagellation is a waste of life energy."

It seemed the whole month of September, 1994, would be about seeking guidance. Again, I ask:

"Leytha, in my readings I've been led to understand there are specific angels who may be called upon to guide us in special areas. You know that I wish to write, to make art, but my greatest concern is to be able, as quickly as possible produce enough income to support myself in a way that does not destroy self-esteem. Is there one who will guide me in this? Of myself, I do not seem able to bridge the gap.

Leytha replies, giving me the name "Dionyn." I feel hesitant to call upon this being, but I must remember that she,

Leytha, has given me only loving guidance. So, I write, expecting a wonderful communication with Dionyn.

"I sense, Dionyn, that you are a very powerful being, male in presence, and able, and willing, to not only assist me to the place I wish to be, but will be my bridge-builder. Is this not so?"

Litheria, Dionyn replies. *I will call you by your light name for this is the name under which you must publish those works which we will dictate to you.*

We will set a place for you beside the other communicators of this age, because this has been your desire from the beginning, to join, rejoin, with those of your own clan. Even now we set in place the works, the energy, the connections and connectors which will, by the end of the year as you perceive it, put you in the position you long for.

Fear not, Litheria. This is just coming home for you. This is where you've always belonged. You have been trudging up a tangled path trying to reach the top of a mountain, but I will lift you with the power and glory of my wings and touch you down safely, in a safe place.

Feel now the unfurling of your own wings. Feel the opening in the sleeping area of your mind. Come daily to this place and open, open, your mind. Fill it with light. Sense the cleansing that is taking place there, the feeling of springtime, of newness, of expectancy. Open, open, your mind. "

This was too much; magical thinking, I decided. A "sensitive" perhaps, but I was not a mystic, and certainly not a "channeler!" In fact I thought that whole process a bit off in la-la land. "These words we'll dictate to you?" I think not. I wanted practical how-to knowledge for my life in the here and now.

I continued to mail off this or that piece of writing to some publisher or agent. I was encouraged by my niece Tambra, who insisted that "hundreds" had heard my poem, "If Only," (written for her younger sister's graduation, when I had no gift to give) the result of her readings of the poem whenever she does some public speaking. She suggested that I create a series of small art-card-books with the several encouraging poems (composed mostly for others, and scarcely absorbed by my own self) I had written. She also gave me a couple of assignments to write some marketing copy for friends of hers. At least I would paid a small amount for this.

Attention to the "here and now," however, disconnected me from my inner life. Was there no way to merge guidance and action that would lead to something?

I'd gone to another waterfront cafe, this time in Tiburon, California, to apply for work. After turning in the application, I sat at a table in the outdoor patio, eating strawberry blintzes and espresso coffee and staring across the water at the San Francisco skyline and picked up my pen again and thought of Leytha.

"So many things which interest others do not concern me. I want to find my place, do something worthwhile in life. How shall I pray? What do I do? What do I look for?" The sense of Leytha's presence was instantaneous.

When the iron is too hot, came the message in my spirit-mind, *it strikes the material and destroys it.*

When desire is too strong, it can warp the fabric of creative spirit by imprinting a stamp, a design, on your life force which is not truly your own.

61

Desire is good, but it can be harmful when it evolves from a need to please others, to achieve security based on the world's standards, or as a substitute for love, relationship, peace of mind, or quietness of spirit.

It is not greater desire that you need to foster but rather deeper relationship so that you will come to know that all is already yours.

Be at peace. I will not give you that which harms you.

Be at peace. Release those for whom you are concerned.

Release the tension that binds you to the past, to limitation, to familiarity.

Look up. Look out. Open your heart, mind, vision. Expand your world.

You are concerned about your health. If the temple is in need of attention, repair, refurbishment, you must give it that attention. Focus on beauty, flexibility, joy, elegance, simplicity. Find time to be outside among my growing things.

Know that I creation is an on-going process. You do not grow "old." You change.

Join with others whose focus is on restoring the temple, of the body, so that you might receive example and support and so change the mind, emotional patterns and programming which bring forth the physical effects which are now hindrances to you.

In your concern about having made many mistakes, and wanting to see the pathway to the future with more clarity, you are

62

looking into the surface of a pool marred by ripples. These ripples are the past, present, and future.

What you are seeing is movement, change. In order to see, or experience clarity, you must look beyond the surface, beyond the pool, to the very source of life. Go now to that quiet place and listen for my voice.

One day, I felt particularly exhausted and frustrated. I had gotten the job at the Tiburon café, but my life was still the same. I didn't make enough to live on my own in this high rent area. Wondering how I could ever move away from my sister's apartment, I wandered out to the back of the property to a wooded area, and sat at a picnic table there, paper and pen in hand.

"I'm working so hard, but it is only busy work. Why am I "called" if I cannot find the path of my calling? My heart cries out to you with longing!"

Child, sister, came the impression in my spirit-mind. It was the voice of the "prism" message. I began to write.

Be at peace. I am providing a place for you, a place of shelter, a place of pleasing, a place of peace. Enter in now. I await you with open arms. I am that which you seek. I am that which calls you. I am in the now of your life.

I was astonished by this message. In a meditative state I looked into the inner theater of my mind. I had studied, experienced many religious and philosophical beliefs. Why was this coming through a Christian lens?

Back in the house, I rummaged through my papers. No matter what happened or how many times I moved, I would arrive with a suitcase, and boxes of my books, some art pieces, and my

63

scribblings... years and years of scribbling! I found the piece I had written in that daydream state at the religious school in San Diego. I had left the lecture hall and walked to Balboa Park. Finding a quiet place surrounded by green, and wrote:

You are like a precious child, spirit sister, mother, daughter, friend, disciple. I honor you as you honor me.

Come, we go our to Father. Prepare to receive the Light.

Fear not.

Here, take my hand.

Come, the time for your anointing is appointed.

Come closer anointed one. Walk through your vale of tears and come into my presence. I would anoint you with the life-light of my own being.

You are now to know my presence in every waking moment. You are to hear my voice in night dreams.   You are to go forth holding the light of my spirit in the midst of darkness. I will go before you. You are not alone.

I enter in...Black Christ, Brown Cristos, Hebrew Jesus, the Light which appeared to Abraham, to Confucius, to Mohammed, to Buddha.

I enter in...Mother Mary, Catholic Mary, Mary the Jewess, Mary Magdalene, Maria, the Our Lady of all nations.

I enter in....John, brother, friend, journalist, watcher

I enter in...Peter, father, worker, carer, stubborn lover

I enter in...saints and soldiers, shepherds and streetwalkers

I enter in, and through.

They make way for me to enter in...into the garden...rolling hills. so green...gentle streams...so fresh.

I enter in...birds singing, clouds laughing, trees waving. Creatures watch, still and wise.

He comes. He looks like I remember Him......tanned skin...strong hands...wide, open smile. He takes me by my shoulders and holds me...arms length...takes my face in his hands...suddenly I am small, child-like in his strong presence. His eyes...so intense. say, "Hello dearest friend, you've been missed. But I've not forgotten you."

I feel... peace. He touches my forehead. I feel - whole. He turns returns - takes my hand. "Come, we go to our Father."

Yet we do not move. I am surrounded, absorbed in love. I weep, overwhelmed. I am light. I am no longer body. I am, yet I am not. I sense He is there...watching, pleased to have given me this gift.

I turn, hearing the cries behind me. I must go back, I explain, share this. He understands. Especially He understands.

He walks with me to the edge of the garden. A great, dark vortex confronts me. I cannot go, I cry out, wanting to cling to him and stay!

Suddenly He is there before me . Come, He beckons, I go before you and prepare the way. Suddenly I am born. Soon I forget. Has He designed it thus?

Several years later, after reading Carl Sagan's book, *Contact*, and seeing the film, I thought how what I had experienced in that brief moment in my mind seemed very much like that of the woman astronomer, on the beach in the "first contact" scenario.

A long periods of time would go by before I would, overwhelmed with a sense of wanting to go "home," take up my pen, hoping I might enter into my parallel world and hear His voice. I sense his presence. The garden is once again springing into bloom.

"I will never leave you, good and faithful friend."

I longed to hear these words again, to walk with Him in the garden The earth is too much with me, Lord! Refresh me! Recreate me that I might love, might experience love. Then, He is there in that place in my mind. It is as if no time at all had passed from the last time I had written.

Walk with me, He says, through the winding streets to the hill. I was not without terror. The spikes wrenched my body with agony tearing screams from my throat. I was not without sorrow when I saw the heartbreak of those who watched me suffer.

Now go with me further. To the Body. Still unwilling to leave my friends without understanding of Eternal Life, I took up the Body again and lived among them.

Behold the eye of the storm. The bud of a flower, the depth of a forest. In these places all is quiet.

As one moves out from the center, the flower unfurls, waves crash against the shore, winds swirl wildly, and trees, whipped by the wind, appear scraggly and barren.

Attend to the center. Your source.

Remember who you are. You are not your environment. But losing sense of your centered place will create a chaotic environment around you.

Take responsibility for your life, but not the burden. For the presentation, but not the outcome. Watch where the light falls and walk there.

In the spring of life all things are fresh and new. Revitalization is not necessary because creation is still expanding. In the summer of life creation is still, not absent, but sleeping.

To revitalize the creative force, meditate upon spring and the sense of newness, expectation, youth, beauty.

Dwell on these things. I would have you be calm, at peace, and know that all which burdens you is about to drop away.

I release you! You may now come into the sunlight. You may come out of hiding. You may bathe freely in the renewing spring of grace, peace, love.

Child! Your conversation with me is as a flickering lamp, so desirous are you of lighting up the room, of displacing the darkness, of bringing light and warmth. Yet the winds of anxiety threaten to extinguish the flame.

Be not dismayed. Let the flickering lamp bur brighter.

67

Be patient. In time the wind will still and the flame will burst high and proud. The light will outlast the darkness. The warmth will dispel the cold.

Patience child. Pray, study, be.

I come in the midst of the night to light the lamp. I come in the midst of silence to speak the word. I come in the midst of chaos to bring order. I come in the midst of loneliness to bring love. I come to bring life in the midst of death.

I had understood little of this inner vision experience. The words were beautiful, but it still seemed as if I were, though no longer going from bad to worse, not going where I wanted to go. I constantly experienced emotional and financial pain. One day I asked Leytha about it.

When antiseptic is applied to a wound it sometimes stings. When healing begins there is sometimes a curative crisis which may hurt even worse than the wound.

If you could look into the world of the spirit, you will see yourself tied by hundreds of strings, tethered to earth. These are the little things which have wrapped strings around your life, easily conquered one by one, but collectively, they have an awesome power to hinder, hold back, hurt.

If you were satisfied where you are you would not be sensing any frustration. What you feel are growing pains, stretching pains. Since most people do not acknowledge this urge to grow, change, move initiate, affect, they make excuses or create reasons or assign a false diagnosis. Or, in the name of "principle," they teach earth-bound, man-made techniques for dealing with pain.

The pain is, because you are a spirit struggling to make sense of life on an alien planet, as it were, wearing a life-suit, your body, which is subject to its laws. Do not judge the pain too harshly.

Continually remind yourself that you are not the life-suit, not the body only. You are the life which makes it work, and are the life which it protects.

You chose to be a mountain climber, beloved, to be an obstacle runner. You chose to do this so that one day you could be an encouragement to others whose experiences have been difficult but who do not know consciously their choices. You made the choice. You have made a commitment to it.

What you need to know, also, is that you do not need to continue to struggle. You are at the top of the mountain and you are running around on a level place looking for another incline.

You have overcome every obstacle set before you in the race, but you have not looked up to see that you have arrived. Now is the time that you set before you. Now is the time that you reach out your hand, your love, to others. Now is the time to concentrate on the inner world.

This too is a path you set for yourself. If you are ready, we will make a place for you.

"But Leytha!" I wrote sorrowfully in my "own" voice. "I do not know where I'm going, or how I'm going to get there. I'm so bogged down by my life. I wish I could just go on a life-time retreat and talk to you of heavenly things!" But it was not Leytha I heard, but that of my patient Teacher, the voice of the prism.

69

I am with you. I sensed the presence. *Closer than your breath. Be patient. Do not run, or panic. Your dream is on the horizon.*

The moon seems to rise only when it can be seen against the darkness of the sky. Out of the darkness you will see light, see it coming, expanding, growing, until it lights your path and those around you.

Spend your mornings in preparation. Rise early and pray. Because the outer life is so loud upon your ears you sometimes do not hear the soft sweetness of my voice.

I have called you to simplify your life. Do not doubt that your calling is true. Nothing that I have set forth can fail to be created. Nothing planned apart from me will have abiding reality.

This is faith: to turn moment by moment from the world out there to the inner world where there is life and learning, peace and healing, comfort and wisdom, love and wholeness.

6.

I am the daughter of earth and water,
and the nursling of the sky
I pass through the pores of ocean and shores;
I change, but I cannot die.
~*The Cloud*, Percy Bysshe Shelley

It is the end of January, 1995 and I have "published," my little *If Only*, poem, as a several paged, "book-card." The cover is a rough textured re-cycled paper, with pastel parchment interior pages. Each card is hand-decorated with a line design—hearts, flowers, lamps, sailboats, etc., then a swatch of fabric for accent.

I took twelve copies to work with me at the cafe in Tiburon, and with some unusual promotional courage inspired, I think, by the little poem itself, I showed the cards to several regular customers, and soon the cards were all sold!

The reaction within my limited circle was pleasing. The partner of a writer for the local newspaper bought two. That night, I attended a little theater production with my sister, volunteering to help out in the kitchen. Suddenly I heard a man calling my name.

"Claudia," he said, rushing up to the coffee counter. "We didn't read your little book-card until we got home. It was wonderful!" It was the man from the newspaper.

A couple from Sacramento bought the last three, and I gave them the sample copy as a gift. He asked if he could write me a

71

check, and when I went back to the table to pick up the check, he pushed a napkin towards me. On it he had written, "Congratulations! Raise your prices!" Then he'd drawn a little ladybug, with a cartoon bubble saying, "You kin do it!" His partner asked me to stay in touch as they'd like to buy some cards for graduation gifts.

My last table of the day, two older women, received rather poor service from me, as distracted as I was by then. I apologized and explained about the *If Only* book-card. One of the women asked to see a copy, and I had to tell her they were sold out. She reached in her purse for money.

"Your poem is wonderful. Could do me a favor. I take care of an aids patient, a Black lady," she said, "and her birthday is Wednesday. I wonder if you could mail me a little book-card in time for her birthday?" That evening, I designed an *If Only...* especially for the woman, and sent it off in the next day's mail.

John, Rosalie, and niece Tambra are wonderfully supportive and feel there's a real business potential here. John has written up a vendor agreement for consignment as well as outright sales to retail shops. I have to find a source for the cellophane sleeves in which to insert the cards. Tambra suggested the use of colored stock envelopes to accent the color of the fabric on the cards.

So, as soon as I have these two sources, I can make up samples to take to some retail outlets. I'm going to start with just ones which are nearby, so that I can service them easily, while working out the retail distribution plan. The book-cards might sell nationwide as easily as here, but that will take a fabrication and distribution plan, as well.

My sense is, however, without much common-sense nor knowledge of the business aspect, the "next" in any of my creative ventures, I'll soon be discouraged. Still, I've four more poems in the works: *Saying Goodbye*, S*aying Thank You, What If*, and *Why Not,* so, "why not?"

I had an odd dream last Friday night. (As I proof this combined version of my several "inner-vision" journals, it is September 11, 2010. My dream was in January, 1995. I think, reviewing the dream today, it may have been prophetic, and I wonder how many others in the world were dreaming such dream. At the time, as the "dream interpretation" session that follows indicates, the dream seemed purely personal).

In my dream, I looked to the left and saw an unearthly and beautiful pink light rising from behind a mountain. A male companion stood to my right, and I said, "look! Isn't that amazing!"

Then the light became brilliantly white. We became aware that some phenomenon was taking place in the skies and looked directly overhead to see a world-like, huge sphere breaking apart.

We seemed to need to get away, and there were two old, 1940's planes. Someone took off in one, to the right, and crash landed. A man came running back to warn, "Don't go that way. It's disastrous."

My companion and I got into the old plane, with him piloting, and we took off from a woodland road, straight up through the trees. I had no sense of the sky, nor clouds nor height.

Getting out of the plane, I look to my right and see a man on a blanket with a dark haired little girl of seven. He looks embarrassed, and says to the little girl, "What's wrong?" The little girl gets up, ignores him, looks around, and wants to explore the woods.

I am in a motel room, where I've apparently stayed after arriving in the plane. The tenants around are very loud and brawling.

I want to leave, but notice I have a lot of my personal things in the room. I start to clean up, and start to water my flowers so they won't die.

There are three plants, two small ones, like chrysanthemums, and a tall one, like a tulip or daffodil, all brilliantly yellow. I wonder where to put them, how to group them.

I place the tall one near a window, as I think it needs sunlight. I think I should put the other two in the kitchen. I pick up two containers of water, a glass, and a measuring cup.

The little girl comes in and asks for a drink of water. I think this might be my daughter, but it could be a child I don't know. I look at the water containers in my hands, and think, these hold dirty water, I'll water the plants with them.

I tell the little girl to go into the kitchen and get a drink of water. I look around the room, and think, even though the tenants outside are annoying, I have my things here. Maybe I'll ask the manager if I can just stay on by the week.

I had already made an appointment with Susan, a tenant here at the complex, who does dream work, to discuss some of my other dreams, in order to get a different perspective in this "search for my self." With a folder of ten recorded dreams on the table between us, I suddenly decided to tell her this most recent one.

After listening, Susan responded, "If this were my dream," using the *if...* method as a means of interpretation, "I would feel the pink, then white sunrise or light coming up from behind the

74

mountain, indicated something spiritual coming up in my life. That I perceive it as beautiful, tells me it is something to look forward to.

"'The world breaking up over my head,'" she continued in her first person intuition, "may mean some obstacle which has been over my head is breaking up." She paused to question me about my own interpretation of the planes.

"I love things from the 40's," I explained. "The music, the old movies. And I admire Richard Bach, who is both a writer and loves flying. Flying in these old planes symbolizes courage, independence, flying "by the seat of your pants," by your wits."

"Well, then," Susan resumed, "I feel the man coming back from the first plane is a guide, clearly warning you not to take a certain direction." She saw the yellow flowers as aspects of my creative, and intellectual self. That I am trying to decide which of these to nourish—the tall yellow flower is my writing, the two smaller ones, photography, and my personal life.

Finally, Susan suggested that putting the two smaller flowers in the kitchen was also a nourishing move, as well as placing the tall flower in the window, where it will, I will, my creative and intellectual self, be exposed to the outside, and the sunlight.

My questioning whether to stay or leave the motel room, seemed a simple reflection on my own situation here, staying with John and Rosalie and wondering how, when, I'll be able to have a place of my own.

The remarkable thing about dreams is their continuing action. Yesterday, I reread some dreams, and communications from my guides recorded since 1988. I see much in them that was prophetic, and understand them from a far different perspective today. It is almost like going back to kindergarten after graduating from high school. One's perception and understanding is considerably changed.

I'd talked with Susan about the dream on Friday. Saturday I worked at the restaurant, after staying up half the night preparing the *If Only* cards, and of course had the remarkable experience of selling all the cards, and receiving so much encouragement. But on the way to work at 6:30 in the morning, I looked over to my left, as in the dream, and saw the most spectacular sunrise I've ever seen in my life.

It seemed as if the sky were the ocean, with wave after wave, and millions of ripples of the brilliant hued pink gold. By the time I turned off the freeway, and towards Tiburon, the fog swept across the sky. Where it curtained the sun, a pure white light flamed.

On Sunday, following a Saturday wedding, the cafe's owner had brought in the flowers from the event. The vase was full of tall, yellow tulips. I brought one home and placed in a vase of water. I'm astonished to see that it still lives. At night, it bows its beautiful golden head to sleep, and reaches up towards the light at daybreak.

Sometime later, when, as usual, my "project" enthusiasm had ebbed with the realization that I didn't have the financial means to develop the cards, I received a note in the mail. "I think you need to read this," my niece, Tambra, had written. Inside was a copy of my own *if only...* poem.

If there is anything we learn by growing up or older, it is that we could have achieved our dreams, if only...

If only...we'd known that a dream can be so big as to elude us but that every dream can be managed in cat nips and cat naps, one step back, one step forward and a little bit of help from our friends.

If only...we'd known the way to begin a thing is not at the beginning, but rather with the solution.

76

If only...we'd known that life is a game to be played joyfully, with rules that could be learned and skills made our own; like learning to skate, or 2 plus 2, or "I can write my name!" and that living had its rules and we could learn them before life taught us a lesson.

If only...we'd known that it was o.k. to ginger-paint a sky green, have a secret dream, or trade sandwiches with a new kid in town; that growing up wasn't supposed to be about being the right sex or shape or shade or age, or making a living or having stuff, but that growing up was supposed to be just about being.

If only we'd been taught that we had gifts and talents which were built in, like the color of our eyes and fingerprints and by honoring these, we would honor ourselves, inspire others, and heal the earth.

If only we'd known that we could be practical and idealistic, logical and artistic, individualistic and caring, all at the same time, all in the same package, a special concoction of humanity that has no age and is never too young nor too old.

If only we'd known about love, then, like forgiving our folks and getting off our own backs, and loving life enough to fill our days with laughter, and unashamed hugs and tears. If only we'd known that!

And if only we'd known that going straight ahead is not always the best route; that tangential thinking often leads to the rainbow, our skies would have been as full of color as a box of crayons.

If only we'd known that people who'd already achieved what we admired would be as open as the public library if we'd

77

just ask, and that if we each shared what we knew, everybody would learn to fish.

If only we'd known that we could change our thoughts and attitudes, our words and moods as easily as we change our socks and more often.

If only we'd discovered that we didn't have to know it all, then or now and like shining galaxies we'd go on harmoniously learning, correcting, expanding forever

If only we'd known we're uniquely unique in the universe and the same Life that created us will continue to guide us, each by our own star. If only we'd known that!

And as for growing up and older, if only we'd known that life could be about saying "what if," and not "if only." But now that we know, what if we told the world?

There were many bridges, I thought, which one must build, and cross, in the process of transition. I came across a meditative note I'd written sometime earlier. I had closed my eyes to meditate, and unable to concentrate, turned to paper and pen.

I am standing in a desert place. I reach down and pick up a stone. There is writing on the stone, which says that although I have been alone, and have sought my happiness in going from person to person, place to place, group to group, I will find my happiness by looking within.

The stone becomes a golden egg. The egg cracks open, an a small, brilliant blue bird flies out, bidding me to follow. I approach a pond, which seems to be made of air. Floating on the pond are hundreds of brilliant blue books, with titles in gold.

78

People come eagerly to the pond and pick up the books, pressing them to their breasts like found treasures.

When all the books are gone, I reach into the pond and scoop up a handful of sand. When I raise my hand, the sand, now pure grains of gold, flow through my fingers.

The yellow tulip that I'd kept in my room for a week, finally began to drop its leaves. I took it out to my "forest" this morning, and dropped the petals into the waterfall of the stream, offering each petal as a prayer, for my writing, my family, the earth. It was a lovely ritual. It made the busy harshness of the crowded restaurant almost bearable today.

It is March, 1995, and I've finished another poem, *Dare to Dream* and updated two stories for children that I'd written in the sixties, *Old Dumpling*, and *Shmadiggle,* and I continue to try to find ways to market my little book-card poems.

I find myself wishing for a sometime companion too, but for now, consign that wish to the same dream wishing-well that holds my own cozy home and waking up in the morning with enthusiasm for the day of creativity ahead

Meanwhile, I'm grateful for being here, rent-free with my sister and brother-in-law, their acceptance of my "leave me alone" lifestyle, which actually fits in with their own lives, the gift of the use of John's word processor, and my woods in back of the house. Even my work at the restaurant, with it's beautiful sea-view, has become   endurable.

So much rain. Am I the only one who doesn't mind? But another tree in "my forest," in back of the apartment property, fell, uprooted by the raging stream and wind of this real storm. One of the senior residents, accompanied by her shaggy little dog dressed in his red raincoat, placed a left over holiday wreath on the tree.

I've finished another poem and readied it for card production" "saying goodbye." And I've revised a book proposal

79

and sent it off to a publishing company that accepts direct submissions. I should be happy. But I am not.

Perhaps it is so much time spent getting the card production going, and not so much time writing, with the exception of the poems.

Perhaps it is the expectation, always an expectation not realized, of having my work accepted in a way that provides me an income allowing me some independence.

Perhaps, probably, I am lonely. But not able to "relate" to relationship, my aloneness seems to be the safer way.

Leytha, are you there?

Claudia, I am as close as your breath. Your discontent is caused by expecting too much of yourself, and mal-nurturing yourself rather than nurturing.

You need to give yourself credit for beginning, following through, correcting, improving, being patient, and being willing to expose yourself, and your creations to others as you have done.

You've received enough feedback to know that your idea is good and that people are reacting to it in a positive way. But even when fame and fortune come as a result, you will be unhappy unless you acknowledge yourself.

And you know that you are denying yourself socially, feeling unlovely and unlovable, but you must take a risk here too, just as you have in the past. It is time to move on with your life. Your recovery period is complete.

Now is the time of your life. Now is the time to live, to love, to laugh, to share, to be, to become. Risk. In risking you will overcome fear, and soon you will be living your dream fully.

I keep trying to come up with ways to bring in an income from the card business. But when I come home from a day of waitressing, I am both so tired, in physical pain, and at a low self-esteem ebb, that it is difficult to proceed. I miss the hours and hours spent writing, but still am getting in a few lines here and there which will eventually add up to more poems for the little book-cards.

All I want is some reasonable income, so that I can keep writing, and have my own place, the fireplace, the trees, a garden, and a little time off now and again to walk the planet.

I've tried, despite my fatigue, to nurture the artist in me, and have spent time at the library looking through art history books, and bought season tickets for some musical performances at the Marin auditorium: American Indian Dance Theater, the Irish Rovers and a men's choral group from Russia.

The reading banquet table at which I was gorging my mind and soul the past few months has, recently, seemed to have nothing on it but empty plates. But yesterday, wanting to swim in someone else's thoughts, I took Ray Bradbury's *Zen and Writing*, off the shelf. To not write daily is to die, he says.

I find myself grumpy though, and feeling frumpy, and sad. Only when I sit, stringing alphabet beads into words on the computer screen, am I, if not happy, content. I have decided, (I, who've never bought a piece of *real* jewelry in my life), am going to put a gold bracelet on layaway. Perhaps one day I'll be able to buy a little charm to represent each published work.

Driving home exhausted after work this afternoon, hemmed in by commuter traffic now further harassed by hail and gusty rain, I looked off to my right, below the freeway, and saw, for the first time in my life, a rainbow touching the ground. It seemed to grow right out of the marsh. I looked through the gauzy strips of color, and, the trees, hillsides, houses, were paler and multi-hued.

Cars were slowed almost to a halt, from the usual traffic jam, and the storm. Perhaps the drivers were also staring in awe at the incredible painting in the sky.

Glancing as far back as I could and still focus on my driving, I could see the bow had formed a perfect 180 degree arc up out of the marsh, diving down on the other side of the sky, into the center of the bay. Suddenly I felt the words, "I love you..." surge into my mind and my fatigue fled in an instant.

I felt like laughing, wanting to jump out of my car and dance towards the rainbow. I caught one last glimpse of the colored   arc   before   the   freeway   made   a   sharp   curve.

"I know...," I said aloud, turning away from the gift of sun and rain and sky, to watch the bumper to bumper traffic ahead of me. "I know. I love You too."

7

Those shadowy recollections,
Which, be they what they may
Are yet a master-light of all our seeing...
Our souls have sight of that immortal sea
Which brought us hither;
Can is a moment travel thither.
Ode on Intimations of Immortality
~William Wordsworth

It was the fall of 1995. I had come to the point that I knew, like the proverbial frog who hopped into a pot of cream, I could not get "out" of where I was without a helping hand, or a big dipper of helpful insight.

I placed a tape of Glenn Miller in my car cassette player. For all these years I've loved big band music and had never bought a single record or tape. My sister would say I was beginning to "think pink" in beginning to nourish my self, and my soul. I drove towards Fairfax, a little town nestled at the foot of tree covered hills. The reds and golds of falling leaves, the narrow main street and small non-franchised shops transport one out of California and into a some small New Hampshire town. I seemed to be a planet away from the barren, potholed streets of Tijuana, but I wondered how far I had come in terms of listening to my own voice. I parked my car, walked down the quaint main street and stepped into a small cafe for coffee. In half an hour I'd be meeting with Claire, an art therapist to whom I been drawn initially after seeing a flyer announcing her "Women's Circle" group.

If I were to follow the inner guidance I'd been receiving, I knew it was time to deal with whatever obstacles were holding me back from manifesting my "Litheria" self. Now, I had doubts about being able, I who had never had a woman friend, to accept the gift of personal power in the midst of a group of women. I felt the way an untrained climber might, on arriving at the foot of Mt Everest. Still, it was something I had to do.

I was, however, scarcely prepared for the multidimensional world I was about to enter, or for the synchronicity which would, along the way, introduce to me to the works of authors Sandra Ingerman, *Soul Retrieval*, and Jamie Sams, *The 13 Original Clan Mothers*.

In my inner-visioning journeys, I had met guides, both amusing and profound, in a mental conference room. I had undertaken hypnotic time travel to explore past lives. I had crossed a bridge into a magical, mythical world peopled by ancient wise beings. And I had gone, in memory, to a favorite childhood haunt where, in my imagination I would meet a loveable power animal.

These experiences, were quietly healing my fragmented life. I was eager to participate in a non-writing method of getting in touch with my Self, but nervous about the acting out process.

Claire welcomed me into her cozy studio, offering me the option of sitting on the floor, or on a comfy palette, or stretching out on the couch. I immediately felt comfortable with her. She seemed to be a tall, solitary tree with deep roots reaching down into underground springs. Long brown hair framed her face like a weeping willow, her eyes wide, intense, and inquiring. She seemed to be asking questions even when saying nothing. Her voice, soft, with an undercurrent of woundedness that rendered her incapable, I suspect, of ever hurting anyone.

I took the big drawing pad she handed me and settled on the couch. I was to begin, she directed, by relaxing, then using any of the pastel coloring sticks which appealed to me to paint a picture of my energy pattern.

If I were uncomfortable with her sitting opposite me, she suggested, she could busy herself at her desk. I indicated I'd be happy to have her as witness, as one of the reasons I wanted to do these session was to make connection with myself as a woman, and with other women. I'd only known myself, I'd finally realized, as mirrored in a man's eyes, or when lost in books or writing, or in days filled with anxiety. She asked if I'd like to clear anything first.

"I feel like I'm at a doorway looking through, but can't quite get to the other side, to being where I want to be with my life," I paused. How could I put this concisely and not take up all the time talking? I wanted to be open to a new experience here. "What I'd like to do is get in touch with myself, and in the process, perhaps dissolve some of the blocks which may be still holding me back."

Claire agreed and quietly suggested I stay tuned to my inner voice as I selected pastel drawing sticks, and make a drawing of my energy pattern. After about 15 minutes, the drawing emerged, an abstract, feather stroked, varicolored pastel with no particular pattern nor meaning to me. Claire then asked me to identify the various parts of the drawing. While the form before me was abstract, my inner self seemed to be comfortable with the pastel shades and forms. As I spoke, Claire took notes.

The brown feathered outer rim of the drawing represented earthiness, I told her. The sharp, arrow-like y shape in the center was definitely the pain I've been feeling in my chest area, and in the center of my shoulder blades. "It feels like an area of expression too," I mused, "of my voice, that I'm holding back, choking it off."

The top of the drawing was open, blue, wing-like. The bottom, gray enclosing a white void...emptiness. Bright golden yellow surged from the blue wings, indicating the guidance I'm receiving from the spirit. The center of the drawing was divided by wavy green sea, and seemed to me to represent nature, and a way to connect the upper and lower portions of my body, and the spiritual, physical aspects of my life.

Claire summed up my comments: green for me meant nature; blue, healing inspiration; yellow gold, pure joy; red, pain; pink, brown—love, nurturing and earthiness; gray, my memory, lack of memory, the unknown; the white center in the midst of the gray circle—what I can't get in contact with, space, things to come. And the pale blue at the bottom of the drawing...cold, part of memory, wants to anchor but only floating there.

Claire suggested I might take a more comfortable position on the pallet on the floor, where she would guide me in an inner vision to explore some of the drawing. I did not like sitting on the floor, but did so, by leaning against the sofa. I was drawn immediately to the red sharply pointed arrows at the center of the drawing.

Curious to explore the source of this pain, I closed my eyes and saw an enormous red neon letter Y against a vast sky of black. I am at the foot of it, no bigger than an ant, a small child, dressed in buckskin - like bulky clothing, looking up at the Y with awe. I am lost, but not scared or alone. The image reminded me of one of the "life" regressions I had experienced with Mary. The neon Y is surrounded by a pulsing yellow light.

Claire asked me to be aware of smells or tastes. I smelled the outdoors, as if I were in the mountains. In response to Claire's question, I answered that the Y seemed to be the question "why?," and was also the first letter of the word "You," referring to myself.

Going back to the inner place, I envisioned the gray of the drawing, and found myself inside a small cave, shaped like an egg with knobby protrusions and a flat floor. It was dark except for

86

light coming from the small opening. I could hear a roaring like the ocean. I sat in the middle of the cave, but my "self" kept changing, flitting back and forth between a fairy like creature, and finally the substance of an Indian maiden or princess. The cave was a safe place, and I was there meditating.

"What does your guidance tell you about the cave and your experience there?" Claire asked, as I continued in the inner place.

"The cave is alive," I explained, "and it is there to protect me." I saw myself getting bigger, still the Indian maiden, but so tall now I was bending over. "As I grow," I continued, "the cave won't be big enough for me. It's time for me to leave the cave. It's a place I love, but it's time to move on." Suddenly, I had a realization: that my lack of memory for the past was a protection against the pain of childhood, and that, if I chose, I no longer needed this protection.

I was pleased with the images I was experiencing. It felt awkward to express them to someone else, as I had done with the reincarnation experiences, but I felt that Claire, too, was giving me the gift of listening, or witnessing, as she put it.

There was time to look at one more aspect of the energy drawing, and I was attracted to the streams of golden yellow at the top of the picture.

"Go into that inner place," Claire directed softly, "and see the golden yellow light growing and growing, then step into it."

I saw myself in a shimmering bubble floating and spinning in a river of light. I felt happy, a kid's happiness. Suddenly my eyes popped open.

"What was that about?" Claire asked. "What happened?"

"The bubble burst. There was light all over the place and no place for me to be," I explained, not really understanding.

"Can you go back there?" Claire asked, "And tell me what you feel?"

I turned back to the vision, but the little figure me felt numb, floating and whirling around, but with no feeling.

"Do you hear anything?" Claire asked.

"A music box."

"What is it playing?"

I laughed. Of course. "A Bird in a Gilded Cage," wondering at how this Gay 90's song had popped into my head.

"What does your guidance tell you about this?" Claire suggested.

I waited. I do not "hear" guidance as clearly, as when I can write it, but the impression came forth that when I feel joy I feel disconnected and vulnerable. I tend to want to put bubbles or cages around me in order to feel comfortable. I want to experience joy, but it is outside of me.

Another client knocked at the door, and I hurried to put my tennis shoes back on. I felt refreshed and was already looking forward to the next session. Claire suggested I continue to work with, meditate on these images and ask for guidance from my guides, higher self or Holy Spirit.

Outside, the fall air was swirling with dancing leaves. I pulled a sweater from my car, wrapped a scarf around my neck then walked back to a funky little cafe featuring Greek food and rock and roll music. Between mouthfuls of humus, feta cheese and stuffed grape leaves, I quickly made notes of my hour's experience, then asked:

Higher Self: You know the meanings of these symbols, and how they relate to my life. What is the meaning and significance of the red neon letter Y?

The letter represents a "letter" to YOU from your self. You are in awe of the grown-up You and see the responsibilities and pain of adulthood as awesome.

Thank you, but how does this relate to the pain in my chest, esophagus?

88

You need to give care and healing to your throat, breathing, stomach, through breathing, and nutrition.

You need to place yourself in a learning environment which will enable you to give expression to your voice.

Thank you, I said, not really liking the tone my "guide" was taking. What else would you have me know about this inner vision?

The neon red sign represents the city to you, a child of buckskins, mountains, and the enormous night sky. You are in awe of the city. The Y also represents YES to you, that you need to learn the city ways, the ways of business, which of course seem overwhelming to a child, especially a child of nature.

This conflict causes you pain, physical pain. We suggest you continue to bring your life out of stressful situations and into the natural environment. From this place, you can do the business required of the adult You, but with the same peace, comfort, sense of awe and wonder as the child You.

Higher Self: What is the message of the grey, memory, egg cave symbol and its application to my life?

It is time to come out your shell-memory, the past. Like the surrounding membrane of the egg, it was there to nurture, protect the past, but you are yearning to live fully in the present and this necessitates coming out of the safe womb of memory which has kept you, protected you.

You saw a void, a space in your drawing because you are no longer in the cave. You have come out, but when you feel

89

threatened you want to go back there. But as you can see, the light, the joy, is outside the cave. Memory plays no role there.

To experience the joy of light and being in present time, you have to look at memory and your memory blocking as functions which protected you. But now, as a full-fledged huntress (this is why you were meditating as an Indian princess so that you might receive power for the hunt, to fulfill your role in life), you may clothe yourself in the power of light, rather than stay in the cave of memory.

I understand this, but how can I utilize this message in the area of generating income from what I love to do? God! This plea is becoming obnoxious to me! Why can't I see clearly other options?

These symbols relate your need to "come out" from the past and, as the adult Indian huntress, to not only join the hunt, but lead the hunt. The "kill" will not come to the door of your cave and lie down and say "here I am", your income. You need to look at how prepared how fortified you are, and when you have determined, realized this, and you are clothed in power, go out.

Thank you. Now, please tell me the significance of the golden yellow colors, the river of light and the bubble vision.

You feel guilty about being happy. Again this comes from the past, and will be resolved by the end of these sessions. You can look at the bubble or golden cage in a positive way by seeing them as contexts within which you experience joy in your creative endeavors.

Yes, thank you. But how do I apply this to my life and my current desire to earn a living from my creative endeavors?

Well, you can stay in the bubble and be surrounded by joy, or you can merge with joy. Or you can be content with confinement within the golden cage where you sing, but feel you are safe. The choices are yours. How much happiness can you accept?

If you choose merging with joy, then you'll have to give up outmoded ways of thinking that have kept joy flowing around you, but not touching you. Be gentle here. The Light loves you. You've been bobbing, swirling in that river of joy for a long time now. When you are ready you can merge with the light. It is ready for you.

My physical and emotional health suffered more and more each day I spend waitressing, some eight to nine hours without resting or eating. I needed to know what to do now, tomorrow, this week. I called on Leytha, but was surprised to sense the impression of a group experience:

To Litheria we say that your path is becoming illumined and you will begin to walk in the experiences you now see in the light. Extend this energy to your identity as Claudia and bring her into the light. She feels abandoned in the harshness of the earth plane.

We have guided, inspired, protected your earth plane personality, but now it is you, Litheria who must take the final steps. You must reach out with unlimited, boundless love and mercy and take the personality Claudia into the realm of light so she may merge with you and no longer feel terrible loneliness and alienation.

We suggest you do this, Litheria, by entering the dream plane of the soul, to prepare the personality for this merger, but to utilize the healing atmosphere of ritual to bring this personality

91

into oneness with the spirit. This process will be empowered by the Holy Spirit, who oversees us all, and to whom we are in obedience for eternity.

We suggest the personality Claudia accept our guidance to go to a place of ritual where the presence of the Holy Spirit is sought and received and respected, and receive this healing of personality and merger with the spirit which is Litheria.

The day after another session with Claire, I'd taken the ferry to San Francisco. I found a small cafe in Chinatown, managed the slippery noodles with my chopsticks, and pulled Sandra Ingerman's *Soul Retrieval* out of my bag. I sipped my glass of lukewarm tea to soothe the ever present pain in my throat, and opened the book, noting she suggested that an isolated pain could be the caused by a spirit "intrusion."

Immediately an image of my little cat Chickiada came to my mind. She had loved to sleep in the curve of my shoulder laying her head across my throat.

When my sister and brother-in-law, and my daughter had come to move me from Tijuana, we'd returned from lunch to find my little kitten, Chickiada, curled up under the sink, weak and ill. I thought she might have been hit by a car, or eaten some poisoned food, as it was common for people to kill stray animals in the street that way.

My daughter had stroked her tearfully, having such a heart for cats, telling her she would live. But the kitten had died. Unwilling to put her in a garbage bag, we had made a little coffin out of a shoe box, and buried her in a vacant lot.

When we drove away from the house, I was full of grief, for the loss of a relationship, and the loss of my little house and one more writer ex-pat dream, and the loss of my kitten. Now, I actually felt her presence!

"Chickiada! You've come with me!" I exclaimed silently, pressing my hand at my throat. I'd almost said it aloud.

I paid my check and walked down the street looking for a blue crystal to keep in my room to remind me of the vision I'd had about a place of inner healing, and stopped in front of a small antique shop to consider a blue alabaster egg, and found myself having to hush Chickiada's insistent spirit, rubbing at the pain in my throat and chest.

"Shh, little spirit," I whispered inwardly."When we get home, I'll take you to a wonderful place where you'll be happy." How she would have loved the woods in back of my sister's apartment building.

The previous day, I'd wakened exhausted from a weekend of waitressing, but looked forward to an intense afternoon session with Claire.

Despite my misgivings that there was "really anything there," in the rather abstract pastel drawn "energy map" I'd drawn during the first session. I followed Claire's direction, and focused on the drawing until one of the areas seemed most important. I kept resisting the impulse to consider the the horizontal brown swipes on both sides of the bottom of the drawing, finally realizing that this was the area I must deal with next.

"Make the image as big as possible in your mind," Claire said, "so that you can just step into it."

I wondered whether there was enough substance in these brown scribbles to discover anything. Still, I closed my eyes, and let the brown swipes fill up my innervision. Claire asked me to step into the brown area, and tell her where I was.

At first I couldn't define the space. The sides of were soft, but ribbed like corrugated tin. When Claire asked what I heard, it seemed there was the roaring of a great wind, coming from outside.

"I'm inside a tornado," I concluded at last. "It is quiet inside. The sides are warm, and alive, but outside the wind is roaring violently."

"Can you see yourself?" Claire asked. "How old are you?"

It was hard to tell. I felt very small, suspended somehow at the bottom of the tornado. As I looked up, I seemed to grow a bit. It seemed as if I were twelve or thirteen. Not at all an unusual age to feel caught up in a tornado, I thought.

Claire asked what I was doing.

"I have my hands against the walls, trying to maintain some balance. I feel," I continued, in response to another question, "...a kind of 'wow!' feeling. Like I'd found myself on some wild carnival ride.... I'm wondering, gosh! How did I get in here?" I sensed the tornado was moving across the land, but somehow I'm safe inside.

"What does your guidance tell you?" Claire asked.

I waited a moment, wishing I could write my journey, rather than describe it, as verbalizing anything, is clearly much more difficult for me, and speaking seems to put a kind of stop-action on the inner movie.

"I see a ladder that leads to the top of the tornado," I said, finally. "There's a light at the top...I'm impressed that I can climb out if I want to." I paused and considered this option. I felt too tired to climb. "For now, it seems too far to climb...I'm going to sit down and read a book...As I do this, the tornado dissipates...I'm sitting on the ground...under a tree, reading my book."

"When you are ready," Claire guided, "open your eyes, and look back at your drawing. Tell me what this now symbolizes to you."

It took a moment to come back. I looked again at the brown pastel swipes at the bottom of my map. "Disturbing energy in my environment, Claire," I said.

The brown tornadoes were on each side of the gray, empty circle I had designated as my memory. "It's energy outside of my memory, a very tempestuous period of my life. But I found a way to be in the center of it, rather than be destroyed by it."

I knew, though I did not express it, that the single saving grace during those ghastly days of adolescence and emerging young womanhood, had been my books. Later, on reflection, I wondered if perhaps both the "cave" experience, and the "tornado" experience had been pre-birth ones.

In my drawing, the center of the energy map is both dissected and connected by a waving green river, which represents the connective energy of nature for me. Again, I found myself questioning whether I'd find anything here.

Soon after closing my eyes, and letting the green waves fill my inner room, I found myself inside a single cell of a gigantic leaf. I sensed a breeze blowing, rocking us, the leaf and me, gently. I felt us assimilating, breathing in the sunlight. I could feel the sunlight pulsing through the veins of the leaf.

"You are within a cell of the leaf," Claire acknowledged. "What do you look like?"

I could not see myself as a body. "I'm just a glow, a tiny little presence within the leaf...I've come here to visit."

"What do you feel?" Claire asked.

I looked out from the transparent cell of the leaf. "Joy. Absolute joy!"

"And why are you there, within the leaf cell?" Claire asked. "What is the purpose of your 'visit'?"

I laughed. "I'm a dewdrop...My purpose is to be assimilated by the leaf and go into all the parts."

It was a joyful vision, but when Claire asked me to looked again at the scalloped waves on my treasure map, I was left without much insight.

"I can't really tell what it symbolizes, Claire. It seems something wants to be expressed, but won't come through."

At the very bottom of the energy map, somewhat intruding into the dark memory circle, were some vertical blue lines which seemed to me to be the feet of the drawing. They felt cold, some part of memory. As I entered the massive cold blue in my innervision, I sensed I was outside of a glacier. I saw an entrance, a crevice, and moved into it. The sides of the glacier were alive, warm to the touch. I continue going further, and seemed to be looking for something.

"There seems to be a room off in the distance," I said aloud. "In the middle of the room...is a blue orb...It is small like a marble... As I pick it up, it grows. I can hold it in the palm of my hand."

I began to feel wonderful here. I was inside the glacier room, but it was warm, and glowing. Music, like the sound of flutes and harps and glass chimes seemed to emanate from the living walls. I could smell gardenias everywhere, and taste lemon drops.

The blue orb began to glow, and seemed to send out vibrations of love and healing. I felt absolute joy, as though I were surrounded by pure waves of love energy. I felt tears come to my eyes.

The music and joy of the orb seemed to enter my body as well as surround it, and I, a graceful spirit being, raised the glowing orb over my head and danced. When there was nothing else I could say, Claire suggested I ask my guidance for an interpretation.

"This is a place I can come to, to experience the gift of healing." I responded easily.

"And looking again at your drawing," Claire directed, "what does it now symbolize to you?"

The blue lines at the bottom of the drawing had seemed so insignificant at first. Now, I saw them as pointing the way to a deeper, more eternal place of memory, where I could encounter my real self. There was time for one more journey, and I had no choice but to turn to the white, empty space within the gray memory circle.

I did not want to go there. I closed my eyes, with Claire's words of guidance that the experience would be safe. Immediately, I saw a blinding white light, like a huge searchlight in front of me, moving wildly about, as if trying to find, or illuminate something.

I glimpsed the edge of a white staircase against the side of building, and opened my eyes abruptly, shaking my head "no!", and holding my hands tightly against the pain in my diaphragm.

"I felt as if my life were threatened," I told Claire.

"What does your guidance tell you," she asked gently.

I looked, listened. A blank. Nothing. Turned off. I could not recall a single life-threatening instance as a child, though one may have happened that was worse than than those that happened as I grew older. Of course I knew that I could have closed off this memory room in order to live in present day time, without the constant intrusion of the physical violence, and verbal abuse I had experienced throughout my life.

Reflecting later, I sensed this was my real birth experience, that of a Caesarian birth, where the bright lights, and white "staircase" of the gloved hands and cloaked figures were lifting me out. Such an experience would indeed seem threatening to a new being who'd prepared for nine months for a different entrance to the planet.

I was drawn back to Claire's words. "You can use the blue orb from your healing place to fill up the painful space in your diaphragm, and to heal your memories. Would you like to do that now?"

I closed my eyes and let the blue orb, glowing, warm, alive, enter my diaphragm, and the pain dissolved. I allowed it to float upward through my body and into the space in my mind where the closed memory vault was located and allowed it to fill up the whole space with glowing blue, healing light.

"Can you ask your guidance for a way to ground you, so that this experience helps you in your daily life?"

97

I laughed, opening my eyes. "I saw myself 'grounded,' wearing fluffy, blue teddy bear shoes.

The afternoon that I got home from San Francisco, I took my little spirit kitten into the wooded space behind the apartment building, opened my arms and let her leap happily onto the branches of a tree. How I wished that someone could take me in loving arms and release me into my "forever" place!

The previous session with Claire had been so intense, I'd put the energy map and Claire's notes away for the week, and had not explored them further. I was, instead, preoccupied with a book my sister Rosalie, had given me, Sandra Ingerman's *Soul Retrieval.*

My sister's chiropractic practitioner had recommended the book to her, and she'd scanned the contents. Opening to a page listing the probable symptoms of soul loss, or fragmented soul, she read, she said, a perfect description of conditions *I* had struggled with all my life.

Rosalie hugged me and handed me the book. "This," she said, all too familiar with hearing me say 'I can't remember,' "was obviously meant to be given to you." I read the book in two days. As I followed along with Sandra's reported shamanic journeys, I intensely felt parts of my "self" crying out to me.

I seemed to have a sudden understanding of traumatic happenings in my childhood. I knew, suddenly, that somehow a part of my soul had fled from during the trauma of my caesarian birth. The tiny girl soul of me, plagued by whooping cough and tonsillitis, and impetigo, chicken pox, and severe colds, had fled during a tonsillectomy at age two. My six year old soul, terrified at the funeral ritual for my mother, got caught in a dark, nightmarish underworld where I would forever be afraid of going down stairs.

In her book, Sandra cautioned that it was difficult to conduct a soul retrieval for oneself. And with the exception of reading her book, *Soul Retrieval*, it was true I knew nothing of the ritual, the drumming, the rattle, or the various realms in which these soul parts might have hidden or in which they might be trapped.

Still, I'd already traveled to inner-visioned conference rooms, talked with ancient wise ones, and received guidance from the world of spirit. I would just ask my guides for protection, and take my Bear Hug power animal along.

I had met my big bear friend on an inner journey to a forest area outside a mountain camp I had attended one summer as child. She'd come, she said, because she sensed I was lonely, and needed someone to play with.

Sometimes, Bear Hug was a powerful grizzly, other times, just a friendly brown bear, or maybe a polar bear. She always chose just the right manifestation. I knew Bear Hug was the perfect companion for my soul journey.

I closed Sandra's book and closed my eyes. I found myself in the midst of a dark forest. Together Bear Hug and I began to explore the area. Almost immediately, I became aware of a fairy like presence. The baby soul saw us and immediately jumped into Bear Hug's arms.

"Claudia has come to bring you home," Bear Hug said.

"I don't want to go with Claudia," the glowing little one protested, shaking her head. "It's not safe."

"But it is safe now, little soul." I tried reassuring her. "I'm an adult now. You don't have to be afraid any longer."

"But she's not strong enough to care for me," the tiny soul said to Bear Hug, ignoring me.

"That's because I'm missing parts of my soul," I told her gently. "I need you to come back and live with me. Together we'll be strong."

"She'll come with us," Bear Hug told me, sensing her willingness. "I'll carry her, while we continue our journey."

We walked deeper into the forest. It was darker here, but not frightening; lonely rather. We soon discovered the two year old soul in a tree, clinging tightly to one of the branches. When she saw us, she recognized her baby soul, and they both laughed happily, reaching towards one another. Bear Hug handed me my baby soul, and reached for the two year old.

"I've been lost here for so long," she said. She fell asleep in Bear Hug's arms, then took the baby soul from me, cuddling both into the protective folds of her furry coat, and we continued our journey.

The scene changed and we were inside a house. I felt frightened, anxious. We went to a doorway, and down the stairs to a dark catacombs. The six year old was curled up asleep on the top of a coffin. My heart cried out to see her here in this nightmare world which had visited me in night-dreams for years after the death of my mother. I lit a candle, and Bear Hug scooped the child soul into her warm, huge arms.

In an instant I was aware of being in my bed. I breathed deeply, three times, asking each of my soul children to return to me and be safe, and whole. "Welcome home," I said aloud, following Sandra's advice, and almost immediately fell asleep.

"Something definitely happened," I told Claire as I reviewed the experience with her before our next session began. "I feel as if the space inside my mind has expanded." I searched for words, "Feels fuller somehow, more complete. And my voice is stronger," I laughed, knowing how that would please so many people who'd been irritated by my soft, quiet voice.

On the way to Claire's office, I'd stopped in a toy shop, in hopes of finding a small fluffy stuffed bear I could hug while I embarked on a memory void exploration. I found nothing I liked or could afford, and went on to my appointment.

Then, inside Claire's office, waiting as she finished a phone call, I turned to see a loveable pink stuffed bear perched on the back of the couch. Claire said the bear had been there during the previous sessions, but I had not noticed. I hugged it me, where it stayed for the whole hour's journeying.

100

Already my energy map seemed to have changed, or perhaps it has brought about change. "But, I sense that my body still wants attention," I told Claire, "so that I will not be limited by pain, or by reactions which cause pain."

I would still have to deal with memory. Even now, my stomach aches with anxiety each time I try to imagine a non-waitress, unlimited financial and professional future. I am tied to my poverty by unforgiving memories of the way it was being the way it must always be.

"Can you name your energy map?" Claire asked.

I looked at the feathery wings at the top and sides of the drawing, the heart shape of the memory void. "Heartwings," I answered.

My final session with Claire, our fourth, was to be an acting out of the previous three sessions' innervisioning impressions. She asked me to consider one aspect of the pastel drawing energy map, and again, let it become as large as possible in my inner theater.

I looked over the abstract scribbles. Even after three previous session I still wondered that there was anything of substance here to deal with. I kept returning to the pink, which indicated self-nurturing for me. Claire said that this "acting out of the pink," would bring in the other aspects of the drawing as well. I was scarcely prepared for the profound experience which would follow.

I closed my eyes, and saw the pink color growing until it became a large blanket, my "baby blanket" actually, but now adult sized. I stood in the midst of a clearing in the woods, with the blanket wrapped around me.

"Who are you, and where are you, wrapped in this pink blanket?" Claire asked.

"I seem to be standing in the center of a circle of stones." All was quiet in my mind. I seemed to need Claire's prompting to describe aloud what was happening, to continue."A ceremony is

101

about to begin," I concluded, as the impression came to me. "And I'm waiting....waiting for my power to come." I searched the darkness. "I...have a feeling of becoming."

Claire asked me to hold that vision, and to open my eyes, and find a place in the center of her small office where I could enact what was occurring. I felt awkward, much preferring to sit, but at the same time reminded myself that it was this very discomfort, this reluctance to stand in my place of power, that I wanted to overcome.

Claire offered me a Mexican blanket woven in blues and pinks. I draped it around me in the fashion I saw in my vision and closed my eyes. I seemed to be standing in a circle surrounded now by Native American wise-women.

"One of the women," I said hesitantly, sudden tears coming to my eyes, "is bringing a bundle of... something like kindling wood." I felt my throat constrict, and began to cry. There was little acting out I could do. In the vision, I simply stood tall, waiting, as the ceremony progressed. "The woman wearing a blanket of stars...she is called Starwoman," I stammered, unable to stop crying.

Finally I could speak again. "She is placing the bundle of kindling at my feet. It is becoming a fire....a blue fire...I am becoming the fire... becoming taller and taller as the fire...a single blue flame...it's night time....the flame is reaching....I am reaching all the way from earth to the sky." As I reached for the sky, I dropped my blanket in real time. Several minutes seemed to have passed as I experienced being the flame.

"The flame is coming back down... I am coming back down to earth...I feel myself planted...firmly...on the earth...on the ground...but very strong now. The fire is gone."

"And what do you hear, or smell, around you?" Claire asked quietly.

I smelled pine trees. I heard the sound of humming, a monotone, many voices humming. "Another woman comes now,"

I reported to Claire, looking across the circle to the ancient grandmother next to Starwoman. "She wears a blanket of deep, forest green and carries a gourd of water." I saw the wise-woman dip her fingers into the water and touch my eyelids. "She says....she says..." Again I cry, trying to continue. "She says the tears that I cry in the future will be tears of intercession for others."

Claire interrupted quietly, and suggested that I allow her to take my place, and that I become Starwoman, so that I might experience all that Starwoman had to offer me. I felt extremely embarrassed doing this acting out, but knew that the embarrassment was something that was holding me back in life.

There was a basket of dried flowers in a corner of the room, and I picked up a sheaf of dried Indian corn to use as the bundle of kindling. When the enactment was complete, I felt impressed to use the sheaf of corn to brush away the ashes at the feet of Claire (as me), and send them to the four winds.

We exchanged positions. Claire became the Starwoman presenting me with the bundle of kindling. I felt too self-conscious to experience anything at all, but Claire said this was O.K., that the acting out was just a way of solidifying the inner experience.

When I returned again to the inner vision, Claire asked why I had dropped my blanket. I looked down and saw the blanket on the ground at my feet. "I do not need the blanket now," I said. "When I became the flame, I dropped the blanket...The warmth I needed from the blanket is no longer necessary." I had felt cold, actually, and seemed to be looking back on my life, vulnerable, transparent even. As though everyone could see through me. I needed to wrap myself in the blanket to have some substance.

"The flame is inside of me now," I realized, feeling the warmth in my diaphragm. "The warmth comes from inside of me." I looked up and saw Starwoman rise above the clearing and return to the sky. "Night is going," I said. "The dawn is coming." I knew

103

our time was drawing to a close and I was reluctant to leave the clearing, feeling so much more was to be given me.

My inner-vision resolved the conflict."The wise-women are becoming a circle of trees," I told Claire, with surprise and deep appreciation. "They've left their gifts at the foot of the trees...I can go to the trees anytime and receive their gifts."

"And where are you now?" Claire asked, "now that the wisewomen have become trees and left their gifts for you?"

I stood in the midst of the clearing as the sun began to rise. I felt a sense of peace, and joyful power. "It's strange. I...I feel as if I've been initiated...accepted into this circle of women." The thought flashed in my mind that my original intention had been to participate with a group of women in Claire's "Women's Circle" workshop, but could not due to time and money.

"What does your guidance tell you about this place? This experience? Do you leave there?"

The thought crossed my mind at how similar Claire's questions were to those of Mary. I searched the clearing, and watched the early dawn cast light beams through the trees. "I am reluctant to leave this place," I said, longing to be there in real world. "I'm not sure what I'll encounter when I leave here...I have to leave here alone...but I'm leaving clothed in power...still, I sense the unknown...I feel I've been initiated with my power...but what to do with it?"

"And what do you hear? Do the women tell you something? The trees?"

I listened and heard happy giggles surrounding me. "The women are laughing...like...like happy children. They are telling me...just to be... be who I am."

Claire's next appointment was waiting. I thanked her, still wiping tears from my eyes. I hurried out and drove straight to a bookstore. Perhaps I would find something in the section on Native

American beliefs which would explain my rather remarkable inner vision.

I scanned the shelf, and put my hand on a book, *The 13 Original Clan Mothers* by Jamie Sams. I went into the snack area and ordered a steaming mug of 'Goddess Tea.' Why not, I laughed to myself! I opened the book and read:

"Becomes her Vision stood inside a circle of Sacred Stones that comprised a giant medicine wheel. She faced the first moon cycle position of the Wheel and saw her Sister, Talks with Relations smiling back into her eyes...In silence, Talks with Relations presented her sister with a gift and then returned to her place on the outer edge of the Medicine Wheel."

I was astonished at what I was reading, as though this were a description of me, and my sister, as *Talks with Relations.*

Each in her turn, the 11 remaining Clan Mothers present *Becomes Her Vision* with a gift, each representing a special symbol, and special wisdom. When the gift giving is completed, *Becomes Her Vision* has a personal experience involving the *Great Smoking Mirror,* and the *Eternal Flame of Love.*

"Becomes Her Vision was drawn inside the fire until she became the brilliant flame inside of all things."

Author Jamie Sands concluded her chapter with these words: *"Becomes Her Vision sings to the hearts of all of the Children of Earth, reminding them of the Whirling Rainbow Dream and their roles in manifesting that vision. She can be called on to assist any Child of Earth who seeks the light of the Eternal Flame of Love in order to be the truth and become her or his vision...Becomes Her Vision's song of wholeness reminds us: "You are, the moment you decide to Be."*

I was astonished, awed, as I read these words. Throughout the three previous envisioning sessions I had, in one scene or the other, perceived of myself as either a child in buckskins, or a young Indian huntress. Somehow this 'child of earth,' had entered the world of the clan mothers.

I was not familiar enough with Native American myth and legends to have either recalled, nor imagined these scenes. Had I then, somehow, connected with a realm of ancient mysteries? Had I experienced a coming into my own power, not as *Becomes Her Vision*, but as *becomes my own vision,* with the very Clan Mothers of whom Jamie Sams had written? There were answers to other symbols too, the dropping of the robe, for instance, indicated the dropping of the physical body to *"return to the Heart of the Earth Mother."* In fact, the description of *Listening Woman* coming into her human form was similar to an earlier innervisioning session I had, in which I saw myself as an Indian maiden inside a dark, but alive, cavern. The blue orb that I found inside a glacier is not unlike the one given *Becomes Her Vision* by *Looks Far Woman*.

"This pastel blue mineral," Jamie wrote, in the voice of *Looks Far Woman*, "represents the gift of prophesy that comes from clear seeing..."

"I was taught," Jamie writes in an afterword, "that any two-legged could access the wisdom held by these *Grandmothers of the Turtle Council House* if she or he had an open heart and a desire to tap into the feminine principle."

Even though I had not been able to participate in Claire's Women's Circle, somehow this two-legged had wandered into a circle which existed in non-ordinary world. But how? And why?

Oddly, I felt the simple soul-retrieval journey I had embarked on after reading Sandra Ingerman's *Soul Retrieval* was significant in preparing the way for the circle of clan mothers. No doubt there could be even more healing for me available through the guidance of a qualified shamaness. Still, apparently enough wholeness of soul was present to allow me to stand in the midst of the wise-women.

In becoming *their* visions, Jamie, Sandra, Claire, Mary, and no less my sister, had midwifed a major event in my own becoming. I would be forever grateful.

106

But, having experienced the inner place of power, I still was unable, I felt, to make major changes in my outer life. I was so irritated with *me*. One afternoon, I again took pen in hand to ask:

Leytha: dearest friend: please advise me about the things which are so bothering me today. Is there a way for me to have money to live on while I am writing?

Dearest one: Claudia cannot, because she is still patterned in the past, but Litheria can. Follow the way of your spirit. Determine to love and nurture Claudia by releasing, letting go of, and conquering limitations in your life. Love your Self!

Well, perhaps I needed to translate *love* as be patient, and to let Litheria be until "Claudia" can become.

I had one more session with Claire, a kind of summing up. She set up a small microphone and cassette recorder, so that I might listen to the account of my journey later on. I'd told her how difficult it was for me to verbalize the inner journey, preferring to write it, reporting as the scene and script unfolded, so she thought that recording my last session might provide a reminder notes for me to write later on.

Following Claire's direction, I closed my eyes and tried to see if I had left anything unfinished. I tried to visualize the pink and brown wings of the drawing expanding in my mind.

I saw a ground beneath me, the brown colors, but the pink would not grow. At last, looking up at it from a small child's view, I saw pink cotton candy on a tall stick. Around me swirled the music and noise of a carnival.

"I seem very small," I said aloud. "And it seems as though I'm lost, or overwhelmed by a crowd of people."

"What do you smell?" Claire asked.

I sniffed the air. "Popcorn!" I said, screwing up the corner of my mouth in half a grin. How I loved popcorn! I felt someone pick me up to see the cotton candy. "It shifts," I told Claire. "Now it's a pink balloon."

"How does it feel to be picked up to see the pink cotton candy and balloon?"

It felt wonderful. I was lifted out of the press of the crowd, high, where I could see. "It seems as if the person picking me up is my father; I feel very cared for and safe."

"What is happening now that you are in your father's arms, above the crowd?"

I reached for the balloon, but it flew away. I felt lost again, sad, empty. When I reached for things, they flew out of my grasp. My happiness flew away.

Claire waited for me to continue, and when I did not, she suggested I ask my guidance if there was anything additional I should know here. It took a few moments to sense the change of 'channel' from my observation and experiential role, to that of listener open for guidance.

"A child looks... to an adult to nurture them, and give them things that make them happy," I verbalized to Claire, my witness. I hesitated. Was there more? "If you continue this into adulthood," the guidance continued, now more personal, "happiness will fly away from you, as it is dependent on others."

I followed Claire's instructions to open my eyes when I was ready, and to again look at the pink and brown feathered pastel lines.

I tried to put into a sentence what that aspect of the drawing symbolized to me, but could not. Claire agreed that I would benefit from returning to the void of my memory, but I would best take a guide. But for now, we would complete my exploration of the energy map.

I closed my eyes to envision the bird-like blue wings at the very top of the drawing. In a second, I saw myself astride the back of an enormous bluebird.

"We are just going for a ride," I answered in response to Claire's question as to why I was there. "To see the clouds...the bird wants to show me a view of reality from a bird's view," I said, listening to the sound of the wind whistling through the great fan of the bird's wings.

I felt safe though the bird was flying very fast, sometimes moving its wings, but sometimes gliding on the currents of air. There was no way I could fall off. I could smell clean, pure air, and found myself breathing deeply in reality.

"Are you on the bird, or are you the bird?" Claire asked.

"I could be the bird...I can go where I want to go. I'm not directing the bird, but it is showing me possibilities." I had a great sense of freedom, feeling wonderful, open, soaring with the kind of power that comes when one is moving in one's own energy.

"And what does your guidance tell you?" Claire asked, after a pause. I was reluctant to end this journey. I looked, listened, for the thought.

"If I feel limited," I said, still searching, still trying to hear or feel. I can't see the whole view...I stopped. These were my thoughts, not that of my inner guidance. "That isn't quite right," I said. Then I felt the surge of energy I'd come to know as that which expressed itself as true guidance.

"Now I can see more clearly," I spoke aloud. "I do have more power. I can experience freedom of flight." I looked again at the blue wings at the top of the drawing and laughed..." Like a magical power bird, I can rise above limitations."

We had completed this phase of exploration, having journeyed to each section of the energy map. How did I now see the whole drawing? Claire asked.

"In only a few sentences?" I laughed, Claire joining me. She waited patiently, however, for me to summarize my impressions. I saw that my *self* was fragmented. Pain and sadness connected the parts like grout connecting the pieces of a mosaic. Once this grout was dissolved, I knew, the picture would be whole.

The red arrow-like bouquet in the center of the drawing had all but disappeared in its manifestation in my physical body. Two chiropractic treatments had relieved the pain in the center of my shoulder blades.

The chest area pain, and the pain in my throat and esophagus ebbed somewhat, but part of the experience with Claire would make me aware of another area of my life which could use some healing but it would be some years before I encountered a doctor who, with a tiny pill for acid reflux, gave me relief from the pain in my throat and esophagus. But the dreadful cough would continue.

I had expected to feel joy, to feel a sense of fulfillment and hopefully a sense of direction on completion of the sessions with Claire. Instead, I walked back to my car feeling the familiar loneliness. Perhaps it was friendship I longed for. Not just shopping together, eating out type of socializing, which, in the first instance I didn't like, and in the second, usually preferred the company of a book. But there was definitely a sense of loss.

Someone had glimpsed into my soul, even walked in my soul rooms with me, and now, out on the street, where all was busyness, and business of the day, I felt lost and alone on a planet of beings who shielded their minds, and had no interest apparently in knowing mine. Perhaps somewhere, some day, I would again find the circle of the wise women.

8

"If I am not for myself, who will be?
And when I am for myself, what am 'I'?
And if not now, when?"
~Rabbi Hillel110BCE-10CE

My "angels" had indicated I would see a plan unfold before the year's end. Alas, it seems to elude me. I continue to write, but have no clue as how to function in the world to earn a living. I long to be in my own space, with my own favorite things around me. But how to earn enough money to live independently when I don't have the stamina and well-being to do waitressing forty hours a week?

Leytha: Why do I not see the plan for my life? Why am I so impotent in the area of producing income? When will I have my own home again? Is there some way I could be making a difference in the world, in people's lives?

The truth is, I had never had "career goals" that were other than creative, writing in one form or another, making art; finally leaving theater and music behind. I simply did not do well when working with others; hired as I was at some entry level position

111

that took specific skills when what I knew how to do was, create, organize (people and projects), cause to happen.

Litheria: When we began these talks, our communication came out a deep need to forgive yourself. You are again returning to self-castigation. Release this now.

Accept the life you created for yourself as being the very one you most desired, the one designed to teach you the lessons you most desired to learn. Accept, do not fight life.

Look around you and accept the beauty, the reality of life. Do not retreat from it. Live deeply. Attend to details. Do not retreat into forgetfulness. Pay attention. Be where you are. Look again to dream time. Look again into your inner visioning. Dare to create   your   reality.

You are afraid to challenge the reality you are experiencing by replacing it with a more fulfilling reality. That is understandable. But test it, as you might any new process.

Make a dream happen. Then you will believe, and from this greater and greater confidence in your new gift of power will come. •

It is important for you to find a way to commit to the spiritual, the soul path. Your joy is the proof here. Do not be afraid to help others challenge their realities. Test your power. Do not compromise. Want what you want fully and without reservation.

You need not fear your desires. When they are bounded by love and the need to live more fully, and to be of service to others, your dreams will find reality in which no regret exists.

112

And what do I want? To write, to have an income to meet my needs. To live in the mountains. To make art as I wish and have the funds to support this. To publish, or as Jane Austin is to have said, "make a living with my pen." To experience health. To relinquish confusion. To laugh. To make a difference in the lives of others. To inspire, and encourage people.

To daily have a deeper knowingness about the spiritual and soul life, the life of the universes, the life beyond this physical one. To have a soul-mate companionship. To have my family find their life purposes. And the world? Well, to contribute by no longer feeling useless. Goodnight self. It is late and I must waitress tomorrow.

I don't know how to assuage the loneliness. I need my "off" time to write, read. And, thanks to the traveling pain which this last week settled in my jaw and created a six day migraine headache, I've been immersed in depression. Depression always follows a migraine headache however, thought it's been sometime since I've had one this severely. My job-money situation has not improved, and though I keep sending out resumes, no one returns calls. So, as in my dream, I certainly feel trapped, a hostage to circumstances.

I've been reading Thomas Moore's *Care of the Soul.* He suggests that when "Depression," given the respect of a capitol "D", comes to call, that one might, instead of struggling desperately to recover a state of sunniness, ask Mr. Depression what message he brings.

All right Master Magician Depression, you've enveloped me these past few days in a doomsday mantle grayer than the darkest rain cloud. Why have you come? What do you want?

There are many things I would say to you, he answers, *since you have never asked before but only wrestled with me in a most inhospitable way. I come to weave a web around you beneath which you may retreat from the world. At the same time, I weave*

113

this web from the substance of your own thoughts, and the world thoughts which intertwine with your own.

See me not as an 'I am,' as in 'I am depressed, but as a single actor/teacher who has emerged through a crack in dream-time, drawing on your soul and body energy in order to sustain the identity you call 'depression.'

I am almost always a catalyst in re-birth, and may even be the cavern into which you retreat to give birth, or be re-birthed. I do not bring with me any light. If you would lift my mantle, or disengage my web, or find exodus from my cavern, you must do so with the soul's energy. If you cannot summon this energy, be willing, then to borrow with permission, some other soul's energy.

Know me then as the dark-time, the time of unknowing, the time in which your soul cycle is at is lowest ebb, the time of rebirth. Do not, then, assign guilt to me, or anxiety, as these entities only insinuate themselves into dream-web, thought-mantle, re-birth cavern, and obscure the vision gift of hibernation my visitation brings.

Giving me your complete attention and respect, will bring forth my message quickly, The sooner, and more intensely that you acknowledge me, the sooner you free me to return to dream-time."

Well, that was interesting. Especially the part about acknowledging your presence, and not feeling guilty. Now, as I am now acknowledging you, will you tell me the personal message you have for me at this time?

You feel a sense of loss, a death, a going away from you, with the completion a project, such as a proposal for a book, or the dream closure of something you want to do but can't afford to make happen. You have, as in your dream, put your 'child' in the hands of others, who now hold it hostage.

Recently, you felt a little death at not being able to continue the weekly visit with your art therapy counselor. With her, you could bound from rooftop to rooftop of imaging experiences and thus free yourself from the captivity of the past.

And, your illnesses, the chest pain, the chronic cough and sore throat, the severe pains in your teeth and jaw, the headaches, which, without health insurance, you are unable to see a doctor, have once again made you face the dependency of your life, a gain, another death, the death of the dream of independence and pride in one's effort, accomplishment and financial freedom. It is not my role to tell you so, but grief repressed will make the body ill.

I sigh. While I'd gained yet another insight, I'd received no "this is your way out" message. But then, what could I expect from Mr. Depression? And now, if you don't mind, I'd like you to go. Your role is played. Your time is up. And I, for one, want to feel joy again. I am going to begin by smiling, right now, and watch *Northern Exposure* tonight so that I can laugh.

More rain. Perhaps I am the only one who does not complain about this weather. I could live amidst rain and snow and wind forever. I love the songs nature sings! Brother-in-law John is convinced we underwent some major earth shift and we're actually in Seattle or some other rainy northern clime. But for me, writing next to a window where I hear and see the rain is nearly heaven. My *If Only* chapbook (a combination of several poems) is ready at the printers. I'm both anxious to pick it up, and nervous. I so hope it looks lovely!

I've realized my self abuse must stop. Were I to criticize another the way I do myself, I would consider myself most cruel.

Wonderfully, since my dialogue with the master magician Mr. Depression, I've had some relief from the shadow of his dark cape.

Weekly, have been doing job interviews, mostly in San Francisco, which not only cost me the price of the bridge toll, but rewarded me with parking tickets too, but no job offer. A San Francisco literary agent left a message for me, that a proposed book was not right for them. To my surprise, he said he had forwarded on to another agent in Santa Monica. Encouraged. At least he didn't think it unpublishable.

Am lonely for a companion. Someone I can talk to about about books, thoughts, writing. Need a holiday. Need to travel. Need my own place, some funky little apartment in the woods! I'd like to jump into the T.V. and *Northern Exposure*, and live in the fictional, Cicily, Alaska.

Have had a flurry of two or three months creating and trying to market hand-made book-cards. People bought them where I worked. I placed them in a few shops. The poem-thoughts encouraged people. But, without sufficient funds to really develop the cards, I've had to shelve this one more dream. I suppose I could learn to not start, if I didn't have funds to continue, but my magic thinking always kicks in: "This is it, this is the answer," until I see it isn't the answer, just another improbable.

Have signed up for some college classes, determined once more to get a degree. I liked being in school. How I wished I could just go to school, though, for once in my life, without having to work.

9

"If something is difficult for you to accomplish, do not think it impossible for any human being; rather; if it is humanly possible and corresponds to human nature, know that it is attainable by you as well...Regain your senses call yourself back, and once again wake up. Now that you realize that only dreams were troubling you, view this 'reality' as you view your dreams.
~ Marcus Aurelius (Ad 121-180) Emperor of Rome.

Sometime in 1996, I moved to a small town in Southern California to make a place for my son who was ill. It is a story that needs to be told all for its own sake. But in the process, of being supportive to him, I began to feel more focused as well. I wrote many articles for the local paper, waitressed, and managed, to put on a dinner-theater musical show I'd written back in the sixties, with the support of local actors and service clubs.

I was finally able through the encouragement of a young pastor in a small church I attended, to move from waitressing into a retail job. There, though the position required me to work longer hours, and caused me (and the manager) great anxiety every time I approached the computerized cash register, I was awarded second in sales for the year. Still, despair dogged at my heels, nipping away at self-confidence and of any sense of a future fulfilled.

"The days are just moving past me," I at last cried out to Leytha. "And I'm accomplishing nothing!" It seemed unnecessary to outline the morbid details of my life. Did she not know all that I am and am not? "How do I regain the joy of life and belief in myself and that which I've been given to do?" What had I done with the life I'd been given? Through my glasses, darkly, I could see nothing but failure strewn behind me.

Dear one, Leytha replied. *How long since we have communicated! There are times when you must force the dance of life, hear music that is not there and sing a song that does not want singing. In the process, joy begins to trickle through the thought rubble with has blocked this cleansing stream.*

What is difficult here is dealing with a veil of emotions entwined around your spirit from past hurts

It is time to give up the idea that the other, any other, would wish, in spirit, to hold you back, thwart you, or in any way abuse. The more than you can perceive, indeed see, others, as spirit, borrowing only for such a short while earth bodies, the easier it will be to understand, to know, that you and others are as sisters-brothers in this life cycle and have pledged to balance one another in the working out.

You and others in your life are one in spirit. Resisting this, you feel separate, alone and apart.

It is imperative that you give expression to the spirit through creative endeavors, through the putting together of words, of sharing through communication, with others. See this in a time of going within, and you will experience less harshness and abruptness.

Gentle spirit, you've been tossed about in the rough unyielding surf until your sharp, stubborn edges have been worn

118

away. But do not for a moment believe this means defeat.

You are no more a stone than the sea is but a pond! You must <u>risk</u> being! Your means of receiving from the source is not the same as those who see money as the beingness of their lives.

This is not to say one way is better than another. Both, and many, channels are available to provide you with material goods.

But this is to say that just as eyes are different colors, and bodies are different heights, inner urgings guide that which you know as talent along different paths. Each being has a different way of responding to the source.

Joy, creativity, discovery, insight; these are your channels. Do not be afraid. We will not abandon you.

Rise above your love. Release others to release you.

In 1997, I enrolled in a small university in Riverside, California with plans to begin in the fall of 1988. Somehow, I'd become determined to get my college degree by the year 2000, but I was also trying to show my son that we could overcome our circumstances.

What I would do with the degree, never occurred to me. I thought first to major in psychology. Instead, having already taken a number of theater classes, thought to pursue theater arts as a major, and perhaps teach. I finally settled on art, finding both peace in the long hours I spent in the studio, and supportive friendships in the two art professors.

One morning, again over coffee in a small cafe, I again called on Leytha.

Dearest one: You are *moving forward, but like a boat in the river it is sometimes difficult to tell if the water is rushing past you or you are moving forward in the current.*

Remember that manifesting the material, requires spiritual, mental and physical knowledge, discipline and insight. Channel money into your life through ideas concretized in a way which will improve the lives of others or benefit them financially, materially.

As you become a source that others are drawing from, benefiting from, the Source from which you draw will widen and flow freely into your life.

See an open channel from the Source, from Creation itself, flowing through you into a star-burst of beneficial showers flowing into, and through the lives of others.

There is no limitation here other than the mental one you've placed on yourself by saying you do not care about money, or that you are not deserving of it.

Open your whole self to the Source. Be the channel, flow with the channel, be the receiver through whom the blessing passes. As it filters through you into the lives of others it will supply all your needs.

But dearest friend Leytha: I am so tired! I am making little progress with my art or writing or my life, only chalking up courses at school. My relationships and finances are so difficult! I struggle so everyday, but make no forward progress. I paused in my writing "communication," to re-read something I'd found, that I'd scribbled down while still in Mexico, asking the same questions.

Do you know you have a spiritual name? It is Litheria.
Perhaps you can understand this as "gentle light."
We know you, have protected you many life incarnations,
have brought together the realization of your creative works and
we will not abandon you now.

We, others here, would have you know that you will not be
abandoned by us. We know your pain, and urge you to see a
healer skilled in the spiritual body arts."

I paid little attention to Leytha's announcement re my special name. Perhaps I had heard it in my spirit before. What I desperately wanted was some practical advice; some way to get from "here," to "there," there being a more stable place from which to live my life. As to seeking out a healer, I could, most weeks, just manage to keep a roof over our heads, and food on the table and gas in the tank, generally living in terror that the car would suddenly require a healer itself!

"Will you connect me with a guide from whom I can receive material guidance," I asked one day, more worried than usual at the challenges of continuing to make my own way and being so ill prepared. Just as suddenly, I sensed a "presence," a guide, angel perhaps, *Mithra.* I don't know why this inner world, other world, or parallel world's beings do not have names like James and John and Paul, I thought. I laughed at myself a little, wondering once again, how much of what I was writing was my imagination. Then, I sensed a male presence, that of *Mithra.*

Litheria: You are able to share your many gifts by healing
the relationships you have with others. See these as spirit beings,
not as personalities manifest. Ask us for guidance in this matter.
Through this connectedness you will find yourself on the pathway
which will supply all your material needs."

121

It was years later before I would see the wisdom, the power that could be released by following that guidance. At the time, I only wondered, but how, and when? This was the first time I had connected with a presence other than Leytha and I sensed Mithra's presence as different from Leytha, more weighty as it were. In fact, Mithra, and others, "spoke" as *we*, and I felt as though I had just had an audience with a counsel, as compared to the gentle, loving touch of Leytha. I knew, logically, I was hearing only my own inner voice. But if that were so, why the gap between what I received as wisdom and guidance, and my actual life?

I continued to communicate with Leytha, determined somehow to overcome what I saw as an embarrassingly dreary and defeating life and outlook. When I had considered going back to college, to finish, finally, and graduate, I knew I would be struggling with money, time, distance and in fact my own health and energy, all the while "standing by" my son in his own difficulties. How would I cope with all this? And to what purpose?

Enter into the place where you become the center of a star. Let the energy absorb you, be you, heal you. Then you will radiate this healing energy to all whom you contact.

Litheria: Money is the fruit of many labors—ideas, efforts, actions which benefit others. Visualize! Visualize!

Each moment you spend in inner visioning will reward you with energy manifested as money, or that which you need. You need not fear your relationships with anyone now. Bless others and they will find ways to bless you materially.

Surrender your Self to our Selves and all will unfold as it is to unfold. Trust is the guidance here. There is a need here which finds, in you, a solution, greatly valued.

122

Show how valuable you will become, while retaining your own self and interests. We would have you come into a place of maturity in the area of negotiation, finance, and working cooperatively with others.

See your challenges as an opportunity to experience this. This can take place rather rapidly. You will just pass over a barrier and be there. Do not think this a burden, but rather a grace.

In praying for healing of others you are healed. In praying for abundance for others your own prosperity increases. So it is with wisdom and guidance. In praying, envisioning for others, you seem to step out of your own way, removing the obstacles you've set up in your own path.

As you see prosperity, healing, guidance, wisdom, opportunity, love, peace, manifest in others, it fills your life as well. Is there more you wish to know?

More? I wished to know everything. How could I presume to seek grand wisdom when I was still trouble about the "what do I do with my life," business. At last, after some time had passed, I turned, with some embarrassment, to Leytha.

Dearest one: I have never been far from you. But I could not intrude into your life or into the negative life force which held you bondage and it was necessary for me to allow you to let this dissolve.

Her presence seemed to be outside me now, swirling around me like a soft spring breeze. I felt like breathing deeply, just to inhale the sense of what she was telling me.

The past is as a leaf fallen from a tree. The leaf is disconnected from the life force which gave birth to it, but does not die. It becomes part of a new life line, or other life line. So the past is no longer part of the "tree" that is you.

The memories you hold are selective ones fueled by emotional energy.

To turn off this energy merely bless the 'leaf," thank it for having grown from your "tree," and let if fall from your branches, to join with the earth.

In letting go, and blessing these leaves of the past you past, you release your "tree" energy to produce new growth. Release the idea, bless it, let it fall away into "fulfilling potential."

Walk among the familiar where you are, as a healer. Teach, share what we reveal to you.

If you so choose, you can change the patterns of your life now, by forgiving yourself and taking a new path.

In truth, forgiveness is unnecessary, as the progress of human life is through, to go through—fear, doubt, self-awareness (consciousness), striving, comfort, pride, and regret.

However, because you have become "stuck" as it were, in a mire of regret, resentment, and self-criticism, forgiveness is necessary to heal your soul.

I felt Leytha's "voice," like the whispering of wind, of a many dimensional stringed instrument echoing in the empty halls of space. It is rainbow colored. It springs forth from pure light.

In this life, you must learn to deal with regret. It may seem odd to you that this is so, but even in the angelic realm we experience these learnings, these lessons.

Again we urge you to know your Self as not separate from the light, but a vibrant being in through whom beauty and healing may be expressed.

Even now, dear one, you are reluctant to think you are worthy of this. All are worthy.

Focus on the light and let it heal your wounds of regrets.

Emotional flagellation is a waste of life energy.

About six months later, Leytha replied to my request to communicate with another, by giving me the name "Dionyn." I felt hesitant to call upon this being, but I remembered that she, Leytha, had given me only loving guidance.

I addressed Dionyn, and sense a very powerful being, male in presence, and able, and willing, to not only assist me to the place that I wish to be, but who would act as my "bridge builder."

Litheria... I call you by your light name, for this is the name under which you must publish those works which we will dictate to you.

I thought this quite amazing, and a little unbelievable.
I have not allowed myself to either "receive," nor publish such works. Perhaps the time is not right.

We will make a place for you because this has been your desire from the beginning, to join, rejoin, with those of your own clan.

125

Even now we set in place the works, the energy, the connections and connectors which will, by the end of the year as you perceive it, put you in the position you long for.

Fear not, Litheria. This is just coming home for you.

This is where you've always belonged.

You have been trudging up a tangled path trying to reach the top of a mountain, but I will lift you up and touch you down safely, in a safe place.

Feel now the unfurling of your own wings, buoyant with light. Sense the cleansing that is taking place there the feeling of springtime, of newness, of expectancy. Open, open your mind.

At another time, Leytha introduced me to "Orinthion," whom I perceived as a Greek athlete. He too speaks to me by my spirit name.

Litheria, you are in contact with the spirit of the body. In asking for this guidance you express willingness to confront, deal with, this area of your life.

You are looking at the physical through the eyes of your past experience in not only this lifetime, but others, in which you have concentrated on aspects of the mind - teaching, music, art, rather than the physical.

For this reason, attention to the physical seems foreign, laborious to you. However, because of your desire for completion in this life-time, it is correct for you to confront this area of your life at this time.

126

While you are highly intuitive, you still need to train yourself, open your mind, to the intuitive flashes, thoughts, that your receive, and recognize these as guidance.

While you have asked me for advice on the physical realm of your life, it is important that you begin to listen to the wisdom of your body.

Listen to your intuition with as much respect as you listen to those of us who guide you through the words you receive.

This will assist you in transforming what you now identify as physical; pain, growing older, fatigue, etc., into joyful expression of the sensory life.

Becoming aware of, giving attention and respect to your intuitive self, and following through on these visions, insights, images, will make your days as full of joy as the moments you spend among the trees, the leaves, the earth. These are living things. You are a living thing.

Do you respect the tree, the plant, the flower, the bird, the deer, the dolphin, more than your own physical self?

Listen, and respect yourself. You chose the physical manifestation of life energy that is yours, and yours alone.

Are you not, unique, and wondrous?

Life and time, and struggle continued. One day, after re-reading these earlier entries, I finally asked again: "Leytha: what is the next step I need to take? Where is home, for me on this plane?"

Litheria: time is non-existent on the level from which I speak to you, and it may be difficult to understand that you are trying to bend time in an attempt to establish a place of self-esteem for yourself.

We have tried to share with you before, who you are, who all humans are, so that you can be relieved of the need to prove anything to yourself, or to others.

How can God's creations prove anything to God? You are the created from the Creator's breath, hands, heart, being. How can there be any lack in you?

If it is love you want, envision it. If it is accomplishment you want, envision it. If it is well-being and peace of mind you hunger for, envision these.

If you can understand that which is manifest in your life, in the lives of others, in life, is only that which has been created, or brought into manifestation by creation dreaming itself!
Envision that when you wake in the morning you know exactly the direction to take!

Envision that you meet the people you are longing to meet who have come to understand their relationship to the light. Envision a fulfilled life.

When you spend time in envisioning, creation begins to take on the form of your visions. The key here is "begins!"

Behold the laws of nature. All things evolve, and circle, from seed to plant to seed again, from seed to life to transformation, to the next cycle.

So it is with changing a condition in your life. If it seems to happen instantly it is because the seed of change, of transformation, fulfillment, had been planted in some past time.

At any time, you are unconsciously "sowing seeds" which will, unless you consciously pull them out of your creative "ground," will come up either as flowers or weeds in your life.

This is not new to you, but you need to take greater caution. Do not allow negative thought to float around freely, unchecked, and even indulged in.

There were times I felt the guidance was so ethereal! I needed something concrete. I needed to know my life work and to get out from under the burden of a lifetime of poverty and struggle! Leytha responded to my tantrum.

The same principle applies. If you will let go of your self castigation and give the same energy to envisioning, all that you can envision will be manifest, will be created.

You must hear what we are telling you at a deep level. Look again to your dreams. Give your power only to God, not to others, not to circumstances, not to self-castigation, not to frustration. God will reflect your power back to you, light magnified in the Light. Power given to, directed to, any other source will be used up, distorted.

You are not far from experiencing the birth of these manifestations in your life. The problem lies in thinking you are not worthy to live and love and create and be safe. Remember dear one, who you are... a spirit being who has chosen to live in this life plane, in the body and life you have chosen. Become conscious of this!

This is not the same as saying you should not live in the moment, but you can have a sense of safeness in all that you do, when you remember, first of all, who you truly are, and what your purpose is in this lifetime. Do not let the circumstances of days and weeks and years define or defeat you.

Morning and evening, go into that place where you can envision what you feel you are lacking and create that. Come into the Light and be restored. The waking life is not the fullness of life. It is rather, a level of life, a degree of life.

To experience greater fullness, or fulfillment, you need to walk comfortably in more levels of life—the inner, the past, the yet to come, and especially in the level of life where we communicate. Even in these brief moments when you connect with me, with us, with the Holy Spirit, you are restored and set again on a straighter path.

Alas, your world has never been an easy one to navigate for those called to the light. What you think is confusion is just an indifference to the things of the world. This causes you to pay attention only, when, like neglected children, they demand your attention. This is a short time of frustration, considering eternity, and a time that will end.

What you leave behind in this lifetime, who you encourage, who you inspire, there is your garden, your worth, your value. When you join us, you will work for them here, as we work for you, and then you will see how insignificant the material world is, and how very important is the development of the soul.

I had felt some finality in Leytha's words. Meanwhile, I had begun my studies at the university, and moved my son and myself from where we lived sixty miles away, to a senior apartment complex a few blocks from the school. Looking back, I see so many "earth-angels," in the real world who befriended us on this difficult path; the Native American landlords who'd first rented to us, understanding my son's illness, a formerly competitive retail associate who loaded up her pickup to help us move, the service clubs in the small town who gave me support, then awards for putting on the dinner-theater project, the newspaper editor who paid me to write stories, so many others.

We had much to do to settle into our new life in yet one more town. We went through the complicated process of finding new medical connections for my my son. A new waitress job required computerized ordering and I feared it would make me the slowest employee there. I signed up, in order to graduate in two years, for twenty-one units. But finally, there seemed to be some hope for a better future.

One day, seeking out a favorite writing environment, a little cafe, I ordered bacon, eggs, fruit, biscuit and coffee, the soothing breakfast food of childhood. I took out my pen and called upon Leytha one more time. Her words were full of encouragement.

Be at peace, dear one. You often reach into the pond of the universe without knowing what you are reaching for.

When you come up with something unpleasant, you wonder why. But what has taken place is natural, the result of not knowing, of lack of clarity. But lack of clarity is not a symptom, it is a cause. Clarify your desires. You are born with destiny, a chosen path, but on the path, you have made choices which now define you. Now, make choices which nurture you.

In the coming times, you will see fulfillment of all areas of your life dreams. You have persevered. You have honored God and others. The storehouses of heaven are about to open to you.

Open your hands and heart and mind to God so that your touch may become as anointed as the thoughts which flow from your heart-spirit.

Give of yourself, until each talent, each hope, each dream, each desire, is attuned to that which God would have for you. Prepare once again to receive joy.

The two years at the university would prove happy ones for me. While the burden of my responsibilities did not let up, I eventually was able to work only part time in the restaurant, and part-time doing work study in the department of art, where I had "found home."

The two professors became good friends, I spent long and peaceful hours at night in the studio exploring art-making which I'd left behind during the sixties. My son enrolled in school and manged a semester or two studying music, doing well.

Graduation at last, with my son, sister and husband, her middle daughter and family, attending. What next, I wondered. I had no plan, and enrolled in a masters program at the same university. Practically, I should have enrolled in the teaching credentialing course, but personally, I doubted my ability to handle a public school classroom.

Meanwhile, I quietly applied to the Arts in Education masters program. The school? Harvard University.

TRANSITION

Going through it? Will it never end? Listen, transitions are nothing more than the determined pushing up through frozen winter earth of thoughts and dreams, hopes and challenges persistent in their need, urge, purpose to see spring rains and spring suns, and grow into wow and wonderful. Look where I am now...gardens and meadows, hillsides and mountains, full of dreams realized. ~ One of my own poems, *Transition.*

The two years I spent getting my degree from the university in Southern California, and the next two years will, one day become part of another type of book. In a nutshell, though, not really expecting to get accepted to Harvard, when I finished the semester in the education masters program at my alma mater, I had more or less accepted my "fate," to become a teacher.

This is not to cast aspersions on this most honorable of professions however, but rather that I could not imagine "loner me" in a classroom. With a professorship, yes, and a quiet, writing, thoughtful life at a University, yes. But I could not stretch my mind, nor my body, nor my energy nor my emotions to embrace that dream.

I had, oddly, taken almost no classes in English, and had I done that, my course might have been different. Instead, I'd concentrated first on theater courses, and then majored in visual arts. I'd found the Arts in Education program during a browsing session one day, and it seemed a fit, if not a far fetched dream, and I had applied.

Meanwhile, a dear friend of many years unexpectedly gifted me with an money for my "education." I was able to buy a car, and for a time, put the remainder of the money away towards the Harvard dream.

It seemed so unlikely though, that I, at sixty three, with a late-date degree, and a Californian at that, would ever get accepted to that Ivy League university, so one day, I impetuously invested in another once-in-a-lifetime dream: a trip to Paris to study French and immerse myself in the world of art for three weeks.

Of course, I did not expect to learn to speak French in three weeks, but I would have three glorious weeks exploring the art and food and mind-scapes of this city of my dreams.

This story too, belongs elsewhere, as it would result in an unbelievable connection later, a man who was to become my "muse," in the writing of my first novel, but someone I would not actually meet until the novel was finished and self-published, some several years later.

I returned from Paris, to have my son meet me at our front door, a large package in his hand. "From Harvard, mom," he said. I immediately experienced resignation.

Surely this package contained all the materials, the "evidences" of all my volunteer activity, and community-level creativity, along with a rejection notice. My son was persistent. "Open it mom!" he insisted eagerly.

That afternoon, I visited my more recent university, dropping in to the office of each of the five professors who had given me a reference for Harvard.

"Do you have a bottle of smelling salts?" I teased. "If so, read this," I invited, shoving the letter in their faces. "Dear Ms Carroll, We are happy to inform you that you have been accepted..."

I, little gal from across the tracks, creative dabbler and "scanner," persistent learner, with sixty four years on the planet, would soon be headed for Boston.

I spent the summer of 2001 teaching arts and crafts at a Salvation Army camp for kids-at-risk in the Santa Cruz mountains. While there, I received a color graphic from an East Coast friend: it was titled, "Gypsy Goes Harvard."

That fall would prove to be a bittersweet experience however. I arrived two weeks before school was to start, two weeks before September 11, 2001.

I'd rented a room in a house owned by a Boston schoolteacher, whom I'll call Betty. This name, and that of her twenty-something aged children, are fictitious names. Originally from the Dominican Republic, Betty had become a citizen, achieved her credential, married, and birthed two children in New York.

I was excited to move my things into the house, which seemed to promise a creative environment as my landlady also hosted artists with roots in the DR, in a friendly and fun, salon setting.

The morning of September 11, I'd called Harvard Medical Center in Cambridge to schedule an appointment for a physical. While I dreaded doctors' appointment, I, who had never had medical insurance, was so happy to finally have the coverage provided during the year of my masters at Harvard School of Education.

"Oh Claudia," the receptionist said, her voice breaking, "we've closed down for the day!"

I was confused. Was this a holiday I'd forgotten to note?

"You mean you haven't heard?" Her voice was anguished.

"Heard what?"

"Don't you have a television?" she asked, incredulous.

"Actually, I don't," I joked. "In fact, I'm probably one of

135

the few people in America who don't ...."

"That's what I'm trying to tell you," she interrupted, almost pleading with me to listen. "America is under attack!"

I was confounded. What in the world was she talking about?

"I'm sorry. I don't...I mean, it is some virus...a pandemic or something...?"

"Oh God, no!" she said, nearly hysterical. "Haven't you seen the television? America is under attack. They've bombed New York!"

I hung up the phone, stunned, still not understanding. Was this some terrible hoax, some "Martians have landed" hoax? I opened my bedroom door and walked into the hallway, where I heard the sound of a television.

I walked towards the open door of the room and stood in the doorway. Betty was at school, but her son and daughter were apparently watching some movie. They did not turn around when I approached, their eyes glued to the television.

Something terrible was happening with one of the Twin Towers. Fire and smoke. Suddenly, something, a plane? God no! crashed into the second tower. My God, my God! What was happening! This was no movie! This was happening! And Jamal and Lilia seemed to enjoying it!

Suddenly, I needed to be outside! That's what I'd do if there were an earthquake. That what I'd always done when feeling threatened inside my house, run for safety. That's why I always hung my purse on the doorknob.

I grabbed my purse, a jacket and scarf. I wanted to go to school, to be with people. Into the hall again. Behind me, I heard Jamal laughing. "Ha!" he said. I turned to see him shake his fist at the ceiling. "It's about time! America had it coming!"

I felt trapped in a bad dream. Numbly, I held on to the banister to make my way down the steep staircase to the front door. Probably the trains weren't running. Of course there wouldn't be school today. Where to go? What to do? I reached the bottom of the stairs, and hurried to the porch, down more stairs, to the street. Automatically, I headed for Martin's, the Armenian family's cafe, two blocks over. There would be people there!

What had Jamal said? Why did he say that? Wasn't his father in New York? Hadn't he and his sister been born in New York? They were Americans! How could they say... vaguely, I remembered their mother and father had been born in the Dominican Republic. I understood. Now, feeling completely isolated and alone, I hurried the two blocks to the cafe, barely missing a screaming fire engine as I crossed the street. There were sirens in every direction.

I stepped up on the curb and stood, dazed, staring at the "closed" sign on door. In the window, an American flag and a hastily scrawled sign: "We're Armenians. Please don't break our windows!"

The week was to prove a bizarre one. With no television, I tried to catch the news via radio, and on the Internet. Switching from a Howard Stern rant on Boston radio, I heard another DJ announce a memorial gathering in Copley Plaza. Arriving there, I saw the park surrounded by police. This was natural, I thought, for a public gathering two days after September 11.

As I made my way closer to the bandstand, I noticed the strange Tee green-leafed shirts many were wearing, and the oddities being sold in varied booths. The gathering was not a memorial service, but a previously scheduled "Legalize Marijuana," meet-up.

Just as I approached the stage, one of the musicians said, "Let's have a moment of silence for New York." I was astounded that he said "New York." Didn't he realize this had been an attack on the United States?

But I was even more astounded by what followed. Not silence. But a chorus of boos! The older hippie tee shirt wearing dead-heads, were booing the idea of a moment of silence for the

137

country that gave them the very freedom they were enjoying that day in the park.

I hurried away, stopping to ask a police officer what he felt about having to be a "peace" officer for this event. Several others gathered around. "We all want to quit and get over to Ground Zero where we can help our brothers!" he said, the others all nodding in agreement.

I continued to journal my 9/11 experience through September and October, an ever present one, while trying to adapt to Harvard and my courses.

In all that time, I never heard a rational voice, except at a panel of some creative people from New York, a New York Times editor, a choreographer, an actor, and a visiting professor originally from Jamaica.

While the New Yorkers on the panel, who had not only experienced the tragic day personally, but had lost friends and family there, counseled tolerance, calm, and sanity, the visiting professor used her time to rake the U.S. over the smoldering fires of Ground Zero. I was furious to the point of tears. I could understand her viewpoint just as I understood that of Jamal's, given the history of the U.S. and other countries in the Dominican Republic and Jamaica, I couldn't understand an attack on innocents nor could I understand this lack of sensitivity.

The moment the microphone was opened for student questions, I was one of the first in line. I could scarcely breath when I realized I was standing in one of Harvard's "sacred" halls of learning, about to counter- attack the insensitive professor. I acknowledged the attitude of all the others, and their loss, something the professor had not done at all.

I reminded them, mentioning my age, and my student status, speaking really to all the professors in the hall, that while we all had a responsibility to pass on an unbiased history of the United States in relation to the rest of the world, that some three thousand innocent people had died, without warning, for no other reason that having gone to work that day, and that the woman professor was totally out of line for using her time in front of a microphone for her extremely insensitive tirade. Today was the time for acknowledging that our country had been attacked, and the lives had been lost. Tomorrow would be time enough to find the answers as to why, and by whom.

I sat down, shaking, hardly noticing that the speakers on stage were applauding, and a huge number of people in the audience had given me a standing ovation.

I was approached afterward, strangely, by a Jewish man, who had lost many family members in the Holocaust. He seemed to just want to comfort me, the first comfort I had felt since the day of the attack.

In November, and December of that year, I volunteered at Ground Zero, working with the Salvation Army, right at the site. Our "job" was to serve food, provide dry socks and personal necessities to the firemen, police officers, and other volunteers, including a group of steelworkers from the Ukraine, who had paid their own way to get to New York.

Mostly though, we were encouraged to listen to those exhausted by the work and emotional toll of digging through the still burning rubble. During my own break-time I wrote in my journal:

Both sites are still about ten story high piles of twisted steel, with some seven stories beneath ground not yet explored. I could only comprehend it by minimizing it: imagining the worst car wreck I ever saw, and then magnifying it by the thousands. I don't want to think about the bodies which will no longer be recovered, nor look long at at those workers still carrying out body bags.

I look instead, with pride, with respect, at the work crews, operating massive cranes, driving dump trucks, working on phone lines, digging down to broken water pipes around the perimeter, both men and women serving, yes, "serving," as firemen, police officers, steel workers, Red Cross and Salvation Army volunteers.

Outside tent, located in the middle of what had been a major street, was a sign, slightly tipsy but still standing: it said, "No U-Turn."

At the door of the tent, stand a couple of tubs of water, with scrub brushes. An off-duty policeman from Jersey, looked up to from scrubbing his boots.

"Every time I wash that ash off my feet," he explained, without my asking, "I do it with reverence...you know what I mean? It's like walkin' around in a cemetery out there. You gotta be respectful."

I sat with another. "I saw something that just broke me up," the older fireman said. "This policeman, a big guy, you know, had come into St. Paul's church where we were taking a break. He had found...." the man stopped for a moment, almost unable to continue. "Well, it's like this. The guy had found a child's teddy bear in the rubble. He'd just stood there in the doorway of the church, then walked over to a chair, sat down and cried like a baby!"

There are a thousand stories to tell, and perhaps I'll be able to put the stories I heard, into book form before September 11, 2010. The story of my own attempt to form a friendship with a Muslim woman in one of my classes. The story of a priest, who'd lost so many members of his congregation. The story of Christmas eve night at the Ground Zero site, when a midnight mass was canceled, when another firetruck was found.

And the multiple stories the firemen, police officers, soldiers and volunteers who sat around their tables as they ate their meals, could have told, thoughtfully answering the hundreds of hand made cards and letters sent to them from children, not only from New York, not only from the United States, but from the world. They wrote, to assure them they were safe, even if they could no longer really believe that.

140

One evening, working in the Salvation Army tent, I handed a fireman a pair of new, dry socks. He pulled his boots back on, asked me for a couple of packet of tums... "Pretty hard on your stomach out there," he apologized.

"Take some for your buddies," I said.

"Hey," he smiled, grabbing a handful, "we really appreciate all you guys are doing for us!"

"Oh no, it's us who appreciate all of you," I insisted. "Have you been out there every day?"

"From day one," he said, with a trace of complaint in his voice. Then he turned back to me. "I meant it when I said thank you. At least we're getting paid to work out there. You people are doing this for nothing...."

"Not for nothing," I insisted. "We're all in this together."

"Yeah," he smiled, closing up his jacket. It was raining out side. "Yeah, that's what I meant. We're in this together."

I would write about this year, using my e-mail journal entries to California professor friends to tie the story together. I put it on a shelf along with a folder of mementos and forgot about it. Recently, looking through my stack of "what next" manuscripts, I found the story again.

Someday, before 9/11/11, I will put it between covers. For now, I'll skip to after graduation from Harvard, and another summer of teaching arts and crafts to kids at risk, then the decision, finally, to take myself, and my son, to the small town with the big skies and awesome, spiritual landscape, Taos, New Mexico.

I'd rented a mobile home advertised on-line, sight unseen. My sister, once again playing her role as "earth-angel" had helped us move there. No sooner had she left than I was out searching for a waitress job.

In Taos, I would learn, I was among my own kind—people with university degrees who were, often simply because they too, like me, preferred the land, the skies, the space to some other part of the country. They washed dishes, or cooked, or worked at the ski lifts, or adopted a retro-hippie life-style. At least in Taos, I didn't have to apologize.

In time, I was acquire a substitute teaching license, and was able to sell a few paintings and craft items at the popular open-aired art shows in Kit Carson Park. We adopted a stray dog, whom I called Lady-dog. We found, for the first time, more or less caring medical services for my son.

For a while, it seemed as if life was going to get better.

10.

After all, I don't see why I am always asking
for private, individual, selfish miracles
when every year there are
miracles like white dogwood.
~Anne Morrow Lindbergh

After a few months in Taos, I opened a tiny studio where my son could teach guitar. I decorated the walls with a few of my own paintings, and when people expressed an interest in these, we moved into a larger space. There, I painted, showed and sold some of my own work. With my son teaching guitar lessons, and I doing substitute teaching, we managed to stay afloat in the midst of an economic down-slide..

I loved the shop. There, I would paint, or write, enjoying long conversations over coffee or a glass of wine, with local friends, or with internationals who found my little cave of a space in the back of an adobe building. Sometimes I would take long drives, around the "enchanted circle" route, and return, refreshed by the awesome beauty of trees, mountains, skies and just sheer space.

Alone one afternoon, I reread parts of my journal, reflecting on my past few years. Not one, but two college degrees, one of those from Harvard, achieved at age sixty-five. Standing with my son his struggles for mental health in a world that had little understanding of what he went through, nor the causes. Seven summers teaching arts and crafts for kids at risk. Volunteering at Ground Zero.

Now, in one more gypsyesque move, making a home, and a studio, month to month, for sure, but in Taos. I seemed unable to give myself credit for any of this, having a penchant for pain and regret. I picked up my pen.

Leytha,: I feel once again, in a box, with my only window to life being my computer, my e-mails, my writing, my Internet searches. I had a masters degree in, I felt, a discipline that I had little talent for: education. While I have great respect for good teachers in the classroom, I've never felt I was thus gifted. My life is too interior. What then? Surely this is not all there is to my life? Once again, I don't know how to move forward.

Litheria... in your time, it has too long since you've contacted us. We have watched, guided, loved you. Know this, that you have not been, are not, in the greater realms, alone. As to your hopes and dreams, you have already planted seeds which will bear results in the spring.

You move through your life so intently, that sometimes you do not see the miraculous changes taking place in the development of your soul. Now, it is time, once again, to envision, with clarity, blessing the past and the present, and envisioning the "next" in your future.

It is not necessary to answer the question "how." Simply be clear, or allow clarity to evolve, and allow the "how" of these experiences to come to you, by intuition, by synchronicity, through people.

144

Let go of the past. Embrace the spiral of time. Let it cycle, circle, weave a new dream, a new place, a new level for you. Ride it easily, with joy, anticipation, expectation.

Let, the key word here, is "let" your dream manifest. Only clarity is required. Go beyond your present sense of aloneness and sense of poverty.   These are but 'grounds' to be seeded with life...Receive, dear one, at long last...just receive.

Let all of the love of which our realm is created, flow around you and into you, embracing you, healing you, energizing you. When you sleep, know that you are loved. Wake into that love. Live, knowing that YOU are love, and not alone.

Remember the light, dear one. Remember who you are, giver of light. The time is now. Time is eternal in the Light.

I am at peace with your guidance, I replied gratefully. Will invite healing, prosperity, guidance, and wisdom to manifest. I will expect miracles. Thank you. It was the first time I had said thank you.

By the spring of 2008, I had found a wonderful on-line publishing process, but new to the process, had no idea how anyone would find my writings. I felt I needed to "connect" again. I decided to just be quiet, as I had done so often before, and, with pen and paper in hand, just wait.

Daughter, continue to seek guidance, and communicate with us. We have no time sense here, so do not feel you are either imposing, nor too early nor too late. Simply be still, listen, and ask. Do not fall into a sense of despair regarding personal love in your life. Look back on what good has come to be in your world in the past years.

There is a fulfillment coming to you, a coming together with the one, the other that you've so longed for and sought, your own Self.

Do not, meanwhile, be afraid to share our words and wisdom with others. This will bring you a great sense of satisfaction, drawing love ever closer. For those who read these words, we wish to surround them with love, with energy, with healing and light.

Self awareness, consciousness of the Divine in each being, will soften the harshness of these days that speed forward at a rate almost incomprehensible to humans.

Be the peace that the world needs. When harm is done to you, forgive and forget quickly, and move closer and closer to your place of Divine appointment.

When goodness is done to you, appreciate and give to others so that this circle of goodness will expand and change eternity. Peace child. Extend peace, and the touch of love and healing to others. You will do that best, and most easily, through a word of encouragement.

Do not think these are empty words or trivial gestures. That which encourages the human heart, and those who do such encouraging, change the destiny of humankind.

One mind, one heart, one body, one soul, one personality, one dream, one dreamer and on into infinity.

Watch the changes, as you would watch the changes in the sky or the seasons, and rejoice. Give then, and expect then, love. We are ever with you, ever one with you. Rejoice.

11.

As you sit on the hillside,
or lie prone under the trees of the forest,
or sprawl wet-legged by a mountain stream,
the great door, that does not look like a door, opens.
~Stephen Graham, The Gentle Art of Tramping

For a time, my son and I had shared an apartment not far from our shop. When he decided he needed to live on his own, I found a small cabin in Questa, north of Taos. It was a long drive, but the beauty of the landscape, at any season of the year was breathtaking. So it was, in Questa, appropriately name for my continuing "quest" I began a different type of journal, in which nature itself became my "angel."

One: I will sit in the sun, mornings, facing the mountain. Outside my cabin, old adobe, dead bark, I hear the river call. Up close, my view is ugly, like life sometimes, a carelessly piled up barrier of old tree stumps, warped, castaway wood, bits and pieces of rusty metal. The barrier is partially a fuel-bank for Mrs. Martinez' fireplace. The Martinez', a sweet 3rd generation Northern New Mexico family from whom I rent the cabin, live in the front lodge when not in Albuquerque…But mostly, the barrier protects my cabin against the possibility of a winter river overflow.

147

Behind the wood and junk pile, like a second story-high sapling building, charcoaled denuded branches backlit by the sun, and hiding partially from my view, houses higher up on the hill across the river.

At the top of the trees, the third story level, skeletal multi-fingered cottonwoods part to frame the pyramid shaped mountain beyond, already salted with first snow. Beyond the trees, the river flows, neither asking my permission, nor dancing for my applause. It calls, but not yet, not yet.

Two: I drink skillet-warmed cappuccino from a brown, speckled tin cup. Looking over its rim I'm surprised by the sight of color, patches of green and yellow-green in this dull, muted, not yet stark winter landscape.

I see lavender flowers, standing up smartly, dancing carelessly in the light breeze. I fancy them, the flowers, determined, like me, not to surrender to winter's cold. It is, after all, still November, but I am cold in my heart and soul. Once again, or still, I am broke, indebted, praying for a sale of one of my paintings waiting patiently in my shop, where no one at all comes these fall days. I am not alone in this. Others, with greater inventories, and paying higher rents, have no customers either.

Sometimes I think He is not listening. Hopefully, He has the better picture in mind. Still, when I pass the little Catholic church here in Questa, I wonder if I should stop by, to kneel and ask His Mother Mary to get His attention! The Lord's Prayer will have to do. I have never been a true believer in anything except survival and up by the bootstraps.

Three: The river calls, flowing downward, always in movement, never static, always changing, seeking. Sometimes I am like the river, but the river knows its source and finds its destination simply by continuing onward, downward toward the sea. I could spend my days here, making art and writing, drinking coffee from a tin cup, here in the morning sunlight, listening to the river's call.

Four: The area surrounding me is the Martinez' private property, but available to vacationers as a summer campground, with RV hookups and painted red picnic tables; a fence on one side, the river on the other. There are no RV's now, and no people; they come in the summer.

This is my kingdom now, for the fall and winter and I see only what I wish to see. A floor of ground covered with rug of leaves, a mountain for walls. No apartment walls!

How I hate apartments, thin walls that let the base and brassy tones of recorded music seep through. I fear one night the dike will break, and all the noise of television, CD's, videos, DVD's, and conversations, disagreements, accusations I should not be hearing, do not want to hear, do hear sometimes do anyway, will come flooding in to drown my sanity in the pollution debris of noise.

Listening to the river's call, I hear the songs of a whole band of birds. I open the door to my kitchen and go outside. The music from KTAO follows me. A rain-chant. But neither I, nor the birds seemed to sense any sign of rain.

Five: Snow has fallen overnight, the first snow. I surrender to the river's call, and find an easy path through the reeds. I step carefully over sand, rock and pebbles; snowless still beneath the umbrella of thick, tall, red reeds.

All this, path and reeds, with winter melt, disappear for a time in the onslaught of the rushing, widening river. I push aside the reeds at the edge of the water and experience awe.

Nature's white, cold hands have sculpted ermine polar bear paws hanging from the ends of tree limb bridge. Each branch drips with crystal prisms; sharpened, glittering fingernails, befitting an ancient Asiatic potentate; and over all, a softer frosting of frozen diamond dew.

I walk back along the bank, but linger, wanting to just camp out there for the day, with no concerns for things to do, money to find. My head aches, my mind's door is shut up tight. The nagging call to be back in the world brings tears to my eyes.

Six: Saturday. The world slows down in this mountain valley, abandoned today by its mainly Hispanic populace, joining the masses jockeying baskets at Taos, or Espanola, or Santa Fe. Shopping is, for me a punishment. Books, paper, art supplies, a computer and printer with lots of ink cartridges available, two pairs of jeans and shirts. Something pretty and black to wear on the date of my dreams which never happens. That, and eats, is about all I require. A car that runs and insurance I can afford is good too.

This morning, I am content to be a part-time hermit, but the river offered me no peace today. Maybe it did offer but I, pregnant with concerns and cares could not accept its gift.

Tufts of cottonwoods caught in branches of red reeds, a croaking frog... a whole symphony of chirping birds. I climb into my car. It's time to head into Taos.

The great open vista along which I will drive, (glimpsed cautiously from side to side), will fill my mind and heart, with glorious appreciation for my New Mexico sky.

Seven: A rare, delicious day off, no substitute teaching, and the weather threatened snow, making it unlikely to expect anyone into my shop. But no river walk this morning, and no responding to the call of St. Anthony's chimes, though I intended to do both, having made a list: attend Mass, walk the river. Seeking, hoping to be touched by the sweet Spirit...of either Mother Mary's Son... or Mother Nature...or the Spirit of the River. I am not Catholic, but sometimes, the peacefulness of an empty church soothes.

Instead, I linger on my front porch, listening to the birds in the big tree over my head. I talk with B...Mr. M's good looking, shy, 50 something son. He putters with the well of the cabin across the road.

I love to see a man working! It must be the country in me. I offer him a glass of water, from the well. It *is* from a well, actually, from outside my house, though I take the water from the faucet. The well water comes from the river.

He accepts and I invite him to see how I've fixed things up. Looking round, at my cluttered walls, he apologizes, to know nothing about art, but admires my industry for sure and promises to replace the leaking propane kitchen stove with an electric one with a big oven. Maybe I'll bake apple dumplings for the shop. He leaves and my house seems emptier than usual.

I wish a man would come into my life. I have a bed and love to share, but no man. Will there ever be a man in my bed? A real bed? A real man?

Eight: The snow did not arrive. Now, the sun has already, in a north-east arc, passed the noon hour, and though I've painted poppies on an old shelf retrieved from the junk pile in back; though I've spot-painted an ugly metal cabinet (just right for art supplies); though I've varnished over a table (to cover other people's dirt), I've no urge to make "real" art. Instead, I sit, layered warmly, beneath a tree at a rough, red painted picnic table, nibbling leisurely at a big bowl of salad.

I read leisurely too, Robinson Jeffers... his poetry taking me high with the eagle...flying over California cliffs...sailing the wind... swooping down suddenly...to feast from ocean's banquet.

Somehow, it matters not today, that I have only twenty dollars in a combination of three bank accounts. Instead, I am sad today for the big, old, dry tree which fell during the night. I will make a collage painting of the old tree. *Spirit Tree*, I'll call it... and invite the spirit of the old tree to live again... in my painting.

151

Do not be jealous, my river, of my time away from you today. You have the ages to sing to. I have only the day, and I wander without plan, through its precious moments.

Nine: Before sunset...ah ha! finished, except for varnish, a collage on a found shelf board.

Not knowing what the collage might want to become, I had looked up from the picnic table to see, nested in the hillside, beyond the reeds and cottonwoods, a red-gabled house, the sky all shades of blue and white. This is what I collaged, and brought the river up right to my feet at the bottom of the picture. Being my collage, I, playing God, could put the river wherever I want.

Then, I sought you out, river...walking along a high rocky barrier at the far end of the property; beyond the dead tree; then down an easy sandy path to your banks....standing beside your piled up tree branch bridge, I try to still my mind (already anticipating tomorrow), and just listen.

I hear a waterfall...There it is, no more than a foot in depth, gloriously light footed in its hop, skip, jump and roll, its fingers of air reach urgently forward... to explore the world around the next bend.

Do the rocks bruise you, river?

Do the pebbles tickle your breast?

Do the sudden depths caress you unexpectedly?

Near the bank, stranded limbs have grabbed drifting leaves, wrapped them round their bones thickly; wet autumn colored scarves. A rivulet escapes the main, wandering playfully along both sides of a small islet. My mind wanders too...with the river. I long to go...

                down,
                        around
                                onward with the river.

   Walking back, I stop to watch a fat little black crested bird
persistently at work picking out squirming delicacies from inside a
hole in the fallen tree. She cannot bother with me, though I come
within a foot of her.

   Ten: River...barely threw you a kiss this morning, but I did
stand beside you for a moment, just beyond the pond which you
feed with your winter ice-melts. There, the Martinez' white geese
scuba-dive into the pond's murky shallows.
   Closing the shop in Taos this evening, heading north, could
hardly keep my eyes on the road; spectacular sunset show. Golds
so bright, so pure as to make kings of all earth's ages bronze green
with envy. I embraced the landscape and wish my inner landscape
were so pure and free. I wish I could overcome poverty, loneliness,
complaining.
   And oh, I wish I could shed the responsibility for my son,
just letting his illness fall away from my shoulders, and from his,
an old coat... letting it fall... fiber by fiber, to merge with the
healing earth...But he is my son...and were the coats reversed...I
know he would not, if he were able, shed care of me.
   Inside my cabin, hurrying against the encroaching
darkness, I threw a scarf around my throat; walking, stick in
hand...walking stick I've carved myself. I thought I'd have time to
see another section of the river, just beyond the pond.
   But darkness hid you, river...I heard only your voice,
onward, onward, swiftly onward... deeply, deeply quiet. Oh, that
you could wash over me, take my debris and leave me quiet too.

Eleven: Cocooned this morning till 8:30...snugly warm. Outside, the pregnant, misty slate skies will soon give birth to flakes of snow.

The river's call was clear, expectant.. inviting me, and the snow-raindrops to join its journey. Stood at the bank, and watched in awe as nature's sprinkled dance transformed the rocks below into giant, speckled robins' eggs.

You know, river, I cannot follow, but will settle for your kisses on my face, and the sucking in of great gulps of distilled, mountain air. A few raindrops kissed me, but most dove into the watery escalator and became the river.

I tossed some bark... one, another, then another... into the current, each in its turn, like a duckling swimming round and round, seeking out the soft, safe, feathery wet underside of its mother, headed for the bank... and nestled beside a log!

Then, I flung a short, scrawny stick, another and another, into the center of the river. *They* seemed to joyfully surf its undulations. Moving down stream... became slithering serpents.

I marveled at the way my mind agreed with the illusion.

Twelve: Reluctantly... I drank the dregs of the rest of still warm mocha...hung the tin cup on the fork of my stick and bending down, rinsed it in a rivulet waterfall, feeling ever so human...so basic...so pioneer. I seemed to hear happy laughter of dark-haired sisters who, in years past, had washed their own vessels in this river.

Leaving the river, I go to the school office....where promises made for interesting work, teaching, maybe journalism will, it turns out, not be honored.

Without a state credential, my master's degree from Harvard is useless. I have no gift, no patience for public school teaching beyond subbing, no tolerance for more college classes to certify me in that which I'll never do well. I leave the school... knowing one more dream is dashed.

154

I hurry to my car, the snow is falling with serious determination, and drive, carefully, quarter mile to El Seville for coffee, and an hour with the family Martinez.

The mister M tells me a story of childhood, walking to school in the snow, with only a sweater for warmth, his father, at the Molly mines, the family still living in the same area where his grandfather was once a sheep herder. I feel warmed, and full now, not only from the coffee and toast, but from the stories.

The snow, steady, but not so furious...calls out to me to take a drive, and I, who take no vacations, take time, and drive towards Red River, pulling off first, to walk by the big pond, iced over.

As I re-read this now, I feel twinges of happiness and sadness, remembering my Ladydog... did the pound find a home for her, or, sad, dead now? Cruel to have been forced to give her up. She knew, when we got to the pound that it was a place she didn't want to be. She refused to get out of the car. Finally, a kind attendant got her out. They put her in an outside pen. I was glad for that, as she would rather be outside than inside. There was a blanket, a small shelter, a bowl of water and food. I knelt down to tell her goodbye; tried to tell her how sorry I was; told her I loved her. The tears fell. Mine, and hers.

But how she had loved this pond, romping in the snow, kicking up the white stuff, lifting up her head to... what?
...perhaps to watch the elusive flakes fall back again, then skidding across the ice.

I watch great drops of snow-rain splash into the pond chasing fishermen to cars. The splashing drops create grand, green cymbals on the pond...they vibrate silently across its surface...in harmonic pulses which I, could only see....not hear...

Perhaps Ladydog would have heard the water's song.

Thirteen: Along winding road...up mountain, past the Molly mine, its ugly hillside scars masked beneath the falling snow...Past silent pines and firs...tall, skinny, like fashion models, sleek, slim, disciplined to statue-like indifferent expectation.

But the aspens...their burnt gold leaves a brief October gift bare of leaves and color, now caught snow upon curvaceous arms.

Where, oh where did all the gold go?

where, the open fabric'd leaves that sifted sunlight

where, the golden, castanets of autumn?

quivering in the noon light

whither, went the gold, as winter came?

At the town of Red River, coming upon it suddenly, around a curve and up a hill, I could not see the river, sandwiched, as it is, between the lodges, condos, shops and road. Beyond that, is the mountain....where skiers will care less anyway if they can see the river.

A sandwich at a Red River place which seemed successful doing what I envisioned my shop to be but which was not yet...an eclectic gallery (two packed levels of locals painting, sculpture and crafts) and deli.

The owner fixed my sandwich, talking to a couple of other shop owners about his, and their woes in this slow economy; not even the snow had brought visitors, he was saying, not since 9/11. I read the local newssheet, wondering if I could have more success here in Red River, doubting I could afford the rent.

Sipping hot chocolate, I watch, wistfully, always wistfully, the snow falling outside. It is a lovely, romantic view, this old-fashioned town, the ski mountain rising up majestically from the river banks. I like my own shop better, my own art work showing there, but the reuben sandwich was hot... and good.

Later: I'm home, back to my version of the river; I've walked beside it...rinsed my tin cup at its banks. In truth, the narrow waterway is the boundary between the Martinez' land and houses on the other side. But the river cares nothing for this...so I shall ignore it too.

Fourteen: I sit in morning sun...facing the snow iced mountain, contoured in purple, ebony and white, volcano shaped and shrouded, Sinai-like, in snow-mist. I half expect Moses or some Native Spirit to snowboard down its slopes carrying what?
I do not need laws only a little prosperity....a little love.

I walk to my river, rock gravel path still matted with ground snow crystals. I stand first on a wide raised plateau, that could seem to be, if I imagined it, a circle within which to meditate, but I could not find thought-words.

Instead, I let myself feel the air, still except for the river, feel the sky, purest pale blue except for wisps of vapor, feel the light, so clearly, cleanly bright. At last, my heaviness is replaced with light. Perhaps I'm invisible. There's no one around to tell me that I'm not.

Fifteen: At the rivers edge (another rain or snow and I'll have to walk higher up)...to the bridge of limbs...watching the ground to avoid sinking into a hidden puddle.

I stop, planting my walking stick like a third leg...turning myself into a living tripod, absorb the pattern of the limbs ...covered still in snow...the water rushing resolutely beneath them.

Time to go, but turning back I catch my breath. I'd not looked high enough. The red reeds across the river seemed a gossamer web back lit by the sun…spun by a giant crystal spider.

Away from the river, I stop to look closely at the fallen tree…Its grayed wrinkled bark twisting around its shape as if an old bag woman had pulled and tugged her frayed cloak closer in a vain attempt to get warm.

I wondered if, perhaps last night's collage, a single tree, its roots straddling a rivulet, its leaves, black and tan and gold, seeming to burst, explode even, from within its leafy mass, was not a response to a call from the tree for memoriam.

Sixteen: I walk once around the outside of my cabin, studying its sagging, sloped roof for some explanation of the walking sound I hear briefly, each night.

Looking up, I become distracted, undone by the crisp northern light in the sky. A silhouette: massed, black, tree-top menorahs, reaching, a whole winter's season upwards.

Above the trees, two velvet midnight blue ravens in flight…they, the ravens, flew low, and toward me, then dipped, the way we tip our heads in passing hellos, breath-filled, heart beating planes tipping their wings. I heard their wings, a harmonic swish, swish against the windless air. I want to cry out!

I have walked the snow crust

and watched the river's surge.

I have seen a crystal sun web....

and I have heard

the sound of the wings of ravens..

158

Sixteen: Braved the cold outside to paint poppies on canvas board. I worked standing up at an old picnic table. By end of day I was sniffling; my hands were blue, and the paintings the ugliest things, with no evidence that I've ever studied art at all. I thought to walk to the river but only gazed down at it from above the reeds.

I am distant... distant from the river...
distant from my work...
distant from myself.

Curled up in the worn, but big, yellow armchair, my red and black penguin bathrobe as a comforter, I read Walt Whitman, some Hemingway short stories, then a detective novel.

From my Wal-Mart CD player, the amused chagrin of a country singer...*"some beach, somewhere"* makes me laugh aloud.

No river-walks for four days...only waves of heavy sickness, from the cold, for sure, from worry, most certainly, from exhaustion. Had it been a numbing sickness, numbing into sleep, it might have been a blessing, but my deep discomfort gave me only one day of sleepy forgetfulness and escape between my worn, warm blankets.

Seventeen: Other nights, hours of awakeness and unwelcome flashbacks of all the cold winters and miseries of my oft detoured life:

...the winter in Dallas, when I could only buy mittens for my children's Christmas gifts...the other winters I left them in the care of grandparents or others, frantically, panic'd, chasing some dream that life would be better if I left, got away, had a chance, convinced they'd be better off without me. Did they then, do they now, know, I loved, and love them?

Nearer now, to the end of my life than the beginning... I've made my chances...college degrees... some writing, some art hither, thither and even some good unto the other now and again

But I do not understand... truly do not understand... why the chances some take lead somewhere... and mine lead always, to another cold, broke winter.

If the end came tonight, no one would even know. No, it is not feeling sorry for myself, only wondering, how others... wasted thoughts.

I look around... a painting could be painted, a poem written, a book read. I look in the refrigerator. It is empty.

Eighteen: At my shop. Doors open. Lights on. Coffee made. No people at all in downtown Taos, so no sales. But two paintings by e-mail and phone... I had expected these, from a summer client, buying other collages for his wife. I wait anxiously for those checks.

I made a lunch from the sparse supply of food laid in for my coffee-bar service. A tuna salad sandwich, an apple. I switch the radio on.

The war goes on and the media frenzy and I drift into a mindless listening mode, against my right judgment, to a talk radio show and agreeing, against my sane judgment, that we send every self-righteous sob to fight in every soldier's place, while I want, in my heart's judgment, every soldier and innocent citizen to know I care.

I don't know how to pray in time of war...or in time of peace. What of the children? What can I do? Tonight I am impotent.

Nineteen: I am alone in the shop, this week before Thanksgiving. I'd called a local church: "...be glad to help distribute food," hoping, I must confess, to take home any leftovers

160

for me and my son; but he, living on his own, has his disability check; and prefers pork and beans in cans to turkey anyway.

"We've got enough people, thank you very much," said the church and I didn't want to admit to needing food.

What has this to do with a river poem? Nothing... everything... flotsam jammed up in a curve of the river, waiting for the rain or wind or ice melt to loose it up, sweep it free... send it swirling down, down to the sea or some pond anyway.

I do not know what to do to make things better, so unfit as I am to work to work for others... what do I know other than collaging and painting, poeming and shop making.

Tomorrow, I will just show up, set up the shop for business...and hope for a customer, a call, a letter, a someone, a something, to make the difference I cannot.

The winter has been bad for everyone. All the galleries and little shops, the mom and pop cafes. Only Wal-Mart thrives.

Twenty: Snow! Heavy, since dawn, and I've slept since dawn, finally, after a restive, recriminating night. Dress quickly....have no boots, but need only to walk to car, parked under protective branches, and scrape soft snow off windows. I wave at the river as I drive by the pond...the world in town awaits, but doubt it waits at my shop door.

No urgency though. Nobody cares when I arrive, just me. So, in Questa, pull into the El Seville café and read the Albequerque Journal, gratefully sipping hot coffee, but glancing apprehensively now, out the window as the snow quickly blankets my windows. I wish I could sit there all day watching the mountain receive its confirmation dress.

I skip the usual front page news, and on the second page, Bush, son, Bush, dad, and Carter, smile in rainy day photo beside Clinton, celebrating with him the opening of his Presidential Library.

161

Further down the page, Bob Dylan; his *Like a Rolling Stone*, named as top-ever recorded song. Said the writer of the article: "He (Dylan) changed the whole nature of song writing."

A photo story next, that a replica (able to bestow healing and blessings by virtue of having been leaned against the original) of Our Lady of Guadalupe was being installed in the Cathedral in Albuquerque.

On the third page, Howard Stern blesses *his* congregation in New York's Time Square...bestowing upon them... boom boxes! The photo depicts his fans apparently shouting out noisy bleeps to celebrate his move to cable radio, agreeing with him that the FCC is F-U-C-K-E-D!

Twenty one: At my shop… again, nobody on the snowy street. How do the other shops around, paying higher rent than I do, manage these days of no tourist buying? One artist in town, pays no rent at all: her gallery is on her own land, inside her own bed and breakfast inn.

An odd town, Taos; this "artsy" section, appealing to tourists (when they show up); and further down the main drag, the stores that sell tires, food, and stuff to the families who live here and work, selling tires, food and stuff, teaching school, doing plumbing, painting, fence building, and hauling whatever you want hauled.

I make the coffee, put together some chicken salad, crab salad for sandwiches. A gallery owner comes in to order a couple of sandwiches. Go back to your shop, I say, I'll bring them over. So, the day is not a loss. Then, a woman comes in, buys one of my hand painted cards. Her husband buys a book.

A man comes in, buys two small, purple flower paintings. Wants to buy my latest, a "blue nude" painting on paper, I tacked it to the wall, to get a sense of it; it wasn't even dry. I'll be back he

162

says, throwing a hundred dollars on my counter. I have to have that blue nude.

People like my shop; I like the people. All I need is more people.

Twenty two: An unfinished painting on the round table in the middle of my shop, but not in mood to paint. Having a few people in the shop yesterday, and some sales, I am hoping for more of the same today.

I clear off a space at the table, pour some coffee, make myself a salad, and pick up the two day old Albequerque newspaper.

One story reports that a radio jock labeled Condie Rice, new Secretary of State, an 'aunt Jemima," handing out boxes of pancake mix. Will this never end? Says Linda Ronstadt about no one, or someone, "America is full of Hitlers!"

I glance back at the photo of Clinton: you were all of us...why'd you blow it? Or why'd you let her...well, never mind. Dylan, you're still, gravel voice, my favorite song-writer. But the news? The stuff of pablum for pop, pop, pop America.

Soldier, if I get to Albuquerque, I'll light a candle for you somewhere near Our Lady's replica...if not, may Jesus have mercy. Please, please, have mercy.

Howard Stern, I have nothing to say to you, other than your f...g "free" speech balances somehow the hallelujah jeezus crowd. I actually envy both groups of believers in their belonging "insiderness."

Nope, don't think I'll join either group, nor any.

Twenty three: Late afternoon...a gray sky promises snow tonight.Mr. Martinez, at 80-something, is out back of my cabin, sorting through the wood pile barrier, cutting limbs and logs with a

163

power-saw. Inside, I've put screws and wire in a second finished collage.

The edges of these pieces bug me. I wrap paper around to the back, but still, compared to canvas, they look sloppy. Maybe I should just dump them in the river and float down to the ocean on them.

An odd piece, though this one; tree, meadow, stream. Perhaps it is the slant of the tree trunk that puts me ill at ease; a leaning tower of Pizza tree; full of figures and faces and unintended images which emerged after the piece was dry and varnished. Spirit tree indeed.

I pull my coat around me, wrap a scarf, and to the river. It held no joy for me. Listen, just listen, I hear...? I listen but do not hear.

Walking back, I continued past my cabin. Pulling my paint-splattered jacket closer against the cold, I eased up on the pond. Mallards paddling peacefully, soft feathered creatures pushing through the ice crust like metal-skin ice-breakers.

Later, finishing up my tree collage, listening to sad, funny, dumb, thoughtful, sappy, romantic...and patriotic c & w music. I make some hot chocolate and attack another found board, creating a whole new collage. It's a winner I think.

...Firebird Dreams? A bright, wild feathered bird (a Phoenix?) against a gray evening sky, flying low above black and amber hills and a pueblo, maybe inhabited, maybe not. The colors, energy, patterns please me.

I re-heat my chocolate and thumb through "Time." Somebody selling art work by children as young as three years old for $30,000 and upward. I'm envious. I struggle to put a $300 price tag on my own.

An early evening walk. Crunched through ice-snow to river and walk close, alongside the water. Bank, logs, limbs all covered with snow. Still, still, I try to still my mind, but I cannot be stilled. Is it "I" or what, that will not be stilled?

164

Near my cabin, I see B's footprints nearby, probably checking to see if I had propane. I place my size five in his big prints for a pathway through the snow.

Later, the propane heater turned up to cozy, I paint on paper, having run out of canvases of any sort, three poppies and an adobe scene. They'd sell well enough if matted or framed.

River... stop calling, I have work to do. Before sleep calls, I've collaged a poppy. I like it. It seems painted on clay, jewel-like really, with torn colors from magazines to form the flower, acrylics tying all together.

Twenty four: Felt cheerier this morning. Perhaps due a good night's sleep last. Perhaps the sunny, clear sky today.

Varnished two collage poppies, then walked to river. Oh! The crunch of snow under foot! I follow my own prints of a few days before, fossilized for now in nature's deep freeze.

The tree limb bridge is decorated with exquisite crystal prisms. What was the bear paw of another cold morning...at the end of the limb...has now been transformed into the image of a giant ice sculpture centipede.

Across the river, other branches near the water have grown ice combs. The many fingered sickles seem to comb the water as it rushes beneath. The river runs free beneath the frozen ice. Would that I could run free beneath my frozen beingness.

Snowed all night. So, drove the 20 mile drive from Questa to Taos at a cautious 15 miles per hour. The up, then down, then up and down road looked and felt like a toboggan ride. Happily, what little traffic there was, drove slowly too.

Indescribable beauty on both sides. Mountain, trees, hillside, valley, meadows, all dressed in snow. I breathed in the beauty and tried to breathe out anxiety...about almost everything.

The day most over in my shop and not even a cup of coffee sold, much less the egg nog, chocolate and sandwiches I've readied. No one at all on Kit Carson Road. No one at all in our building. I look at an unfinished painting, and wonder I would bother finishing it. Instead, wrap some pieces to send to my friend in Paris. He's promised to try to get a showing. I don't place much hope in this promise, but at least the paintings will be in Paris.

Twenty five: River, river take me away...take me anywhere. I love my little cabin. I love my little shop, whatever am I asking? An "anywhere state of mind" perhaps, that would be better than wondering how I will make it from one day to the next.

Started out for the river...but snow frozen into slippery ice. Wearing only loafers, turned back. Walked instead, through powdery snow to the pond. Some small animal foot-prints led to the ice. I wondered if some critter had walked across to the other side.

Cold, severely so, despite layering in this 20 degree clime. Walking back, circled my cabin, wondering now at the big prints in the snow, too large for a dog.

Last night, after glass of wine, some chicken, some Glen Miller...painted a green-blue vase of yellow-orange roses on a reddish table. It's pretty, will probably sell. I do not get the same satisfaction from painting these as from the poppies or the collages.

Can I endure yet another day of no sales? If only I could make enough during the on-season to support this off season. With snow most of night with wind blowing powdery drifts onto the porch, have decided to stay home to paint, beginning a big, 36 x 36 poppy.

Making sandwich for lunch, spilled barbecue sauce on small painting of clay pot; probably, being a similar color, sauce enhanced the pot. Perhaps, when noting info on the back, I should write: acrylic, varnish, barbecue sauce.

166

Twenty six: Crunched though soft, but deep snow to the pond: I tossed a rock out towards the center. It landed with a clunk. At the far edge, the pink, plastic flamingos, their feet planted firmly beneath the snow, unflappable, did not react.

More tracks in the snow... tiny prints (a bird) with two lines on each side, as if a fairy creature were pulling a sled. Perhaps the lines were made by the bird's tail? Behind my house and down to the river, huge prints, maybe seven to ten inches long, like two big toes, and a heel in back. Perhaps an Elk?

Looking behind me, I see my own prints, deeply etched. Alongside, a line, then golf-ball sized hole, then another line. The light drag of my own walking stick. How odd, to see evidence that my physical being had walked there.

At the river...no ice sickles on the tree limb bridge. Mounds of fresh powder had turned the limbs and logs into white, puffy abstracts. Perhaps Claes Oldenburg had wandered by, to do a pop art commission for Mother Nature.

To the south, bluing skies... to the north, a dark grey backdrop, hanging high behind the Rockies.

Twenty seven: Hot sun today, hot on my head, urged me to take off of my black knitted cap. The strange, colored atmosphere disoriented me. First, rosy-peach (though no colors like that in the blue-white-gray sky).

Then, when I stood on a wide patch of snow surrounded by rust and gold reeds... the air turned golden. I wanted to bottle the light. I work in dim, unwindowed spaces. An artist ought to have good light. It is though, this odd, Northern New Mexico light, that drew the artist moths to this country.

Worried the 36 x 36 poppy most of the day. Like the shape but not the color; it needs brightness. Illumination some artists call it. I need the same. Time to walk to the river.

167

Longed for my camera: the ice formation draped over the limb and log jam bridge looked as if the elegant translucent creature from "The Abyss" had come to rest. Its color, like ET by the river, fading to purest white in a stage of dying, yet holding to life. The ice sculpture's transparent wings hovered ever so slightly above the rushing waters, seeming to capture bits of the river as it splashed upward.

River, river, absorb and recreate me!

Twenty eight: At last! my camera lens, repaired, has arrived in the mail paid for by a one-third portion of a sold painting! But, I've no heart to go to the river.

Instead, walking around the grounds, find some gloriously curved branches. Spent hours making banisters for my front porch steps, so I won't slip, again, on the glassy, iced stairs.

Caught up in this building process, I create a screen of branches, waxed string and feathers. In the afternoon light, the string becomes gossamer spider webs. In the breeze, the feathers become tiny birds and the branches...wandering fossil-like fingers of nature. I know Mr. Martinez will take my "installation" down when I leave. For now, it's lovely.

Ten days till Christmas and no peace, yet, these 2000 some years, in Bethlehem nor Baghdad. Are you sleeping, Dad in Heaven? Why the suffering? Why the dying? The river will still be there...and ice, still on the logs and along the bank.

Twenty nine: I stand by the river bank, holding my camera close, beneath my coat, trying to warm it...it wants refuge from the cold to function.

I look up...startled at the sound of an animal...galloping down the river towards me. I fumble for my camera switch, but too late. The beautiful, awesome female deer...taller than me...was only a few feet away. I didn't want to move, didn't want to

168

frighten her. We stare at one another, then she... quite as startled as me... turned…

Oh! Don't go beautiful thing, I cried out…but she bounded out of the river up the bank... into the reeds.

Later, drove to the small, and only Questa store...bought ice cream. My fridge has no freezer. So, once back home, scooped up a bowl of snow and planted the carton in the snow ice and the bowl, in the fridge.

Ate my dinner, and put leftover rice into a tin plate and placed it on the front steps. Soon, arrived a ring-tailed critter with big furry body; his behind to me... his eyes watching the yard for competitors, I suspect. He did not notice my peeking through the curtain at the door window... to observe his feasting. I did not share my ice cream.

Thirty: Finished the second of two large, 36 x 36 poppies.
This second one is exquisite, golden, full of light. The first, am not so fond of; reds, and must work to bring in more light.

These are abstracts though; not really poppies. I paint, I think, energy instead. Do I imagine I see faces, creatures in the seacolored backgrounds? In one, a sea seeming to eat at the poppy shore; in the second, a muddy green, billowy retreat.

Well, I shall name them Tsunami one and two, and try, in so doing, honor those who died more than 150,000 now they say…and to honor those who struggle to live.

New Year's eve in my shop, with no place else to go, except a noisy, heavy drinking downtown pub. I stayed open till nine P.M., putting out some iced champagne, should anyone wander in. Someone did. They, the whole family, had been there the day before. Now, they were ready to go home, back to Missouri. They wanted the big, red poppy. Did I have some way to wrap it? I surrendered two sheets I used to protect the floor when painting in the alcove outside the shop. For $1300, I would have wrapped the piece in my clothes.

They would, would the piece was hung in their dining room, they said, send me a photo. I held the check close to me, but did not follow them out. How they got the painting, themselves, their two kids and the dog, into their SUV, I'll never know. I could pay two rents, on my cabin, on the shop, and buy some more canvases. The year had ended well.

Thirty one: The New Year has come and gone, and I... the planet even... face uncertain, challenged futures. What is there to do but create... love, share that which we have to share and not give in to undertow?

I walk by the river and breathe…breathe in the majesty of the snowy mountains…and watch the river...moving....freezing, thawing, changing, reflecting.

Gypsylady by the river...how do you find yourself today?

Weary, yes... carrying the burden of my son's illness; struggling yes, with all the old money ills; grief-stricken, yes, for the world, the planet, the people; lonely, yes... no man in sight to fill my heart and bed.

But what the hell! I will throw my artist's cape around my shoulders and paint another bright poppy…golden, brilliant, deep and pale. I will suck the yellows, reds, oranges and greens into my selves, and warm, from color and creating....will be born again.

I suppose even gypsies get old, but I will, in growing older grow older, become aged wine, and go on, like you river... forever... down, around... and onward. Somewhere out there, river, there is life and laughter… joy even, and maybe love, maybe contribution, somehow, in some small way... to the human race.

Dream me another dream gypsy. I'm not done for yet and the river calls...Take me river… forever onward, down to the sea.

170

12

She who is centered in the Tao
can go where she wishes, without danger.
She perceives the universal harmony,
even amid great pain,
because she has found peace in her heart.
~ Tao Te Ching, Lau-tzu

The late spring economy continued was more daunting than the winter. Teachers were feeling the crunch too, as I seldom received calls to substitute. Impetuously, anticipating a summer in which I could neither pay my shop rent nor my own rent, I closed the Taos shop and returned again to California to teach another summer at the camp for kids-at-risk.

I loved the camp experience, having once wished as child, I could stay at camp all summer, and now, as an adult, I had, several times. I had a huge "crafthouse" all to myself, and gave daily classes to kids between the ages of seven and twelve. My afternoon "free-time" was the most popular activity, (except on a very hot day, when the pool won out), with as many as seventy five kids showing up to work indoors with beads, outdoors painting on cardboard, at a wood table set-up, creating bows and arrows, constructing houses and cars, dolls, and whatevers from the abundant supply of recycle items I'd collected before camp started.

On days off, after one group of kids had left, and before another group arrived, I sometimes drove into Santa Cruz, for dinner and a walk along the beach. Other times, I walked beneath the towering redwoods that encircled the camp.

It was a wonder-filled time, sometimes hectic, with the long, fourteen to sixteen hour days, sometimes frustrating when the powers that be interfered, but the combination of trees, space to teach, and experiencing the joy of discovery on the faces of the kids, always made me reluctant for camp to end, wishing each time that this could have been a year-round job.

That season completed, I moved to the San Francisco east bay, into a Hud apartment my sister had found for me. I felt ridiculous, to have two degrees, and no way, given my age and the general economy, to get hired. Meanwhile, the apartment was quiet and lovely, the rent was reasonable, and I was able to use the time to paint, and to finish my novel.

During this time, I also got to know my sister and her family in a special way. The healing of relationships of which Leytha had spoken to me, was in full swing.

It was unbelievable to finish my novel, and then I set about trying to find an agent. Of course, the rejections came in as fast as the proposals went out. Finally, deciding I was too "old" to wait, in this changing world, for someone to say yes to a first novel, I published the book myself, calling it *The Long Shadow*. Later, I would make a few revisions and re-title the novel as *Code of the Running Cross.*

Joyous to see my work in print, I wanted so much to go to Paris and meet the friend who had become my muse in the writing, but had to take a practical, financial long way around. I finally found an ESL teaching position in Taiwan in the fall of 2006.

It was an adventure in learning, for both me, the teachers, and my students. Keeping a blog, the year I was there, I eventually, formatted that "diary," into a book, *1000 Steps, an ESL Teaching Adventure in Taiwan.*

172

During my Taiwan school holidays, in February, 2007, and again in July following the completion of my teaching contract, I spent three weeks in Paris. So, at last, five years after our first e-mails, I finally met the friend who had made such a difference in my life, encouraging me, on-line, to live my life, to write, to paint, to love. We shared the long awaited bottle of champagne, and the mutual promise to continue our creative friendship.

I had already planned a sequel to the Code of the Running Cross. In fact had already written a few years back, a manuscript that I had made some headway toward convert it, into a prequel of the the novel. Now though, I found that the need to concentrate on the continuing characters of Claudia and Francois, (namesakes of our selves, though considerably different in character and relationship), was too emotionally challenging. My Paris muse now found himself confronting the daily challenges of the global economy as it affected France, and his business there. He had no time, despite his promise, to be the supportive receptor of my e-mails re the two novels progress.

There were other manuscripts to polish up and put into self-published formats: and so I did that: three stories for children, a collection of inspirational poems, and two earlier versions of the Leytha letters, which I originally published as Guidance Angel volumes one and two.

I no longer painted, needing both a workshop setting, or the outdoors, but more, a place to show and sell my work. Instead, partly to cope with the long evenings alone (no car, no going out after dark), began a series of wall hangings, braiding recycled material, and weaving randomly with yarns while I watched television. About twenty-five of these pieces now cover my walls, the old paintings from Taos consigned to a closet.

I could never have guessed, struggling as I was, when I first began my "correspondence" with Leytha, how her words to me would come to pass, or when or how. There are times I wish I could regularly reach into that inner space, or "beyond" space,

173

time, and simply "ask," but I do not. Most days, I simply reach into nature, and listen to the wind, the trees, the birds.

I also waited to hear some response from the applications I've e-mailed, to again teach overseas. I fence-straddled, wondering if instead, I should continue on with the alternative licensure for New Mexico, a process requiring far more paperwork (and some expense) than the easier to find overseas jobs, but which, once accomplished, would give me a sense of "home."

I felt stuck in yet another Hud residence (lovely, but still…), surrounded by senior citizens, some of whom are active with family, but most are resigned, or at peace with retirement, while I was neither. My heart yearned for excitement, involvement, financial success, and love.

Frustrated with my health, nothing serious, but a whole basketful of minor complaints that irritate: insomnia (a life-time of this), pain in my legs, a chronic, wracking cough. Far too many days I've sat at my desk, staring out at the trees, wondering, worrying, feeling alone, abandoned by life, by myself.

13

We have all a better guide in ourselves, if we would attend to it, than any other person can be. ~ Jane Austen

Do I have a choice? Do I have choices? Asking the question, I sense "Leytha." As before, I "access" this presence through writing. I "hear" nothing. I just write what I sense. As before, Leytha addresses me as "Litheria," my name in Spirit, she says, meaning "giver of light." I feel a long way from becoming my name.

Litheria: It has been some time since we've communicated, and we are happy that you've crossed the bridge of time and place to ask and listen once again.

You are concerned with choices you've made, whether by free-will, or because you feel you've had no choice and had to take certain actions, have led you to where you are today.

It is not that you have no choice in these matters, and seem consigned to waiting to see if "they" make up their mind in your favor, but that you made a choice to reach out. Now that you've done that, having made that choice, taken the actions required to

follow through, you're being confronted with other aspects of making a choice.

These aspects, for you, at this time, involve other people, who must also ultimately make choices regarding you, and whether you, your experience and what you might offer, fits in with their own plans.

Making a choice is never a one-way affair. It is like coming to a crossroads and deciding whether to go left, right, straight ahead, or even turn around and go back. But once making the choice, choosing the direction, once you start moving again, new choices will appear.

You'll experience backward looking as well: did you make the right choice; what if you'd gone the other direction; what have you missed by making the choice that you did?

You do have a choice but the making of it is only a part of the larger picture, not static, not a one-time, end- all thing.

The "feelings" you have at the moment are the natural result of wanting some changes, changes you see as improvement, in your life. Bless where you find yourself today, and the choices you made to get you to this place. Find beauty, meaning, love in the place where you are.

Congratulate yourself, in fact, that you made choices in the past, some wise, some which seem, on looking back, not so wise and that you've learned from this.

Encourage your "self" as you would encourage others. Do what you can, while at the same time practicing open-heart, open-mind, with expectation, but without "precise" expectations of what the changes, the flowers of your choices, must look like. The analogy of flowers is a good one, in that seeing "choice" as a natural action, an action of nature, there must be, in your attitude, a real sense of patience, of "in good time," that the results will manifest.

It is so important for you to realize that the outcome of your choices are not dependent on you alone, but are dependent on how you, and your choices fit into the overall scheme of life, and this "fit" may equally be negative or positive.

You may seem not to have a choice, for example, due to responsibilities you value, or money you don't have, but you have the choice to take a walk, or e-mail a distant friend, or look for unique ways to increase your sense of abundance to make the other choices possible.

Embracing this attitude towards choice will also help you become aware of opportunities in your life, environment, that you had not seen before; doors to secret gardens one might say; doors which were there all the time, while you saw only solid walls, prisons of frustration marked "no way out."

Once you begin to bless the choices you've made in the past, and to make choices in the present that can lead to satisfying results in the immediate presence, it will become easier for you to see the "secret" doors that surround you at all times.

They are there, but it is only through changing your attitude, and embracing this new, but more realistic way of perceiving choice, that you will come to see answers that you could not see before.

I watch the news, re Iran today, and wish I had someone intelligent to discuss this with. I read books that I cannot share, and worry things back and forth in my head until, once more I burden my patient sister with a long, meandering e-mail, trying to sort things out in the process. But, writing here, I feel my "angel voice" nudging me.

How did you feel when you shifted your attention from present blessing to future uncertainties?

I felt an inner calmness transformed to anxiety, I answer.

This choice is also yours then: to choose how you wish to feel. If blessing your present reality results in a feeling of wellness, peacefulness, then, do you suppose that blessing your unseen future could produce the same sense of wellness, of peacefulness, of a blessed present when tomorrow becomes today?

The truth of this is profound. Imagine a bridge of light on which you can walk from today into tomorrow. On this bridge are others passing by you in both directions. They greet you and raise their hands in blessing and you return this greeting and blessing to them.

These "others" are your thoughts, some traveling into a yet unseen, unknown, undefined future, some having experienced an aspect of that future (through choices you've made or are making to create, according to the knowledge, desires that you now have), are returning; they too bless you.

Imagine that these are returning to your past, and, in fact, to the greater, universal past, and that they, your thoughts, go there to bring you greater wisdom, a larger perspective, ideas, energy, renewed vision.

178

Imagine that those thoughts, hurrying in front of you are going into that divine country of the yet undiscovered (by you, or anyone), that place called the future, the next moment, next hour, day, year, lifetime, eternity.

Bless these thoughts especially, because they will return, bringing you insights, awareness and guidance, like scouts who hurry ahead on a wilderness exploration. You cannot "beam" yourself physically into some future place, but through thought, imagination and through the lens of yesterday's experience (that of your own personal, world and universal history), discern how some futures (as they are without limit) may unfold.

Recall the experience of swimming, and how you learn to allow the water to hold you, guide you, and how your movements are quite different from those you experience out of the water, standing on the sand, or the concrete side of a pool. "Swimming" in the future, imagining your future, is a somewhat similar experience.

I find these ideas remarkable, since, when writing (as in dreaming, I suppose), even when writing fiction, I actually *experience* these alternate realities. Leytha seems to be suggesting that "mind" sends out "probes" to explore other possibilities. In "basic mode" this is like a preliminary scan, a topical survey of yet undiscovered, no, perhaps it is more like "not yet experienced" reality.

Perhaps thought-probe details are vague, not clear, perhaps because there exits a "there" which exists for itself, or for one or millions of people (or no people at all), but you, or rather "I" am not yet in the scene. Were I to enter the scene, both the scene (the alternate possibility) would change, for me, for others, or for the non-others.

179

I wonder if clairvoyance is not a finer tuned mode of these "thought-probes?" But even here, because there are limitless factors, timings, preconceptions, and movement that unless slowed down and amplified, would seem like so many hills of ants, or fast-motion film. Even the latter though, has a single story to tell. Probing the world of thought, or the future, or merely several possibilities or probabilities would be rather like taking each of the characters in a film, and telling just one aspect of the story, or their stories; the film would be endless.

Imagine Casablanca, told mainly from Ric's perspective. But we also see (as the filmmakers did a great job of suggestion those other realities in each of the colorful characters in what is, ultimately, an ensemble piece), Casablanca from the perspective of many of those characters, if only briefly. It was likely too that the filmmakers continued to ask "What if this character took this path, or that character took another? Resolving that question of course, resulted in the classic ending of the film.

What we don't know, is what would have happened to the characters (and the film), if any single character had taken another path. That, of course, is the advantage (and, to virtual realists, perhaps the disadvantage), is that the characters must continue along the path to which they are destined by the filmmakers.

As fiction, they have no choices, other than the choice (life) given them by writers, actors, make-up artists, costumers, lighting techs, etc, and then, finally the perceptions (multiple) of the audiences.

But we human are not fiction (are we?), nor at the mercy of the filmmaker (destiny, or no?), and so, we apparently, whether acting, reacting, or pro-acting, create our own stories, making not a single choice, but a series of choices, self-correcting choices in some cases (like walking), or self-destructive (indulging in what Star Trek's "Spock" would label as lack of logic).

In the former, we ask "what if," in the latter, it may be " I know, but I must do this anyway," or perhaps we make choices based on "I don't know." Well, enough from me. I will continue listening now to Leytha.

Choice then, based on what you are experiencing today, is not a concrete thing, when you consider that the future (the next second, even) is not concrete, but fluid.

It may be easier for you as you begin to understand this, to consider choice as something to be trusted, something you can trust in yourself, something you can trust in others, but to realize that the "future" or outcome (the first result) of choice is fluid, and can and will be defined only as you and others arrive simultaneously in a moment in time.

For example, today, in this moment, you are thinking of walking to the post office to mail a manuscript to a publisher. You have made many, many choices in the past and many others have made choices which affect this decision. Your personal, and world history, your lifetime of exploring reading, writing, life; finally, the long process of writing the book (and choosing to), and even the many choices you made to live where you are now living, where the post office is within a pleasant walking distance.

On the way to the post office you will make many choices; how fast you will walk, what you will see and focus on, what you will do in response to something unexpected, and even what you choose to think, imagine, bless as you walk.

Once, however, you place the manuscript on the counter, and pay the postage, you have literally sent it, your thoughts, hopes, dreams, into the future and it is a future that will now have some definition. For you personally, you can choose to anticipate with either anxiety or resignation or hopefulness the result.

181

Beyond that, this aspect of your future is now an on-going part of the present of others: the postal carrier, the airline, the deliverer of the packet, the reception, review, and decision of those considering your manuscript. All of this is "their" present, but choices they make will affect your future.

Your choices however, for your "present," regarding the choice you made to prepare and send the manuscript are now myriad; you can choose an attitude of hope and blessing and expectation; you can choose to continue work on the other projects you've already begun; you can celebrate that you believe in your work, and that one more time you have been willing to submit it to someone who has the power to say yes, or no.

And, you can choose to examine the present and create some other future, for some other aspect of your life, such as a willingness for friendship, love, physical health, joy, etc.

14

If you look to others for fulfillment,
you will never truly be fulfilled. ~ Tao-Te-Ching, Lau-tzu

I've now interviewed on the phone with two women administrators of the school in Mexico, but it's been more than a week now and I've not heard back. Since the last question was a request for my age, (on the e-mailed application, but perhaps they didn't notice), I wonder if they'll make a negative decision based on that.

With only six weeks now until the beginning of a new school semester, and my own needs to make decisions whether to update my passport anticipating out of the country work, or to continue on, devoting a similar expense to the stateside, New Mexico license, creates both a sense of urgency and a sense of fence-straddling, since I don't have the funds to do both.

Then, at midnight (morning, in Iraq) two nights ago, I received two calls from the administrators (also women) of the school in Kurdistan—the personnel director, and the principal. These calls also went well, and, in fact, the latter one ended with the principal saying that were I to come there, I would begin at the elementary school level, but with my Masters, it was likely I'd be transferred to their new University.

183

Well, of course, the idea of living and working in Kurdistan is an exotic, adventuresome idea, and the idea that I would be making some contribution to children (and associates), who will be part of the rebuilding of their nation, is satisfying.

I want to be happy, to be enthusiastic, to be joyous in my expectation of this, but have no one, no friend, only my patient, tolerant sister (who this time, has not replied).

And still, New Mexico dangles its carrot in front of me; I can see, feel, the first snow, the sunsets, the open spaces, the small space with a fireplace I would call home, the little storefront gallery I might go to, after school, or on weekends.

But all is not in place for that. I will have to make a choice, when my money is here on the first, whether to continue the teaching license application process and then, see if anyone will hire me, with the semester so soon to start, or whether, if a contract arrives from Iraq, whether to hurry through a passport renewal, and the visa process.

I worry now, too, because I'm experiencing constant, and severe pain in my lower back and legs. Little help from doctors, except to give me non-narcotic medicine for pain, which I seldom take.

What choices then, do I need to make? Perhaps I am putting the proverbial cart before the horse. Perhaps the process I need to be involved with here, is sending out "mind-probes." Perhaps I don't have enough information to make choices right now.

I didn't go to Leytha, seeking answers. It seemed for the moment, just sufficient to be processing "my stuff," but it was beginning to irritate me. I had insomnia again, followed by sleeping until almost noon once I did get to sleep. Being alone, in the sense of no meaningful conversations with anyone was almost intolerable.

An invitation though, has come from my sister, my "real time" angel, to spend a few weeks on her "acre" in the high desert of California, not far from Reno, Nevada. So, here I sit, after a comfortable night in their RV, with my sister's permission to do absolutely nothing for the month of July, and her encouragement just to "rest."

She knows this "rest" will be impossible for me. I've plugged in my laptop and looked at the two typewriter composed manuscripts I want to get onto Word. I've arranged a bit the "fixin's" for a craft project I brought along, that of making some small arrangements from the flowers I've hung above my desk to dry (collected on walks) so my sister might use them in one or the other fund-raisers she goes to in this tiny town.

I've put all three projects on a "later this evening when it's cooler," and returned here to cogitate, and make my ways through the currently cobwebbed maze of my mind, hoping for another light-filled forest clearing, and new direction.

"Fessing up," I keep hoping "new direction" will mean work published, art showing and selling. I hope it will mean continuing to try improving my health. I hope especially, it will mean making some contribution to humanity, and, well, the truth? Love and companionship and a little money too.

For the past year and half, I have lived like a hermit in terms of other people. This of course, is hardly new to me. I love being involved in some activity, such as teaching, or coordinating an event, but then such peace, when I can be alone again.

Out of this aloneness, I have been focused on completing and independently publishing my several books: the novel, some inspirational poetry, some children's stories, an account of my time teaching in Taiwan.

I've gotten much pleasure too, from walking in the wooded area in back of my apartment building, collecting twisted branches and petrified vines, and then weaving on them with yarn.

I've even conducted an eight week writers' workshop for a small group of residents where I live; the youngest was sixty two, the eldest, ninety-seven, published their efforts as *Voices of Sea*

Turtles, and entered it our area's County Fair, where the book won a fourth place ribbon, and two of my little books, *Dare to Dream*, and the children's story, *Shmadiggle and Imagination Asteroid,* won first place in their category.

I am frustrated though by the on-going Internet search for literary agents and ultimately (real) publishers, and or, the wherewithal to promote, as an independent publisher, my own books. And, frustrated that the weaving pieces I've been doing, need to be framed or mounted protectively, to be shown, and I have no place to show and sell, and without a car this past year and half, no way to get there if I did, and no funds to enter art shows in the area. One booth had a $700 price tag.

I'm irritated by television news which seems to have long crossed over to sound and video bites oriented toward popular entertainment, rather than solid, trustworthy journalism, and get my "news of the world" from Associated Press reports on the Internet.

I make some art while watching Charlie Rose, C-Span, and PBS, and wonder how Tom Hanks' movies (or whoever else is in the current spotlight) can show up on nearly every movie channel on the same day?

I want to tear my hair out, or the hair of someone on those panels, where the "authority" or celebrity figures have absolutely nothing to say about everything and easily slide from real issues to discussing the most intimate personal aspects of whoever is in the hot seat that show.

Of course, I don't have to watch, and seldom do, channel surfing through all the offerings until, if I must watch something (in order to hear human voices) I put in some favorite old video. But still, it bothers me a lot, that the tabloid mentality spews forth from the airwaves, influencing, inciting, I feel sure, and for some, providing both entertainment and escape, and for me, irritation with the dumbing down of the national "voice."

15

Each player must accept the cards life dealt him or her; but once they are in hand, he or she alone must decide how to play the cards in order to win the game. ~ Voltaire

I am fence-straddling, being glad that writer me has stayed focused and got so many manuscripts together, and upset because "she" doesn't know how, or hasn't come up with the "right" book, to get the attention of a real literary agent.

Oh, I've read the "how to write a query letter," and "how and where to find an agent" books and on-line advice, and trying all that. But gosh, being alone, and lonely, and without funds (beyond living expenses), nor Paris-style cafes to walk to, or car, or living in an area I could drive around in without being on a freeway, there are times I can't face the search, and what has been one "send me a few pages (but later, sorry…)" and lots of form two-liners e-mailed back so fast you know it's an automated lie: "…after careful consideration…"

But then, in the past, when we mailed things (snail-"mail, if you're younger than me). queries and manuscripts, you could play the waiting game for months. In the past before that past, you could walk into a publishers office and pitch your book. Ah…for those days…

My dearest guidance angel, Leytha, are you there? I sense the reply, as "Leytha," addresses me by the name she had said was my "spiritual" one. Her "voice," not a voice at all but an impression that I sense only through writing, feels like a gentle spring breeze.

Litheria: I am always here, will always be here, as you will "always be," and perhaps it is "time" to let go of the current struggle to "accept" your age, when truly, you know and believe, that age has no meaning in the "world" of beingness, the place where the spirit and soul and the "you" that you have created and defined in this lifetime.

You "feel" it of course, because the body, as we've spoken of this before, is physical, and susceptible to physical laws on this life-plane, but the known and unknown. Still, it is well to remember the body is not *merely physical, but is a manifestation of the spiritual, soul-stuff, and eternal beingness.*

For now, the easiest way for you to experience your body, your physical self in a new way, a way that gives you comfort, energy, and sense of well-being, a sense of eternal youthfulness, (allowing you to phase out what has become, in your earnest attempt to "come to terms with" age), is to image (not imagine, but rather image, since "imagine" conjures up an idea of the not-real), your body as motion, which it is.

For the most part, this "motion," movement, change, renewal, this life within your life, is going on without your conscious attention to it: your breath, circulation, heart beat, digestion, cell renewal, protection from viruses, your abilities to see, hear, touch, taste, smell, sense, process, think, create. For the most part, you do not even have to think about this.

You are, and have been, constantly concerned with the well-being of your body, having been afflicted with pain so much of your life. Here is a path to freedom from the pain: stop telling your body what to do (what to eat, drink, not to eat or drink, what exercise to take, how much sleep to get), and let your body tell you what to do.

I am limited in my ability to describe this idea to you as well as I would wish to, because in truth, "you," and "your body," are not separate, but you live in a time of great duality: life or death, heaven or hell, physical or spiritual, with the physical, due to the admirable research and breakthroughs in what you know as "modern medicine" becoming less and less "whole," but a collection of "parts:" heart, stomach, lungs, brain, muscles, skeleton, chemistry etc, with an emphasis on diagnosis and treatment (or the masking of pain), rather than on prevention of "dis" ease, and "un" well-being.

It may be helpful to you to study, now, some of your Eastern philosophies again, which are more holistic in their approach to these things. For you personally, pause, stop, listen, and respect the voice of the body, and your "wholeness."

We will talk more of the other concerns you have at this time, but meanwhile, embrace all into this concept of wholeness. You are a hard taskmaster on yourself, and a shift is needed from self-criticism, to appreciation for what the soul has chosen to experience in this lifetime, to acknowledgment of what the personality has achieved and overcome, and to continuing forgiveness.

Remember that you began our conversations when you responded to the inner nudge to affirm, "I forgive myself and others." It is a powerful mantra, and leads to love. Loving

189

yourself, will lead to loving others, and experiencing love in return.

You have, Litheria, high expectations for your Self in this lifetime, but your Life, as we've explained before, is not to be compared to another, nor should anyone's.

You still harbor expectations of life acknowledged as fame, money, recognition, and we cannot say these things will not be in your experience, as they well may, (and, we cannot, as you know, either predict the future of a soul's journey, nor direct it, other than to share our mentorship when asked), but now we remind you, that your life is very much about touching others, encouraging others, in an individual way through "showing up," creatively, or contributing, over the period of your lifetime.

It has also been about experiencing life, through agreement to do this, in order to learn, to understand (your Self, and others), to become tolerant, patient, and wiser (another word for remembering, though earth-plane experience, Who you are, from Whence you came, Where you will return or continue, and your True relationship with other humans, and all creatures and that which is Life.

For the moment, relax, stop demanding of yourself, stop analyzing and critiquing the current world as you see it, and wait for an experience of "memory" which will once again heal the separations you feel in your Self and reconnect, merge you with the infinite and eternal.

Today, I write on my laptop, at a small table inside the RV, parked on my sister's high desert property. When she first retired, her husband bought the vehicle, refurbished it, being handy with these things, anticipating trips around the county. A changing economy also changed their plans, and now gardening takes the place of travel for them, and the RV serves as a "stay over," refuge for visiting relatives like me.

I'd anticipated putting together a collection of dried flower arrangements that my sister might sell at one of the fund-raisers she attends, but while the big table outside the RV is perfect for this, the sun is too hot, or the wind comes up suddenly, as it did this morning, stealing one whole plastic bag of my dried flowers and then, playfully depositing it on the other side of the RV.

I read, snack, try to work on a manuscript, a journal kept during three months in Guatemala, and later, typed on a typewriter some twenty five years ago when I returned. I don't want to lose the images, but it's hard to revisit myself of that time, and I keep putting it off.

I check my e-mail, and no one is there, my friend in Madrid is apparently still away on his business trip to Angola, and no word at all from the various schools I've contacted, Kurdistan, Mexico City, China, Taiwan. I celebrated my seventieth birthday in Taiwan, but now, though the first e-mail responses (based on my resume, my Harvard masters), are positive, and the phone calls (based on my "charming" personality…smile) go well, I feel certain that the fact that I now have chalked up seventy-two years of living, is causing the delay that indicates a no.

I have my own doubts, in pain most days from what I now think is fibromyalgia, and walk carefully due to vertigo (probably the result of a childhood inner ear infection) which has, since childhood caused me innumerable falls, some days are better, some days worse In pain most of my life, I've gone ahead in spite of it all, and just plunge in the pool of these overseas job possibilities as though I'd have no problem at all climbing the stairs, and would manage somehow, to conceal the fatigue that comes from sleepless nights. A chronic cough plagues me too. It's made worse in the presence of my brother-in-law's smoking, but sometimes just a swallow of water, or breath of air will cause convulsive coughing.

191

I see, sometimes, just glimpses, of other realities; me, giving talks, or workshops based on one or more of my books; me; sharing a home with someone I loved and who loves me; me; in a studio-gallery-bookshop of my own in some small, tourist town; me; on the Charlie Rose show talking about one or the other of my books; me, feeling like I am making some contribution to someone, or some segment of humankind, for the good.

I "feel," though, removed from all these dreams; as though it were as unattainable by "me" as a trip to the moon. Yet, ten years ago, in 1999, I had not yet graduated with my BA degree, nor gone to Paris (to celebrate that) for the first time, nor met the person whom I came to call my "muse" in the writing of my first novel, nor come home to find I had been accepted to Harvard for masters' study, and "9/11" had not happened and the world had not yet changed.

I flit from one project to another. I feel neglectful of my art, what with lack of funds to frame, mount, somehow present them in a way they can be shown and sold; perhaps I need to give up art-making for now? The books; which one do I concentrate on, of these eleven completed books? Two of them, *Dare to Dream*, a book of encouraging poetry, and *Shmadiggle and the Imagination Asteroid*, just won first place blue ribbons in the creative writing categories of poetry, and stories for children, at our local county fair. I was pleased, but what is that, I complain, compared to "real" publishing?

And love? So many people have passed through my life, and I through theirs. My "muse" friend, now, in this seventh year, no longer answers my e-mails, perhaps overwhelmed with trying to keep his Paris-based business afloat, or perhaps, even having promised life-time, creative friendship, no longer is able to honor that. As for my Madrid friend of nearly two years there are no plans (no wherewithal for either of us at the moment) to meet. I have a hard time imagining a live-together with anyone, actually.

192

I wonder sometimes about how I might make a living from creating more of the writing workshops I gave for the seniors where I live. Their diligence produced enough remembrances for me to publish a little book for them, and this also won a ribbon in the local county fair. I could continue with them, I could develop a whole program of writers groups for seniors, but I've no energy for this. Eight weeks was enough for me, if not for them.

If life is lived in decades, then I have lived seven of them. Whatever I'm given from now on is a gift. How do I make the best use of my talents now? How do I make some contribution to others? How do I find love?

I wait, listening for Leytha's presence. I don't expect "her" to resolve these issues in my life. I only hope for insight, for wisdom, for some indication of action I should take (if I should), that is hiding from me.

Litheria: you are *loved. How can it be otherwise? That you seem not to experience this love that exists for all humans within the greater scheme of existence, nor see it manifested for you on a personal level is an area that requires change in your perceptions.*

When there are expressions of love, you withdraw. This comes from the childhood you have experienced, and relationships as an adult that you have experienced in which love has not been love at all, but a means to possess, control, intimidate, obligate, or require something of you which is not reciprocated.

Mostly, you fear having to give up your freedom, to be, to think, to create, without influence by others.

We know that you know this on the psychological level, but there is a place you can now go to now that will bypass all that, a detour, if you will, around an area which is flooded with the debris of this time of suffering caused you, and caused by you. That there

193

is suffering, chaos, yes; that you cannot play "God" and fix it all, nor return in time to "fix" what was, yes.

But now, since you are exploring the idea of "choice," do focus on the myriad ways you do have choices: to follow your own path, contribute of your own talent and skill, and most important to hold "the whole world" in an embrace of love where healing can come forth, wholeness can manifest, and out of chaos will ultimately come light and creation.

There are areas of "envy," that you will need to heal and clear. This, as you well know, has to do with these ideas: that you have had to work very hard to create, projects, learning opportunities and work; for some, for many, as you see it, "one thing leads to another," and ultimately to some form of success, or relationship, or "place," that feels like home. Since you do not feel this is true for you, you envy, do you not, others who have achieved one or the other of these ends?

Envy needs to be healed. It is an open sore on the psyche, on the physical, mental and emotional body, and to ignore it, is to constantly re-open the wound. Healing envy or not to heal it, is a choice.

Are you now willing to heal this irritation? The process is simple, but on-going. It is merely a matter of consciously blessing, wishing well, the other, or others who, walking through the doors of your mind, now seem to taunt, "I've achieved, but you have not."

Watch now, as the person who walks through the door and says, "You will never have, achieve, experience, as I have." That "persona" is your own demanding self. It is not your real "Self," but a shadow self, a compilation of taunting voices flung at you

194

from various aspects of your world, childhood, adulthood, and the competitive society in which you live.

Love wants the best for you, as do I, and those of us on whom you call to guide you. You can "receive," or experience this positive encouragement, by extending the same love to others. This does not require action on your part.

We are not saying, go out and save the world. But rather, to begin to be conscious when envy is present in your mind, and replace that with blessing and love.

Having done that, you will want to fill that now empty space with something. What will it be? What do you want to experience?

At last, this morning, some relief from the pain in my legs, lower back. Why? The pain was awful the past few days and nights, sharp electric jabs, and just constant, deep, sharp aching, with the usual sore spots all over. And, have seven huge, red bites, mosquitoes, ants or some other insect, we don't know. My sister gets them, her husband hardly at all, and me, painful and inflamed. Topical Benadryl medication helps. Some Chinese salve, oil, relieves the pain in lower back and legs, neck somewhat. I need massage, I'm sure of that, to put my body "back together."

I slept with the curtain drawn back in the R.V., just enough to shield the effect of the glorious full moon, but at the same time to watch the gentle wind dance the leaves in the aspen tree. Nature heals me. I miss my "stuff," but somehow out here, feel less inclined to push towards achievement than I do when alone.

When in the depths of "my" pain, I began to wonder how I could ever go overseas to work. Climbing stairs (hauling myself up by the banister) would be an embarrassment. How would I get enough rest, with my two hour a night, pain filled sleep, to function well in the classroom? Well, it's nothing new to me, as pain, physically and emotionally (less of that, other than my constant prodding of me to achieve), have been with me for as long as I have memories.

But, at this point, working overseas is not an issue to debate, as neither Mexico City, nor another Mexico contact, nor Kurdistan, have made any further overtures to me, i.e., in the form of a contract following their enthusiastic phone interviews of two weeks ago. I can't imagine them making an offer now which would meet their August 15th required arrival time.

The check I wrote to renew my passport (with a new photo, an "in your face" grinning one, to replace the sad sack, droopy hair, old lady look with the wrong glasses, taken for my 2001 passport), has cleared the bank, so that means the passport is likely in the mail to me.

What do I want, Leytha has asked me. Oh to be free of pain, and to give meticulous attention to my body, slimming it, and strengthening it, so I might live these however many years with energy and without complaint. Still, how fortunate I am, compared to others: I am not terribly wounded. I have no fatal illness. I have no addictions, other than eating more calories than I use up.

The terrible migraines which plagued me until my fifties, have disappeared. Pain in my stomach has been controlled now, for several months, with the help of a single tablet, and attention to less spicy foods. When at home, I try to walk often, if my pain is not too intense and I swim occasionally. Dance! I would like to be able to dance again, to care about music, to be in a place where I could be enthusiastic about making art, (and showing, selling it).

And laugh! My sister has an absolute gift for laughing, constantly sending me and her friends some graphic joke from the Internet, especially about the process of aging. I find aging no laughing matter, and think of my age now, only because I feel it will be a deciding factor in whether or not I'm offered a contract to teach, either overseas, (or New Mexico, once I send in the

196

application packet). And age, not able to get enthusiastic (nor even curious) about the men in my age bracket (well, sixty to seventy something), that Yahoo, E-Harmony and Match.com send me, I've unsubscribed to one, and not subscribed to the others. I would like to enjoy my present, make a contribution to others, and look forward, all at the same time.

Some friends have read my novel, DG and his wife, and PM; and where I live, B and M bought copies. And of course, when I first published it, under a different title, I sold the book in Paris, and at the New Mexico bookshop. (Forgive me dear readers, for all those typos in that first edition)!

SB loves my books of poetry. And little ten year old E, thinks the three children's books are "must reads!" Ah, to have the same enthusiasms from agents! But days, weeks have gone by and I've not contacted any more of the on-line resources. The novel query mailed snail-mail to a publisher who handles mystery books returned the packet so fast, I doubt even the paragraph synopsis was read before transferring it all to the return envelope. Twelve dollars wasted.

What do I want to experience, Leytha has asked. I don't know, other than to look back, all the way to childhood, and what I wanted then has changed little, other than letting a few fantasies drop away, and a few others become some aspect of reality.

Who am I, seems to be the question I want to ask now. And how to be, within the context of where I am at the moment. And how to believe that impossibilities can become probabilities: health, love, art and writing income, some sense of making a positive difference. Some give their lives, as wars, strife, protests, marches, conflicts continue. I would prefer to live mine. So much world strife. There are days I cannot even read the Internet news, so overwhelming, so much blame, so few solutions.

I, sitting here, in my sister's RV, parked on their high desert property next to their house, my bills at my Hud apartment paid automatically through my bank account social security income, limited though it is to less than nine hundred a month, have no real worries. But I am deeply discontented. This safety net (of a year and half, beginning at age 70), is not comfortable for me. I want to work, create, contribute, love, live a life of meaning and excitement.

No word from any of the overseas jobs I've applied for. Time to write them off. Surely they would have responded by now, and in their delaying, I have developed doubts of my own. Still, I applied to another, in Saudi Arabia, yesterday.

Meanwhile, Sissy has cleared off a space in my bro-in-law John's workshop, and I'm spending lovely hours there, putting together arrangements of the flowers I hung over my desk to dry this past year. In recycled jars, and thrift shop cups (we picked up a few yesterday), they are pretty, and saleable, but where? Maybe just at some small fund-raising event Rosalie goes to out here. If I had a gallery-shop they would sell (and my books, weavings, paintings, collages, drawings, painted plates and....); where, that I could live and work and pay the rent?

My sister and brother-in-law both work outside in the cooler hours of the morning, John, building a pond, Rosalie, trimming small trees, then she tends to some of her free-lance consulting work, and John is off on fixer-upper errands, or some free-lance building for a neighbor. They relax easily (something I never do) in the evenings, with a book, or nap, or in front of the T.V., watching a show John has taped.

In their kitchen, I pour a cup of John's morning coffee, pace back and forth. Rosalie kindly, seeing the stress mask still on my face from the night before, a night once again so full of pain that sleep did not come until dawn, asks how the morning feels to me.

"Better," I smile wanly, glad to be up and free of fighting the night. She has washed my clothes and hung them up to dry.

"Wear your sleep dress around," she laughs, when I complain I can't get dressed.

198

"But I need to get into a work mode and I can't do that in my pj's."

She laughs, chides me, younger sister by five years, she is, in most ways, my "older" sister. "Relax then! Do nothing. That's why you're out here!"

"But I…"

"I know," she says softly. "That's not the way you think."

It is here, fingers on keys, that I am "happy." It is out in the workshop, sorting sage and weeds and twigs, mixing them with the dried flowers, that I am "happy." Wasn't it always so? Reading, writing, making art? Happier though when part of an encampment – people who do their own thing, and leave me to do mine, and who are there when I surface. But the "next step," that which puts my books in the hands of readers, and my art making in the hands of buyer-appreciators, and my mind in the presence of someone, or someone's with whom I can talk about that which matters to me. Ah, this eludes me.

What eludes me, Leytha? What is the path? Can I live more consciously in today, while building a path to the future? I sense Leytha's words:

Litheria: What do you hear? Birds singing outside your window? The sound of the fan cooling the room you are in? Your sister calling from the porch to invite you to a senior luncheon she's prepared a big salad for

No thank you…preferring my own company.

What do you touch? The keys beneath your fingers, the sharp edge of the table against your arms, the feel of the chair where you are sitting, your feet against the floor? What do you see? The cluttered interior of the RV where you are typing; on your table-desk, a cup of cold coffee, a small calculator, a tall, unplugged coffeepot holding up the window shade, two

199

manuscripts you've brought along to put onto your computer, a
pencil, a mouse pad with a compass design, four rocks.

Isn't this an "environment" which pleases you, has always
pleased you, a place, a space, to put your ideas on paper while the
world moves on around you? What do you feel?

I feel a sense of contentment, amazingly unusual for me.
Being around my sister and her husband takes me back (for better,
for worse, with past memories, images, feelings visiting me this
week) to childhood, to teen years. The struggle to find my own
identity, no, to verify it, justify it, as being different from those
around me (I thought…was it true or not)?   Here, I am "allowed"
to just be who I am, struggling to sleep, getting up late, then
writing, making art, thinking, reading. There is not much I share
with them, nor they with me, other than also just being themselves,
but I feel less alone. That is a good feeling.

But, shouldn't I be "making a living?" Shouldn't I be
"contributing, teaching, earning, saving?" Shouldn't I be longing
today, for news of a teaching job contract in one place or another?
But if it was challenging for me to "fit in" somewhere career-wise
when I was younger, how much more complex the challenge now
that I am old enough to "wear purple."

16

It is neither good nor bad, but thinking makes it so. ~
William Shakespeare

Why do I feel guilty? At this moment my life exists in a bubble of safety if not contentment, not affected (immediately at least), by the swirling tornado of chaos that continues to upend the world ?

The feeling: "good." Take this feeling into your day. If you wish to contribute, if you wish to lay stones as a pathway to your future, if you wish to experience more love, it is this feeling, "it is good," that will build your world. It is so deeply profound that you, and others, on your life-plane, simply cannot fathom it.

"It is good..." or any form of appreciation, blessing, gratitude, sense of peace (even the peace of passionate engagement with others, creativity, work), will both heal you, bring the future into the present, and radiate out into the world around you, intimately, and at a distance.

Today, this is your mantra, your affirmation: "It is good."

Today, my seventh day staying with my sister and brother-in-law, in the desert. Recovering from the insect bites, some quality sleep last night after a dip in the hot tub relaxed the muscles in my lower back and legs, but still had severe stomach pains that affected my esophagus and caused pain in my chest. It is par for the course, of my lifetime; a series of non life-threatening, but painful irritations. Am I manifesting these as irritations with my life? I think not. It is rather the other way around.

John, a year younger than I, recovered from a recent surgery, is off to Reno to complete a building project for a friend. Thin, wiry, and amusingly grumpy, he seldom stops moving unless reading, or scrolling through his evening marathon of crime and mystery shows. Sissy has washed clothes, enjoying hanging them outside the old fashioned way, to save the cost of the running the dryer, and has gone into her office to work on files.

I, convinced now, that no one is going to hire me for overseas teaching, despite the fact that they were initially impressed with the Harvard masters, and teaching, writing, art experience. Once they learn my age there is e-mail silence. My updated passport will be waiting for me when I return to my apartment. But for what reason? Without teaching income, or the miracle of an agent and publisher saying yes, I'll not be able to travel.

It will be August then, before I can send in the application for the alternative teaching license for New Mexico, too late, likely, for the coming year. Will I run into the age thing here too? Probably, with layoffs in the profession, and teachers looking for jobs.

I have put together ten (with a never ending supply of dried flowers and grasses around here to use, and have yet to make a dent in the box of flowers I brought with me) bouquets. Small, in cups, or interesting jars, they've turned out beautifully. I'll package them in see-through cellophane and ribbon, and Rosalie will take them to one or the other of the fund-raisers she goes to. In a shop of my own, the bouquets, and paintings, collages, paper mache, and my books, would sell.

Am I feeling sorry for myself again? I am. I've considered if I might stay out here for a year, (giving up my apartment, and that rent and several of the expenses), saving money, and availing myself of non-distracted writing time, and John's workshop for making things. In her own storeroom, Sissy has more craft making treasures than I could use up in several years!

But the cold weather would make it impossible for me to live in the RV, and there is no place for me in the house. So...here is this dreary picture of a lonely 72 year old with some talent and eclectic experience, without offers for jobs, nor money to move, nor funds to open a shop. On the other hand, here are two people who care enough to let me (again, as I've done so many times before, coming and going), hang out at their place.

So, Leytha, what shall this "giver of light" (as you have interpreted Litheria, my "spiritual name" to do?

Dearest one: your dilemma is real, as real as it was some years ago when we first "met." You struggled then, valiantly actually, to become unstuck from the quicksand of your life. Have you not accomplished many things you would have thought completely impossible at that time?

Your life seems to be lived in plateaus; you struggle to learn, to change, to achieve, and then, there is a plateau, a leveling off place. You find this plateau experience to be boring, without virtue, and you feel ashamed.

Why? Because you are comparing still, your life to others and looking always toward a tomorrow that will, like a Christmas fantasy window, be beautiful, spectacular, causing passerbys to stop and stare, admire and envy.

203

Today, this day, is the day you must live. Here in the desert, you have a quiet place of your own to write. You are working, are you not, writing these words as a follow-up book to your first one. You are making some art that will bring others happiness. And, you are having to confront, pay attention to your health.

Meanwhile, you've followed through with possible overseas teaching offers, and you are still considering, weighing the pros and cons of teaching in New Mexico. In addition to all this, you research, and wonder, with highs and lows, ways to find agents and publishers for your books. Enjoy the nowness of this. There is nothing else you need to do.

Again, in your life there are, have been, many, many paths to take, and paths that have been taken. Do you not see that you have come into a place of quiet peacefulness? This time has not yet come for the changes you seek. The time is soon, but not yet, for change. Live in the present. The time for change is not yet. Stop worrying.

Five A.M., and I have been up for an hour, with only bits of sleep throughout the night, due to so much pain in my lower back and legs. But have uploaded photos of the dried flower arrangements I've been putting together out in my brother-in-law's workshop. It feels so great to have someplace to work other than my living room. I am on a complete sabbatical from television, since my bro-in-law rules this domain.

I miss Charlie Rose, and C-Span, and PBS and the documentary programs, and a favorite video while I do my weavings at night. But, here, at least I'm not arguing with the way the news is covered, as trivial entertainment, nor channel hopping in a vain attempt to find some program that will fill up the void of loneliness in my life for one more night.

204

So, my "news of the world," is gleaned mainly from my Yahoo page, and then clicking to read the longer AP version which still follows some journalistic fact finding and presentation, rather than news for entertainment.

It has occurred to me though, how even this news seems to be "celebrity" focused, in the sense that news "items" are about somebody, a leader of a country for example, rather than about the people per se, unless a protest, or riot, or natural disaster strikes.

And if a quote from the leader, or the star is not available, then we are given one by some bystander, or twitterer, or blogger, or worse, by a paid "authority," likely (shades of envy?) touting his own book, CD's, seminar, workshop. I've not yet sorted it out, not figured out why it is important for me to be so concerned about all this.

Have adjusted to a different routine. Have read, or re-read several books in this week. Has it been only a week that I've been here? It seems I don't even live in Marin any longer; my apartment is there, a few things I care about, but I've left it and set up "living" here. Perhaps moving on to another phase in life is like that. If I can move into a place of comfort re a relationship that is loving, lasting, fun, supportive, creative, passion-filled...and probable, will I not just leave behind the sense of longing and loneliness that has plagued me all my life?

Dawn has come. I did not notice the lightening of the sky with my eyes on the screen. But now, looking up and out through the front window of the RV, I see a cloud streaked pale gray above the mountains. Zeus, the neighbors' big, black dog is moaning for attention. He sleeps on a big, round mattress in the shed when the neighbors are gone. My sister says he searched both properties for weeks after his tiny black and white, feisty companion died, of old age I think. I experience loneliness, but can't imagine what it must be like for creatures completely deprived of the companionship of their own kind.

205

What I "feel" now: a sense of futility; that the struggle to create throughout my life, to make a living doing the most menial jobs, to try (and fail so terribly as a mother, a hard word for me to say, as it doesn't seem to apply to me at all), and finally to achieve two college degrees, and independently publish books and produce art and travel (at last) to Paris, to teach in Taiwan, means nothing, in that it has led to nothing, as usual, beyond the experiences themselves.

Perhaps it is being "with" family, my sister and brother-in-law that does this to me. Do others feel this? That their professorships, or entrepreneur, or community involvement means nothing in the context of just being with family? Or do I speak of a peculiar affliction of creative types, who constantly must be stroked for having achieved, (because it is never enough?) or who must, at least, be in the process of creating or achieving? Or is it just me?

Leytha: this July dawn, do you have answers for me?

Gentle one: appreciate the dawn. You are alive to see it. Are you discovering that simplicity, that peace, that life lived for the sake of just living is more challenging than confronting chaos, meeting schedules, making plans, anticipating change?

Why not practice (if you must "do" something) feeling appreciation for this time of the dawn, for a new cycle of life? In the act of appreciation, the seeds of change that nurture are sown.

Leytha: I am so frustrated by lack of sleep caused by continual sharp pains in lower back and legs. Trips to Kaiser have resulted in no diagnosis, and this or that mild medication to dull the pain in a way that also won't cause me more stomach distress. Is there something in the world of spirit or soul that I need to know

206

to relieve this pain and restore my ability to move, sit, lay down easily and with comfort?

Litheria: from your perspective, the body is a physical entity and subject to the laws of this plane, and also subject to that which is inharmonious to the physical body. You sometimes feel guilty for experiencing pain because what you experience is so much less than that which some other may experience, or the condition is less dire than an other may experience.

Isn't this true? So, for this reason, you do not actively seek ways to relieve this pain and heal your body.

In regard to your own distress, you must seek out alternative methods, such as acupuncture or acupressure, massage and hot baths. Your distress is not permanent. It will also be relieved as you achieve a more natural body weight, and in particular, as you look to your dwelling for greater comfort in terms of where you sit, and where you sleep.

There is a tendency in you, as Claudia, to ignore the more immediate in your life, and to adopt a kind of wishful thinking. It is easy for you to do this, because you tend to have more joy in the world of the mental, of thought, the inner world, and in the act of creativity outside of yourself (things which you create), than you do in your physical being.

The pain and discomfort you are experiencing is not your body expressing that, but is actually your body calling out for joy. We spoke to you of this before.

You must focus on ways to experience physical well-being, comfort and joy. In so doing, you will replace one experience, that

207

of pain, fatigue, weakness, sleeplessness, with another, that of joy, refreshing sleep, comfort and energy.

This may sound harsh to you, but you have been, in recent months, concerned with "quality of life," as the years advance, and as you explore ways to increase your abundance, and to experience a lasting love relationship.

You must give attention to you, to your body, and do, whatever, wherever, and within what financial circumstances you find yourself, to take care of your physical being.

A quiet, overcast morning. My sister has already hung some laundry on the outside clothesline, and she and my brother-in-law sit on their "morning patio," a small platform that looks out toward sunrise on a clear morning, and talk, laughing. They are happy here, working hard, when they choose, on the land, or resting, doing nothing.

I can hear them talking, but at a level where I hear only the sound of their voices, not their words. It is like hearing two birds of a different feather. Somewhere above them, actual birds talk, and I do not understand their words either.

Is it like this with the world of the spirit as well? At times, through writing here, or through creating something, a story, a poem, some piece of art, I "hear" that which is beyond my normal range of sensing: tasting, smelling, touching, hearing, seeing, and think I understand something, or have learned something, or something is revealed to me or verified. At those times, I'm eager to share this experience with others, and in this I feel frustration. My "others" experience is limited.

I make photos of my dried flower arrangements and e-mail them to my sister and brother-in-law in their offices a few steps away from me! I send the same, or photos of walks I take, or things like the country fair, to J, because he is interested in all that

I do, and my "American" experience is so different from his in Spain.

But there is no one else to communicate with. I look through my e-mail list, so long when I was doing interesting things, like attending Harvard, or teaching in Taiwan, and now, it has dwindled to less than ten.

Back in my apartment, my "others" are the seniors who live there, some who have lives away from the complex, some who, I suspect have only their television as companionship, a few others who show up for bingo, or music appreciation, or a health talk. I do not, I am not "old" nor "elderly," I scream to myself! What am I doing there?

My conversation are limited to saying hello on occasion to one of the three staff members or the people I see, but don't know in the Marin JCC deli, or at Bogey's the funky little café I can't afford to go to often because of their high prices, or the anonymous seekers and workers at the Marin Civic library.

My "others" are the people and drivers on the buses I take to the mall, when I don't want to walk all the way around the park, and shoppers and clerks in the stores where I seldom, except at the drugstore, buy anything, or the medical personnel at the hospital, outpatient clinic. In the cafeteria there, the Latino cooks laugh and are friendly, and I wish … I wish… for what? For a neighborhood experience.

But there are no "others" for me to share my thoughts with, my books or art. I don't know how to change this except to continue trying as I have been, to find a job teaching overseas, or get qualified to teach in New Mexico, and to believe (does it require that, belief?) that a lasting, loving, passionate relationship is coming to my life, and that one day, a way to sell my books and art will occur to me and be possible.

There is no other sound around me now. Rosalie and John have finished their coffee and conversation, and gone about their tasks. John is building a large pond, and yesterday bought some water plants for it. Rosalie prepares to go to a fund-raiser of a group determined to turn a former movie theater on the army base into a live performance theater. In the past, I've been involved in such things (building ponds, and community theater). Now, they no longer interest me.

I want only to publish, or to find ways to market my own independently published books and sell my art, and perhaps teach, to the extent that the loss of my safe haven provided by social security, and deferred student loans, and paid Medicare will not seem like a loss, but will, in my new world, (a world of challenging economics for the whole planet), seem like the necessary path to take to experience a greater abundance and the elusive "quality of life" that I seek.

What can I do to bring myself and my books closer to being read? Will write a note to Moby Dickens in Taos and see if they will carry the books. The challenge is, whether they can, (by their own definition), make enough by ordering via the distributor that handles our independent publishing.

This, of course is true of all the book stores. The dilemma too, once I go that route, with the ISBN codes on all, I effectively eliminate any interest at all by agents and "real" publishers.

Well, truthfully, I would just be "happy" with my own studio shop. How can I move toward this? The teaching license in New Mexico. And, and!! focus on feeling better physically so that I could approach this possibility with confidence and joy.

Yesterday, a long drive with my sister to see the local Lassen County Fair. A summer of fairs, apparently! On the way, marveled at how the landscape on one side of the road was sagebrush, and sometimes meadows with grazing cattle, and on the opposite of the road, climbing up toward a mountain, tall fir tree were growing.

We stopped at a small coffeehouse, a rarity in this countryside, with none such in Doyle, though an R.V. park there does serve food and beer, and shared a hot drink; me an Americano (as espresso is too strong), and Rosalie, a double, tall vanilla latte. She, (as am I, plagued with overweight these past few years), has lost almost ten pounds going, with other local gals, to a weight loss program here in the boonies.

Impossibly hot for me at the fair, and could only walk a few feet without seeking shade, neither adjusted to the altitude, nor the hundred plus degree afternoons. But, camera in hand, enjoyed so much taking photos, anticipating a slide show, of this slice of small town Americana. I've just e-mailed it the editor at the Lassen County newspaper, thinking they might enjoy it.

The two (more) e-mailed queries to lit agents have already been met (in less than three days), with a no thanks. My sis reminded me we have no KFC, if the Colonel had not continued despite one rejection after another.

I know this, of course, the challenge: which book to promote, and to whom (with only one "pitch" per e-mail query allowed), or concentrate on promoting (without money, how?) my current crop of on-line published books.

A rare e-note back from my daughter, fifty two this July, who seems happy traveling the east coast via RV with her husband. They plan a trip all the way to Alaska next year. She has (having made choices), abandoned her very real talent for art, and seems to find happiness with her husband and their travels.

A note from a New Mexico woman friend, who has met a younger lesbian companion, and they are enjoying trips and events together, while both take care of their jobs. She continues though, to offer "help" in any way, should plans develop for me to teach in New Mexico.

Returning from the fair, my sis and I stopped to pick up some materials I need to continue the little craft projects I'm doing here. I appreciate her generosity, I think she does this as much to give me some support in my "art-making" such as it is right now, as anything.

I looked around the parking lots of each place we stopped, the super-savers, the WallMart's, the strip malls, and sighed with despair at the dreary sameness of it all. Will I ever get to Paris again, or to Venice, or St. Petersburg, or Madrid, or….? I don't know, *don't* know, how to break through these barriers to get to the lit agents, to get an overseas school (oh, for a University) to hire me, to teach (perhaps) in New Mexico. I just put out the e-mails, and wait, wondering now, how any of them will take me on at 72?

And what of love, companionship, relationship? Is it possible for me with someone my own age, and all the concerns that conjures up about living together, health, sharing, boundaries, physical relationship? I can't see it. I think I was born to be a hermit!

Well, there are some in-coming e-mails re teaching jobs: China, Turkey, Saudi; perhaps I'll just keeping sending my s.o.s.' "hire me" inquiries and applications. Now, I must get out to the workshop and make some stuff, and live in today.

17

This soul, or life within us, by no means agrees with the life outside us. If one has the courage to ask her what she thinks, she is always saying the very opposite to what other people say. ~Virginia Woolf

Should I call on Leytha? I feel I should "know" the answers for my life (ah... if I ask the right questions).

Litheria: It is this asking for answers that keeps you moving ahead in your life, and this is an important aspect of who you are. There are strong forces in your life pattern that, on the one hand have driven you to overcome, to write, to make art, to get your degrees, to graduate from Harvard (and at age sixty five, remember)!

And then, to try the gallery-shop against such challenging odds, to stand by your son in his illness for so many years, to develop the relationship with F., to write the novel, to complete and independently publish all your books.

There is also is a strongly etched image in your mind, that says, no, that is not the reality, but only a dream, and the reality is the down-across-the-tracks little girl. She lives still in you, and is you, and it is her you must celebrate, not retreat from. She / you, have overcome, searched out the wonders of books and learning, longed for travel and knowledge of cultures and the world.

But, it is not "she" who writes your books, or gets college degrees, guides others in productions of plays you've written, or stories they wish to write, or sells art you've created, or applies for positions in Moscow, and Kurdistan, China and Taiwan, Mexico and Saudi Arabia. It is you, the she you have become.

I still feel a sliding into yesterday, rather than an almost reaching of the top of the mountain. I don't know what to do, or how to change this in me. Even as I write, the tears come.

Once Leytha suggested I would one day be brought into contact with "other givers of the light." I've touched a few, here and there, my fingers reaching out to touch their fingertips perhaps, but there has been no "embrace," no continuing of this. I achieve degrees, and descend back into poverty.

I write books and make art, and the ways and means I have do not allow me to do more than flash-in-the-pans; mere summer fireflies, then winter again, and I am alone, and nothing seems to have changed at all. I have to look at the University degrees, the books on my shelves, the paintings in my closet, the art on my walls, to know.

But my friends: two or three. My creative contacts, none. My relationships, long distance. My bank account, filled up once a month by social security and ssi. My e-mails filled with terse, impersonal rejections. Admittedly, there have been "yes" responses this year. Prizes won for writing at my local fair. Appreciation for the writings I helped my senior friends put into their "Voices of Sea Turtles." And the two phone interviews re teaching overseas, and two concrete offers (Pakistan, and Kurdistan), which I turned down because the timing meshed with that of both the changes in our own country, the presidential election, and continued violence in theirs.

But, I feel isolated, with days passing when I feel I'm the only one alive in my "real" world, and long, always to be, as the song says, "a part of it," but what, dear Leytha, is my role, and how do I audition, and how do I find "them" who will say, 'yes, join me, join us?' And do I just ignore this current world economy and continue on with my search (I always ignored "conditions" before), regardless of age?

I have applied for every teaching position on the overseas site to which I subscribe (with the exception of Indonesia, China, S. Korea, Thailand, which feel too volatile to me at the moment. I am, though, feeling more distanced from the possibility of anyone saying yes to seventy two year old me. Bummer!

Having at last achieved my degrees and garnered some teaching experience that they actually recognize, I am now hobbled by this cultural chronological prejudice.

So, am thinking more determinedly about New Mexico again. I have friends there, or contacts anyway, which is more than I can say after a year and half in Marin County, where I only know, by first name, the few people who participated in my writers' group, and the apartment staff.

I've e-mailed my sister (hilarious, since I am, in her RV, only a few steps away from the house, but thoughts come to me more clearly when writing than when humming and uh-ing apologetically, verbally.

My e-mail outlined a possible "get to New Mexico" scenario. Sis worries about my giving up my medical to do so, and about how I would live until, or "if" a legitimate teaching job develops, and can I find a reasonable place to live close to a school so I can manage driving (the car I don't have yet) through the snow.

She is wonderfully practical, and while I, as elder sister, ought to be the advice giver, I have none to give, and she has some life wisdom, garnered partially from her work for some sixteen

215

years managing the very HUD apartment where I now live, and feel tethered to it, as a safety net.

Today, varnished the wood pieces I'm making, and discovered, in two of the small blocks, the most wonderful faces. One of them, which I now call "Woman of the Wind," a craggy, fearsome, old woman face, with wild and flowing lines of hair.

But turn the block around, and the face, like some Rorschach ink blot, becomes a cute smiling face; and above her head, a bewhiskered old man. On the second piece, a Native American-like woman figure seems to embrace the sun (a beautifully swirl of a knothole); but turn it upside down, and one sees, plainly, a serpent; turn the piece horizontal, and I could easily see a porpoise, or perhaps a seal.

I pulled out a large piece of wood, dark, perhaps intended for a short shelf and not used, to see if I could turn it into something. There, in the center, a column, (a slim tree?) reaching up to a very clear definition of an owl's head. Or, perhaps instead of a tree, this was the figure of a cobra, a cartoon version, a friendly fellow, almost smiling.

Humm: wind-woman, a smiling face, a bewhiskered old man, a woman-who-embraces-the-sun, a serpent wrapped round a sun-bowl, a porpoise playing with a ball; a slim tree topped by an owl, a smiling, stand-up cobra. What are these wise-ones saying to me? Or are they saying anything at all? Perhaps just a "thank you for seeing us?"

Yesterday, my sis brought two tiny eggplants from her garden to show me. One of them was clearly shaped like a hummingbird, the other, like a dolphin! Now, we're both intimidated about eating them! "Ah, not me," my sister commented. "Vegetables are for speaking to help them grow. Once done, they are for eating!" I ask her how she might "work with" my images. "As you would with a dream," she says practically. I go to my Guidance Angel: Leytha?

Wind-woman, Litheria, is she who tosses you hither and fro, moves the leaves and grasses and sage, irritates you with her harshness, plays a song on the branch-harp of a tree. Movement, music, aggressiveness, playfulness. These are the voices of Wind-woman.

The smiling face, and the bewhiskered old man, the upside down images of Wind-woman: your sister and brother-in-law; the child you: fairy-like, happy and playful, living in the now, the old man: a hermit, gruff; a story teller, a keeper of memories The young, the old, and all in between are to be cherished; they live within you; cell-memories of the lines of your humanity.

Ah, night, eleven P.M. When I was writing the novel, I used to start on it about now. In severe pain all day, my right leg, all along the outside, and then, tonight the inside of my leg, near my ankle feels swollen and sore and tender to touch. Exhausting.

I'd gone with my sis to an seniors "ice cream social" and don't know if the pain I was already in, or the pain I feel in joining in with seniors gets me down!

Have quickly re-read the little collection of letters I have, in which I corresponded with military personnel involved, some eighteen years ago, in the Gulf conflict. Grateful that I sent those on, in their original forms to the Harvard Library collections, but re-reading them, I so wish others could read them, and wish that these special, very temporary friends, could be known by others.

There are so many books yet to write: I want to reformat *Letters from the Gulf* into a 6 x 9 book to publish on Lulu. I'd need to follow through with the information I got today, in a quick e-mail turn-around from the on-line Stars and Stripes newspaper, as to how, via the Dept. of Defense, I could find out, at least the city and state, of where these people ended up.

How I would love to have one more letter from them each, with what they are doing now. And, how much I long for a real publisher, and not just myself.

The sequel to the novel, *Code of the Blue Rider*, and the untitled prequel: what? Another two years to complete? For whom? For myself, I suppose. Truly, I love to write. What I lack, is someone, or someones to share my word making and art making with, and some dream-time funds.

My sister will be going back to the coast to work for a week, beginning Monday. What to do? Shall I ride along with her and go back home for a week, and continue to stew over whether to stay there, and just write (and continue in my lonely state in that very manicured, well kept up area)?

Or do I (or instruct her to) give notice on my apartment, collect my mail (and new passport, and continue on with plans for some different future overseas, or New Mexico, or here, typing away on my laptop on the table in the RV, until the cold weather drives me into the house. She has no bedroom for me there.

At home I have no decent bed (I sleep on a futon), and my back and legs hurt less, though they hurt still, sleeping on this RV couch, than at home.

But I miss my pretty table, and candles, my lovely bathroom, the view of trees from my bedroom window, my PBS and documentary television programs, occasional swims at the gym and walks around the Civic center pond. It's hard to explain the loneliness of the beautiful area where I live, though.

Today, my sister brought a box full of acrylic paints from her storeroom, into the workshop for me. All I need now is canvas or wood on which to paint. I brought along the tall, twisted vine and yarn sculpture-weaving I'd been working on at home, continuing weaving on it as I watched television. Either task, art making or watching television is boring to me without the other. Writing, I can do for hours, and need silence.

218

This evening, I walked around the property, my camp-made walking stick in hand, accompanied by Zeus, the big black dog belonging to the neighbors next door, and wondered at the incredible molten gold sunsets.

Letters off to Mary C., and Duncan, former professors and continuing friends, whom I plague now and again with letters from the heart, feeling they understand my search and concerns.

I need to get copies of my books off to Moby Dickens Bookshop in Taos, and to my college libraries. I need, at least, my books to at least have the companionship of a few writers throughout the ages, whom I loved, who have inspired me, but whom I know, not one, in real life.

I walk around in a bubble, just as I have from childhood, a bubble that seems to prevent me from having contact with my own kind. Yet, who are they?

Litheria: There is a strong force that pulls you constantly into the world of the past, the small agricultural town you knew until you were sixteen, and the former shipyard town you knew until you were twenty.

You must remember though, the library, the Saturday mornings there, the stories; the books given you by your stepmother, the writing you did, the drawings you made, the songs you composed, the children you birthed, and the longings, from childhood, to understand God and things spiritual.

Can you now let go of the past and free yourself from this force, and take your place in the spiritual realm? In writing, in the making of art, in finding, discovering actually, ways to make a contribution, in these, you are happiest. In nature, being close to nature, you are happiest. You doubt, because you wish to clothe your creations in the garments of success: paintings shown and sold in a prestigious gallery, books on the best seller list.

219

These things take time and effort. Be patient, and continue. For some, it is true, there is discovery of talent that takes the person to where you have always longed to be: for others, it is a synchronistic type of luck that puts one in the "right place at the right time." For others, the fulfillment of talent in this lifetime is not destined.

It is your struggle to overcome, that is exhausting you. Try instead, acceptance of all things. This is not the time for overcoming. It is the time for accepting, for receiving, for appreciating the time, the peace, the freedom from chaos that is yours at this moment. Rest in this.

18

Throw your dreams into space like a kite, and you do not know what it will bring back, a new life, a new friend, a new love, a new country. ~ Anais Nin

I reach, I scheme, the line of the kite always beyond my reach.

Second day "back home" in my apartment, having come along with my sister who has a three day consulting job in a near-by town. Cleaned out and organized my art closet, and set aside some materials to take with me, wondering all the while why I continue to create stuff, with no place in site to show and sell it. I'm already pacing the floor.

E-mailed the school in Erbil, to see if they are continuing to consider me, or if it is a closed door. Tried to progress my way through the teaching, and substitute applications (nearly the same), on the Santa Fe District Schools. Always a challenge trying to fit my eclectic (to say the least) work history into the application forms.

Called Footprints, through whom I went to Taiwan. K, who remembers me, and knows my book (she kindly said it was sitting on the reception desk), candidly answered by doubts about getting hired at 72. "A question of insurance in most cases," she said

221

sadly, "but some countries have an age limit, with even 50 being the high point. We both wondered at my getting hired for Taiwan at age 69! She will though, look at the various options, all countries (with China and Taiwan the more likely to lower the age requirement).

The writing, either finishing up things, or starting again with the sequel to the novel, is nigh impossible when I'm (in my mind anyway), playing a game of "what's next" ping pong. I could have written half the book these three, four weeks, if I could settle down. I did, however, go on-line and send for a proof copy (two, actually, to be sent to my sis' address, since I'm going back with her), of the revised novel, as *Code of the Running Cross,* without my "author" photo on the back. The photos looked fine when I took them, but the process for getting them on the back cover distorted the image.

In fact, I had jumped up from my late afternoon lunch of watermelon, a banana, rye crisp and some smoked turkey, to get on-line and move forward with the book. I'd been procrastinating, for some reason, just doing the final "approved" step. I had switched on the T.V. news, and heard a bit about some Muslim families, in Minneapolis, who were worried sick because there had been attempts to by outsiders to recruit their kids to be terrorists. My jump up to the computer was the result of recalling that I'd written that scenario (different ethnic group, different state), in my novel.

So the novel, some three years now after I actually finished and published it as "The Long Shadow," is now out, ISBN coded, as *Code of the Running Cross.* It will find its way onto Google Search, and perhaps someone will stumble onto the book title, and order it. While ordering the two proof copies today, checked my "storefront" revenue, and someone has ordered "*1000 Steps.*" So, two whole books sold on-line this year, thirteen sold in person here at my apartment building, and two books with blue ribbons from the County Fair.

It's laughable on the one hand, but on the other, they DID sell, and DID get recognition. It is then, a matter of finding ways and means to promote the books. In this regard, I called (a week and half after I said I would, dreading phone calls) the buyer at my favorite bookstore in Taos, Moby Dickens Bookshop, but she works only Friday through Monday.

Where am I in this boxed in scheme of things, Leytha? Too "aged-wine" to be hired to teach overseas then? Well, gosh! I had one fascinating year in Taiwan, and got to Paris twice, so there! Too limited a budget (as in practically non-existent) to promote my self published books? Well, sold copies of that typo-filled first version of the novel, as "The Long Shadow," at a book talk in Paris that same year! And frankly, this new title, as *Code of the Running Cross*, and the small changes, have improved the book I feel. Let's see then, if the buyer at Moby will think my prices (high cost to print-on-demand this way), allow her, and maybe even me, to make a profit.

Sitting here in my peaceful apartment, looking out at the trees, and looking around inside at my art on the walls and books on the shelves; I do not want all of this to just be boxed up to wait for me a year from now. I want to be at home somewhere. Is that New Mexico?

I wait anxiously for my sister to come home from her consulting work, even though once here, I, giving her the run of my TV, glad she can just relax, and watch what she wants to. Tonight though, we may go see the new Harry Potter movie. The last time she was here, we took in the latest Star Trek, hardly memorable trivia for grown-ups.

The feeling of days passing me by, of little value gained nor contributed. I'm anxious to return to her desert place. Even sitting typing away in "my space" in her R.V., I can look out and see that she and my bro-in-law are there puttering with the small garden of squash, corn and eggplant, or making slow but steady progress on the pond, and am lonely for a companion of my own, and some real sense of "place" in the world, but I am not, as I am here, deeply alone.

Litheria: loneliness is to be acknowledged, and changed, and all that you are doing will bring that desired change to you. Acknowledge too, this quiet phase in your life, this time of calm, which, although you call it boredom, or loneliness, in fact, you are not bored, and engaged with your writing and art-making and reaching out to explore teaching opportunities.

It is rather like when people say, "I'm hungry," not recognizing the body's need for a drink of water, or deep breath, or a walk away from the work being done at the moment. What is it you are really saying, when you use this expression, "I'm bored," or "my life is boring?"

The same is true for your attitude toward aloneness or loneliness. Yours, Litheria, is that of a deeper hunger, a deeper longing. To feel your life is of value, and to share your life with a companion, and community of people who are more in tune with you, is this not true?

Yes, of course, Leytha. But even when I communicated you with you years ago, there was an implied promise to bring me into contact with a community of light-givers. And instead, I grow more and more isolated, except for my few e-mail friends, and my sister.

There is a need then, for you to re-interpret, to look again at what this "community of light-givers" means to you. Certainly, your elder contacts at your apartment building, joyous about the opportunity you gave them to write some of their remembrances, must think of you, even if that is not the term they use, as a "light-giver."

Certainly, you have shared the light of life with children you have taught, in Taiwan, New Mexico and at the California summer camp.

Surely you know that even the few who've read your books have felt inspired, encouraged, or at least entertained. And what of the many, hundreds perhaps, who, over the years have taken home a piece of your art-making? Have you not shared some bit of creative light with them?

Yes, Leytha. There have been plays and songs, books, projects, activities, not-for-profit engagements, business and creative endeavors, teaching and sharing. That is true. My life is like a tree with thousands of leaves, each of those leaves is someone whose life I've touched, and whose life has touched mine. But why then, this constant discontent? What do I want, long for? What is this sighing? This waking up in the middle of the night and feeling so utterly, desperately alone?

Litheria: you have walked a path that is strewn with sharp rocks that have pierced your feet, and obstacles that you've had to climb over or go around. In doing this, you've still continued forward. Along the way, you've lightened your pack, as it were, and now find yourself in a place, a state of simplicity.

It is true that nature brings you joy. It is true that the act of creating brings you joy. It is true that giving to others in the form of teaching, encouraging, facilitating, brings you joy. Is this not true?

But it is the area of your own human needs that you must turn to now, not away from them, but toward them, engaging your Self, with your human needs; the need to feel well, rest well, eat and drink in a way that best nourishes the body.

225

Beyond this, is the need to open your Self, your human self, to others, and to allow yourself to be loved.

This is crazy, Leytha! I've always deeply respected what I sense as your voice, but how to open myself to being loved? I HAVE opened myself to others. But where is the evidence of love for me?

Oh, how silly this is. But, yes, it is a deep feeling, this feeling of not being loved. By whom? And by whom would it finally matter to me, satisfy, make me happy? Is it God I lack? How can I, with an eclectic world-knowledge of religion, and personal conclusion that religion is something created by humankind in all its variety to explain the unexplainable, to identify and personalize the unknowable, and to give peace, yes, that above all, to this discontent, how can I make some commitment to religion?

Perhaps though, it is not religious peace, nor personal love I seek, but a spirituality that is not divided between the "real," and the "spiritual," but is merged, one and the same.

Here I am, with seventy-two years on the planet as I write, still wanting to be in the position, place, space where I can say, ah, at last, I am making a difference for the good of humankind, perhaps actually being rewarded (paid, loved, acknowledged?) for it? That is obnoxious of me. One is supposed to be a giver of time and talent without expectation of anything in return. And I want something, something of a feeling I think, of feeling good for having found my niche in this life-time. This, my gypsy self has not yet found.

Ah-ha! Do you see, Leytha, how neatly I detoured around the idea of allowing myself to be loved? By another single person, a partner, a companion? It is true, absolutely true that I cannot see myself as the other half, or the one half of something called a partnership, a relationship, a marriage.

226

All my life I have wanted, longed from the depths of me, to define "me" and to know who I am, in the universe, in eternity, apart from any connection with another.

Litheria: yes, we know this, and this is why you communicate here. Trust me when I say that your search is the search of the soul to find itself face to face again. But that time is not yet.

That time comes for many, it seems, in the ecstatic, through contemplation or meditation or the abandonment of life as others perceive it, of work, family, responsibilities, etc., to become a hermit or holy person, but this is a fiction.

The soul will not completely know itself nor its place in the greater Soul, until shedding the body. It would be impossible for you to live IN the body, and to know your Self as your soul.

There is a "near" path that humans take, however, and that is the path of service to humankind. It may be a path taken within the boundaries of a religious discipline, or a social entity, or a path one takes as a lone individual.

In a sense, while you are still conflicted about this, wanting to have still, some sense of recognition in the world for your writing and art-making, it is this path of service that you've chosen. Perhaps chosen is not the best word, as you often defaulted to service, not knowing, you felt, how to function in the world of money and prestige making. But this was never your calling, Litheria, although your creative work will yet bring you these.

There will be a peace for you in relationship. It is nearer than you think. But the greater peace will come in a moment,

227

could come in this very moment, as you realize you are not apart from that from which you came, and that to which you will return, and in fact that which you are and will ever be. That is the relationship you long for. It is relationship with your Self.

Take a walk now, hear the wind in the trees, feel the breeze on your face, the sun on your skin, the ground beneath your feet. Where you are, is where YOU are. You need not BE anywhere else. "Relate" to who YOU are, and have been, and will become, but focus on the now of your life. Today is beingness, because you are alive on the planet and you breathe.

Some, meditate for others, those who are suffering in the conflicts around the planet, those who are suffering physically, those who are experiencing great economic trials. Some find a path of specialized service to humanity.

Engaged in this Litheria, you could let go of your own pain. It is the pain of guilt. It is this terrible weight that you feel in your back and legs and feet and neck. Let go, let go and live.

19

Twenty years from now you will be more disappointed by the things that you didn't do than by the ones you did do. So throw off the bowlines. Sail away from the safe harbor. Catch the trade winds in your sails. Explore. Dream. Discover. ~ Mark Twain

Here I am back at my sister's place for what, a couple of weeks or more? My apartment felt as lovely as before, but so did the loneliness. On the way back, we stopped in Reno, and met up with my bro-in-law at the Nugget, a casino hotel where they had a complimentary night, and a free show. I joined them at dinner for some soup and a drink, but not going to the show, wanted to just wander a bit, before going to another casino café for my own dinner.

Not much fun really, being by oneself, and finally, fatigued by the drive, and the return to a higher altitude, went to our room and, after a hot bath, fell asleep watching a movie on television.

I feel my life wasting away, without meaning, and following along now, in my sister's footsteps for awhile is diverting with trips with her to Wall-Mart, and Saver thrift shops, and Macy's. She enjoys shopping, (and must shop, for their twosome family), but I don't enjoy it. The people, the sensory overload, and I suppose, my own lack of money to shop for anything that would matter to me, gets me down.

It was too hot to stay in the car, so I tagged along. At a thrift shop though, I found a long black, embroidered skirt and lavender blouse, a rare purchase for me, considering my penchant for simplicity of wearing black. My sis insisted I buy a sun hat to wear when outside here; a nod to my dermatologist, after he excised a melanoma on my arm and warned me to stay covered up.

Looking over my art work in my apartment, Rosalie had commented on a small "archetypal" paper mache figure, draped in a long robe, playing a drum that I'd done on my own time when back at college in 1998, to get my BA in Art. "These would sell," she said, addressing a constant concern of mine, the what and how and where of selling my art work. So, at the thrift shop, she and I both ended up simultaneously bringing some materials to the shopping cart, materials that will make for picturesque costumes for the figures.

Today, I finished up two small projects, some potpourri packets, and some dried flower arrangements, that my sis can show and maybe sell for some cause she participates in out here. And, tomorrow, I'll clear the workshop space and begin laying out the various aspects of making the figures: blocks of wood, wire, wallpaper paste. material cut in proportional squares, yarn for hair, scissors, staple gun, wire cutters, sand paper. I love working with these things, taking bits of this, pieces of that, and creating something new.

This morning, opened my e-mail to a further note from the owner-director of the school in Dohuk, Kurdistan, wanting me to reconsider, after I said no to his offer of a teaching position at the soon to be opened college level school. I was concerned when he'd said no visa necessary, but checking the Kurdistan government web site, I see, in fact, that he is correct re Kurdistan, but a visa is required to enter Iraq, a fact overlooked by the potential employer.

230

I e-mailed the director of the Department of Education in Kurdistan, asking about this person, and new school. Surprisingly, I received a note back, expressing appreciation, as they liked to know who might be trying to hire foreigners to come to their country. He had not, at the time, even heard of this businessman and his plan for a school.

Perhaps the Kurdistan experience would prove deeply valuable, for them, for me, and I would stay, continue? Still, this offer from Mr. "A" doesn't feel right.

So, it is back to looking at New Mexico. I will have the money I need, after the first, to register for the various tests required, and pay the fee for the application, and send that to the Department of Education. I received a call, that it would take about four weeks to process the application, and that would likely mean September, and the positions will be filled by the time I'm eligible for them.

And regardless, since the test sites are in NM, how would I get there, and after, how to be there to go to job interviews. Money needed, yes, and a car there, and place to live, and sufficient income from substitute teaching to maintain me. Nothing seems possible right now, neither New Mexico, nor teaching overseas.

I've finished the dried floral arrangements, about 30 of them. I don't know if my sister has made a decision to take a table at the little local festival yet or not. Her question is, will the locals want, or afford something like I've made?

Ah well, not enough money can be generated from these to make any difference to me, so, perhaps she'll decide to just use them at a fall fund-raiser for one thing or another.

My brother-in-law cut some scrap wood with his power saw today, to make some flower boxes for Rosalie. I was happy to get the leftover cuts, as they are just the size needed for the bases of the figures I'll be making soon. He also cut the ends off some found wood I'd brought along, to make walking sticks from.

Certainly, I am, despite the heat, the wind, of this area,

231

despite my sleepless nights due to the constant pain in my legs, enjoying my space in John's workshop. I've not yet asked him for wood scraps I need to mount some of my smaller weavings, and, in fact, may have to buy some quality wood, have him cut the pieces to the sizes I want.

From the window of the R.V., I can see long-tailed magpies sitting on the posts of the little wire garden enclosure. In the house, John watches over the lamb shank Rosalie put in the oven to roast, before going off to a weight program meeting.

The sun, sifted by trees, and wooden fencing, lays down shadow patterns this late afternoon. The horrors of the daily news are as near as an Internet click, and as far away from this simplicity, as the moon.

I want to communicate with Leytha. But what have I to say? I feel as "stuck" at an entirely different level, as when these communications first began, some twenty years ago?

Litheria: this is a time to engage in the long vision, in what your life, on this earth plane is all about. To continue being concerned with the immediate, and for you, the ecstatic, the high, the "this is it, at long last," is to invite disappointment.

This is not to say that you are to abandon plans, ideas, to change your life in such a way that is more satisfying to you. It is to say to abandon your "concern" for this or that goal.

Continue your search for an overseas teaching job and if one appears which feels right to you, then is the time to make the decision about whether to stay or go. Continue to fulfill your plans for teaching in New Mexico, and the ultimate result of that, being able to have your own shop and a place to sell your art and books.

When all the conditions are fulfilled, then will be the time to decide if that is the path you will take.

Continue also to explore art making at this time, and book writing. It is not always given to you, on this plane, to know what the future holds. It is doing the work that matters.

There is a depth that you have abandoned, Litheria, which is meaningful to you, as you strive so hard to find a place for yourself, still, in this world. Look to that space now, to find peace.

You are, at the moment, surrounded by the night. Think of this as deep, calm pool in which you can immerse yourself and be refreshed. Think too, of the peace which surrounds you at the moment.

Look to the peace that is within you, a peace you have yet to know, a peace you have yet to experience. It is the constancy of life, and your soul's path to experience that which seemed to be outside itself, but is, in reality, only a manifestation of the one life, it is this you seek. But why do you seek something outside yourself when all that you seek is within?

Have you forgotten the power of imaging that which you seek to experience?

The morning brought an e-mail from another school in Kurdistan, the one in Erbil, saying, after our enthusiastic SKYPE interview, there were no positions open that "matched" me. It is the age thing I'm sure. Perhaps I should let go of both love via long distance e-mail and getting hired overseas at this stage of life.

There is a dead-end that I cannot see, or rather, that I cannot see beyond. Perhaps life is merely turning a corner, and shadows block my view of the path to be taken.

I've finished up four small wood assemblages today, as I'm so fascinated by images I see IN the wood, and love the textures of rock and wood, in these little table top sculptures. I will add these

233

to my four small wall hangings in the same style, and stock these, along with the weavings (a new one, on a plastic rim frame, looks like an abstract mask), for my future shop.

At one time, all my life in fact, the idea that I would ever be able to complete college and get a university degree, much less go on to Harvard to achieve a masters at age sixty-five, was much more in the realm of the not probable than my having my own shop, for my books and art, a cozy, working studio where I can welcome people from all over the world, and make my living while still making books and art.

So, this I will stop "longing" for, and (yes, Leytha), image it, and all the ways and means for that to come about. Love, romance, companionship, partnership, relationship? Ah, too many "ships" to sail, and me, a poor pilot and poorer navigator. I toss out my hope and desire, and my hesitation, undefined, to the universe, and wait.

Five more days, and with money in my bank account, I'll decide if I'm going to invest the $230 in fees (test dates, and application fee), for the NM licensure. It's interesting that in seeking an overseas teaching job, one is always warned against paying fees to the school or recruiter. I'm sure I'm not the only one interested in teaching in New Mexico, who finds this amount to be hard to come by.

At this point, I'd really just like to buy myself a real bed, a daybed, I think, and rearrange the rest of my bedroom for art-making. I want to start painting again. But then again, back to the dilemma of no place to show and sell my work.

Once back in the apartment, I know I will again experience intense loneliness. I have no heart for joining any of the on-line dating games again. Nor for association with the older (my age, younger, older) residents at the apartment or in the community. Playing bingo at the Jewish Center next door is not my cup of tea. Whither my tomorrows? Ah, it's too hot, even with the cooler on in this R.V., and too hot in the workshop until early evening.

234

Spent the day cutting the material we purchased at the thrift shop in Reno, into the rectangles I will use for the robes of the little figures I'll make. A total of almost 100 pieces of material. 100 finished figures at $20 (worth more), $2000. The question will be where to show and sell them, with artist space rentals so expensive in the events I can access.

I am awake (the third awakening in a pain-filled night), at 3 A.M. So far I've smashed three mosquitoes and countless other flying critters, and now that my brother-in-law set up a T.V. monitor and video connection, I'd gone through three favorite old videos: *84 Charring Cross Road*, *Chocolate*, and *An Affair to Remember*. I don't really watch them. They are my sleeping potions, keeping my mind quiet while I drift off, watching the movie in my mind. But tonight, there was no sleep.

This morning, during a short drive, my sis listened as I went over, hesitantly, as I do when trying to explain myself to someone verbally, the prospects for New Mexico. I know, and she mentioned again, the safety net of my living arrangements in San Rafael. I confessed to a need to live on the edge somewhat, to have an adventure, to meet people (in New Mexico), who were more like me. From my apartment, I often wrote e-mails to my sis, more of a way of "working out" my thoughts, just as I'm doing here, I suppose, and she, my tolerant, patient "witness."

"Write an e-mail to yourself," she suggested today.

"Dear Claudia..." No, I can't do it. Tonight I have no answers. I am still lonely, still longing for love, still wanting to be in a place where I can show and sell my books and art, and meet interesting people, and be involved, somehow in something compassionate re humankind.

Litheria: Reach, reach, reach for that which you want to experience.

235

An awful night. Severe lower stomach pains, and severe pain in lower back, right leg and foot. Arm and shoulder muscles hurt too, but I knew that would result from the afternoon spent cutting material. When I finally got to sleep about three A.M., I woke, screaming, gasping for breath, from a nightmare. I'd gone into a childhood bedroom, a big room that seemed familiar, but I was as I am now, or a young woman, and climbed into bed with two other girls, one of whom might have been my sister as a child.

A hall light went off suddenly, and I heard the door open. "Daddy?" I called, expecting him, as he would both tuck us in as children, and gently waken us, with a jiggle of our toes at the foot of the bed, so not to frighten us, in the morning.

But it was not "Daddy," but a menacing man whom I could not see at all in the pitch darkness; I was laying on my right side, as usual, when I can face a wall, and I suddenly felt the man's hands on me, trying to fondle me. He was strong and I couldn't push him away. I cried out, but the sound came out in a dreadful, tight mouthed squeak. At last, I was able to open my mouth and make a real screaming sound, and woke up, dreadfully afraid, and surprised to see that I was in the R.V., safe and sound in the narrow, single bed. Looking out the window, I saw that the indoor porch light at my sister's house, was still on.

Later, getting back to sleep after putting a favorite video on, the sound of it lulling me to sleep in the other room, I dreamed, again seeing my father. My "daddy," was not an educated man as far as school goes, he was a great teller of stories, but in my dream, he appeared and handed me a book. The title had something to do with a practical type of mysticism. The word for the philosophy, or practitioner, began with an "e," although it was not existentialism, but was more related to the word, esoteric, I think. But the word which wants to surface in my mind is something like *eridonism*, which, as far as I could recall, means nothing.

The book's author name was that of my father, but not my father's real name. The man disappeared, and I screamed in anger

236

at the crowd around me accusing them of keeping the truth from me, that my father was a writer. Knowing that, had it been true, would have made my life so much easier, so much more directed, and not so lonely and alone.

I opened my laptop, and typed *eridonism* into Google, I came up with "hedonism" first, and then *eridanus*. Eridanus, the River Po in Northern Italy, and a constellation, considered the longest in the sky, figures, as a river, in the myth of the fallen Phaethon, son of Apollo. After recklessly driving his father's chariot too close to the earth, nearly devastating it, he falls, at his father's hand, flaming to earth, and is received by the river Eridanus. Interesting, but gave me little insight into my dream. I called on Leytha:

Litheria: Your dream is referring to that aspect of your being, the male aspect, that you both fear, and revere; the one, an attacker, abuser, a coward, a terrorizer of the innocent; the other, representing your highest aspiration, to be a writer, to express philosophic ideas rooted in nature.

The "father" aspect of your dreams does come from your own childhood, but also from the cosmic "fatherhood," that which can be both the powerful and vengeful God whose name is not to be spoken, and the son-source of life which guides and nurtures.

What is important here, is that in your current experience as a woman, you survived, and even put away, or disappeared (by waking up), the threatening male aspect, and in your second dream, turned on your accusers (was this not a Mary Magdalene scene?) acknowledging the giver of the "book" as not only your Father, but the writer of that book, and practitioner of a philosophy of being that valued nature and harmony.

237

The name that you tried to recall does not need to be reconstituted in your reality. You sensed that it had to do with a philosophy, a practice, a fellowship (did the man in your dream not refer to "those of us who follow the way of e….") which related to nature, to peace and harmony. Then follow this path; it has always, since childhood, been your choice of vision quest.

"E…what?" I still wondered, trying to make sense of the dream: education, exploration, elucidation, environmentalism…?

Perhaps the dream, and the "word" reference to Eridanus, was intended to show me my own impulsive and too often reckless behavior, but while the "angry" father, Apollo, would send his offspring flaming to earth, the reception by the river, Eridanus, indicated a "soft landing." I wonder if the story continued. What became of Phaethon? Did he become the river? Or did the river provide him with an opportunity for re-birth?

What an odd day this had been. I napped until 1 P.M., finally, having not gone to sleep until dawn, about the time my sister gets up. I have referred to us as me, the moon, and she, the sun, and certainly our sleep habits, and our personalities bear this out. In the afternoon, I drove with her to a nearby, very small town, a former military base, where now there is only a library, a traveler's market, a thrift shop and a recreation center where my sis sometimes goes for swim aerobics.

We found some material in the thrift shop to use for the mache sculptured figures I'll be making, but from the moment I got into the car until I came home, I was almost overwhelmed by the heat. Knowing my preferences and even need, for cooler weather, it is laughable I should consider working in the Middle East!

Back "at the ranch" I went to the workshop to put pieces of felt on the bottoms of some small wooden assemblages I'd made earlier in the week. Suddenly, the sky was black, thunder crashed like gigantic kettle drums, and it began to rain. In a few moments,

238

the giant drops turned into hail the size of large marbles. The hail, and the rain continued furiously for almost half an hour. I'd never seen such a phenomenon.

My brother-in-law is in the process of building a pool, which should hold thousands of gallons of water. It quickly filled up to running over. The hail bubbled around on top of the muddy water like marshmallows on chocolate. In an hour, the thirsty, dry desert ground had soaked up the standing rain puddles, and the evening turned pleasantly cool.

Change, I thought, all is change and unpredictable. While the weather may have been predicted by those in the know, we did not expect to go from hundred degree temperatures, to a thunder and rain and hail-storm in just a few hours time. Standing in the shelter of a shed outside the workshop, so I could watch the hail come down without getting hit by it, I worried about my sister, who would have been driving home in it.

Later, she said the two lane road was thickly covered with hail, and when she, moving along slowly and cautiously, saw another car up close behind her, she moved over so he could pass, but that car too then proceeded to continue on very slowly. I was so relieved to look up finally, and see her car in the carport.

Things matter more when nature kicks up her heels, like the safety of my sister, and other things do not, like whether I would be teaching somewhere in September. Rosalie and John looked around the yard to access the damage: poppy plants and petunias flattened, a heavy metal picnic table knocked over by the wind, narrowly missing a window, a dead baby bird near the pathway to the house. Back in the house, we all agreed to a big helping of Rosalie's berry cobbler and ice cream. It was nearly their dinner time, but who cared. It seemed more important to just celebrate riding out nature's show time.

I await a phone call from my friend S, in New Mexico, but it is now an hour later than she said she would call. An e-mail arrived saying she'd like to buy me a ticket to Albuquerque, and the invitation to spend some time with her kicking around some business ideas she has that I might be of some help with. Mentioning this to my sis, she said she could take me to the Reno, NV airport anytime. Both these women are supportive of my dreams and creative endeavors, in whatever way they can. Working women both, they give what they can. Someday, I hope I can give back.

At the thrift shop, my sis had pointed out a "free items" table. I picked up a little wooden planter, a box attached to a three wheel cart made of twigs, painted white, the paint peeling. I immediately put it in my bag. It's on the window counter now, beside the high-topped baby shoe my sis gave me last week.

"If you'd had fancy little shoes to wear like this when you were a child..." she'd said, recalling my reference to the high-topped brown ones I'd had to wear for weak ankles, "...maybe seeing this will help you heal." I glanced again at the little tricycle cart. "It's my gypsy cart," I laughed suddenly. But the cart, having no pedals, is either stationary, or motorized, or moves along by magic. I wonder where, if I climb in, it will take me?

Between sis and bro-in-law, the mysteries of scanning my college transcripts and getting them into my own computer files, was resolved; the process taking much more time than it should have. Why a 30 minute download time for five pages? I needed the transcripts in my computer files, to upload them to various schools when asked, but right now, to complete a registration with Santa Fe Public School District.

The social security money has been deposited in my bank account so now the time has arrived for me to decide for sure if I'm going to spend $235 on the fees to get me going with the New Mexico license. Tomorrow, my sis is going into Reno, and will get the $65 money order I need for the application fee.

Another almost sleepless night due to the pain in my right leg, so, that, and being done in by the heat of the morning, almost caused me to cancel my trip into Reno with my sis. But, she wanted me to go along first, to see the "Doyle Days" parade, celebrating its one hundredth year as a town, established in the railroad days. It was sad, even by my sister's kindly standards for small town affairs. A couple of old veterans carrying flags, some young people in costume on horseback, a tractor pulling a hay wagon, filled with kids, the several vehicles of the volunteer fire department, with both the women and men drivers throwing candy to the kids.

Rosalie and I both had a dozen ideas how it could have been more colorful, with more participation., remembering our own small town upbringing, when our stepmother and us kids spent hours making tissue paper flowers to decorate our family restaurant float.

Still, I enjoyed taking photos which will find their way only to my computer files, and never be seen by anyone. I captured a woman scout leader inviting a rock hound vendor to get involved teaching her kids about the geology of the area, a mom and children giving away puppies, some folks serving up barbecue and Budweiser, and the volunteer firefighter dressed up as Smokey the Bear.

"Must be hard for him wearing the costume in this heat," I remarked to his companion, who was guiding him across the grass.

"Not as hard as fighting a fire," the man replied, with a slight smile.

It is in these smallest of small towns that the spirit of America lives, I thought. Friendly, unpretentious people, trying to make a living, some, off the grid, and volunteering their time for what they think makes life worth living.

We headed on into and stopped at a bank to get the $65 certified check I needed to send in with my New Mexico "alternate licensure" application. My sister, so generous re older me, got the check via her own bank account, and postponed my usual $200 a month payment to her for another loan, so I can, with my limited social security income, continue plowing this road which will hopefully lead me to New Mexico, a teaching position, and places to show and sell my art and books.

Returning home late afternoon, we pulled off the road so I could photograph a striking red rock mountain. I walked through the recently the area recently blackened by a fire resulting from sparks from the tires of a passing truck and I collected some small bits of rocks I can use in the sculpture "scenes."

My sis, as usual, seems to enjoy being supportive of what I do. This morning, working in my brother-in-law's workshop, I looked up to see her cleaning off a gardening table for me to put the "in-process" sculpture on, and realized that for once, I had everything I needed to complete my projects.

I'll call the NMTA number on Monday, and check on whether I can take all three of the tests I need toward becoming a "fully qualified" teacher for both K-12, Art, and Language arts on September 19th, or whether I must take only one test at a time. Then, I'll need to find a way to get to NM, and stay there. Honestly, getting an overseas teaching job was less complicated: a phone interview, an e-mailed contract, a visa and airline ticket arranged, and away I went. But that was when I was sixty nine, not seventy two.

Of course, the same thing could happen in NM; and while "age discrimination" is illegal, there are dozens of reasons they might have for hiring someone local, someone younger, even without saying so. But, enough of that.

I must get my stubborn donkey of Yahoo to open up, so I can e-mail an attachment of the information I want to print on clear labels I bought yesterday, which I'll attach to the bottom of the finished sculpture pieces, and to the backs of paintings.

20

I am not bound for any public place, but for ground of my own where I have planted vines and orchard trees, and in the heat of the day climbed up into the healing shadow of the woods. Better than any argument is to rise at dawn and pick dew-wet red berries in a cup. ~Wendell Berry

Leytha: have you a message for me today? I am, despite pain throughout my body today, happy; being out in "the countryside" like this; having my sis and bro-in-law nearby; making art, working with my hands in the workshop. Without the Internet news, without television news, a sense of a world at peace is possible.

Litheria: you needn't wait for a message, as you know. Simply opening yourself up to the Infinite allows the bridge of communication, like a bridge being lowered over a moat, to make a way for you to enter the castle. You are experiencing the "mysticism of the ordinary," the peace that runs quietly beneath the surface of turmoil, conflict, and all that is not in harmony with the earth and with eternity.

Do not see the lack of communication from your friend as having anything to do with you. It does not. She is in the process of

243

working through some things in her life. While she "means" to call you, she actually cannot, needing to concentrate on resolving these other issues.

There is more than one path to take, more than one way to climb a mountain, more than one way to cross a continent or an ocean. It is time to envision a variety of answers, ways and means, towards the changes you wish to see occurring in your life.

At this time, it will be helpful to just meditate on the infinite variety in all of nature, plant, rock, animal, bird, insects even! Each have found a way, on this life-plane, to exist with the basics given here, of earth, water, air, sun, nourishment, and community of kind.

If that amazing use of what is available, and the more amazing adaptation to it is a law of this plane, why should you, recognizing this, limit infinite variety to the physical?

Would it not follow that there is infinite variety of thought, ideas, methods, creations, ways and means, as well? There is no way for you to comprehend the immensity of this idea, but by relating each: ideas, for example, or paths to an end, to the infinite variety on earth, in the universe, the galaxy, the stars in the sky, the sands of the seas, the leaves of trees, you will begin to open your mind and heart to infinite possibility in your personal life.

Were you to come to "practice" this way of seeing life, you would one day extend this concept to include all that comes into your consciousness: world events, the economy, human health, and even, or perhaps especially, the matter of love and relationships. The possibilities, in fact, the probabilities, are infinite.

There is no box around you. No room without doors or windows. All is open, all is porous, all is in movement, all responds and reacts when responded to, or reacted to. In a single moment, all changes. There is no permanence, only movement and change. Embrace this concept with an open mind and heart, and see not one pathway, no one person, no one "ways and means" but an infinite number.

I will soon be on my way to New Mexico. My friend S., has kindly reserved a one-way air ticket for me the end of the month, less than three weeks. She will make space for me at her place until I can get my act together there. Once this came together, my excitement gave way to "am I doing the wise thing?" Translated, this means, as I mentioned to her, "I have cold feet!"

She replied, much as my sister might, "Then put on your boots!"

Meanwhile, knowing now that I'll be in New Mexico in September, I registered with the NMTA, on-line, for two of three qualifying tests I want to take: basic skills, which is required, and visual arts, which is needed to acquire an "endorsement in that subject, in order to teach art. Taking a test for an endorsement requires that one already has sufficient course credits in that subject, which I do. Later on, I'll take the "language arts" test. While I did not concentrate on English in any of my college work, I did take a number of theater courses, and this would qualify me. Once I registered, I was able to send off, with the $65 certified check, the application packet for "alternative licensure" to the New Mexico Department of Education.

So, that, plus the fact that there was no follow up from any of the other overseas positions I applied to, has narrowed my focus. My sis will drive me back to my apartment couple of days before my flight, to pack a suitcase, and will take me to the airport. I'll delay giving notice on my place, and moving whatever personal possessions I want to keep, after I have a job.

Busy this week, with finishing up some thirty five dried flower arrangements, wrapping some weavings and small assemblages, and printing out, with my sis' help (and my brother-in-law, who programmed my laptop to be able to print to their office printer), some fifty photos of local scenes, particularly amazing desert sunsets, as post-card size images. All of these, we'll offer for sale (I say "sale" but wonder at the prospects, in this low-income area), at a senior event tomorrow.

Whatever does sell, I plan to give the money to my sis, who not only provided some of the materials for the crafts, but whose electric bill almost doubled with my use of my laptop, refrigerator, cooler, heater, in the RV where I've been staying. Of course, they would never even mention it, but I happened to see the bill!

After arranging our table at the senior center today (fun, at least, to see some of my stuff on display again), we all went to a tiny Pentecostal church nearby to stuff ourselves with a Mexican menu potluck, a fundraiser for the church. The wife of the pastor, (they are an older couple), had also baked up a variety of pies for sales and my sister bought a cherry one for John.

We sat in old, folding church chairs, at oilcloth covered plank tables. In the middle of the room, a big, black wood stove. In the back of the room, a crib, a few drawings by kids on the shabby wood walls, and a huge flannel board. I remembered the flannel board from my own childhood; Bible stories illustrated by laying cutout flannel backed figures on the board.

Last evening, I watched the second half of a Woody Allen film, "Alice," trying to get through the shallow story. As I sat in the church, downing a mouth-watering piece of chocolate brownie, I found myself comparing the two environments: that of Allen's rich, bored, philandering New Yorkers, (with the exception of "Alice," whose angst led to her ultimate salvation, dramatically abandoning it all, volunteering with Mother Therese, and finally, a simpler life alone, with her children), and these very poor people.

246

Perhaps they are happy, if it matters to them, prosperity and happiness being less important than community and a certainty about eternity.

Tonight I type in the house, rather than taking my laptop back to the R.V., just wanting some company. But, company means my sis and bro-in-law in the other room watching television. I will miss just living in the proximity of family when I'm gone from here.

I drove home from the church with John, while Rosalie went back to the senior center to help with final preparations. Back in the workshop, I sanded down a pine branch I picked up the other day when my sis and I stopped to take photos of the beautiful red rock mountain formation. It will, I can tell already, make a beautiful walking stick. I will miss the workshop.

Perhaps I should be wringing my hands and heart over the conditions of the world and the sufferings of so many, so many people. And, deep down I do. But just for a little while, it feels so good just to be at peace within a small, small world.

A day of sleep (a sore throat), and reflection. Wondering if I should ask my sis to drive me back to my apartment this week, to have couple of weeks there to think about whether I really want to give it up. Does everyone do this? Second guess themselves? Even if I were going overseas, I would have, at least, a job there.

But there is good reason for my second guessing. New Mexico is all speculation. Despite my finally getting the licensure application in, and registering for required tests next month, and having both S' invitation to stay with her, and the gift of a plane ticket, I now am concerned about whether, in this economy, and at my age

I suppose this state of mind has been brought on partly by the sore throat and the no-sales of any of my dried flower arrangements, paper mache dolls or weaving projects at the little "flea market, crafts sale" event yesterday. Really a mistake I think to have mixed "flea market" and "crafts sale" together. There was only one other craft maker, a lady who made knitted hats. I exchanged a floral arrangements for one of her hats; a beige one to match my coat, in preparation for a New Mexico winter. A few people bought copies of the photo cards we'd printed out, views I'd taken around this area. I suppose we "broke even," with my sis buying a few "flea market" goodies.

I feel so removed from this world that my sister is comfortable in. My world is one of thought, of ideas, of making stuff and stringing words together. Will there ever be someone I can talk to? A community of people who are active and excited about life, life as I see it, life as I seem to lack experiencing?

Litheria: You are experiencing life; you are not outside of it, this is merely life. For weeks now, and months before this, you have written, or created some piece of art.

You have shared what you know with others. You have reflected on the way the world was, is, and becoming. You have experienced time with your sister that many wish for and never achieve.

You've been surrounded by growing things, and even now, looking out your window, you see a ring of mountains, acres of sage brush and sky with changing cloud formations.

This is merely a time of peace for you. Can you not accept it as such?

But Leytha, what value do I have to anyone just now? Without looking forward, without having something daily to "report" (if only to myself) as accomplishment, I feel lethargic, useless, without joy.

We have talked of this before. Having planted the garden, now is the time for nurturing it, the time for patience, the time for expectation. Can you not image, imagine, what you want your life to be about once you leave for New Mexico? Now is not the time for looking back, for wondering if you made the right decisions.

Now is the time for celebrating yourself for refusing to accept the status quo in your life, for daring to push boundaries of age and experience, for believing in your talents and skills, and for knowing that you have love to give in friendship, and are willing to receive love in return.

I'm back at my apartment, courtesy and generosity of my sister, who drove me home, stayed overnight, and headed home at dawn. Now, anticipate my flight to New Mexico in twelve days. The application for alternative licensure was waiting, via return mail, when I arrived home, with an attached note re items I'd left out. But checking through it, I think the error is theirs not mine. So, will deal with this in person after I get to New Mexico, since the Dept. of Education is in Santa Fe, and S. can take me there.

It is strange how smoothly, how easily, some transitions are, and how challenging are others. I don't take these edu license obstacles as negative scarecrows though, rising up to shout, turn back, turn back! Perhaps instead, having fought the course, I'll come out a winner.

I've cleaned my house, and as I look around, there is nothing extraneous here. I wish, as I could with some savings, just make my move now, my art and personal stuff going with me, the furniture going with my sis to whomever she wants to gift it, perhaps to herself. Instead, I'm holding on to the apartment for at least another month, to see what New Mexico holds for me. I don't like this fall-back position.

It is certain though, into my second day back here at my apartment, with no one to talk to, that I feel as though (by choice),

I am totally alone in this huge building. As for the "neighborhood," it is one of cars going and coming to work, to shop, to pick up kids at school. Walking a few blocks to the neighborhood grocery an hour ago, I passed no one but a Latino man, working on his car, parked across the sidewalk.

While I criticize the phenomenon of a "national conversation," based on the info-as-entertainment spewed forth via television, radio, the Internet, perhaps I could be more sympathetic and engage with this trivial conversation with others, but what "others?" After a year and nine months in this apartment, I know no one except those few who participated in my remembrance writing workshop.

If others, trying to function in an anonymous world over which they feel less and less control, sense their loneliness as I do (for community, for tribe, for meaning), then this may be one of the reasons they turn to the electric and electronic media, speaking of celebrities, anchors, hosts, authority panels, bloggers and even the President's wife by first name, as if they knew them personally. In fact, it is likely they do know these people better, likely, than those they work with, pass in their cars, or interact briefly with in shops and service centers.

But then, this is why I want New Mexico. I want a real town, and real people, and real opportunities to show and sell my books and art, and maybe, just maybe, real friends. This is not to say I did not have some miseries when I was in New Mexico before, with the very short tourist season of art buying, and with landladies and restaurant, retail and hotel supervisors screaming at employees in the Jerry Springer or Donald Trump ("You're Fired!") modes of communication. Still, within my own shop, and within the context of occasional substitute teaching in the elementary school, and especially within the embrace of the New Mexico landscape, I was happy.

Litheria: We wish for you to acknowledge your own Self in making the decisions, taking the actions, taking the risks, reaching out to climb this one more mountain. And we wish for you to surrender worry, concern for how it will all play out for you.

But now is the time for a further step. Now is the time for you to step out of the role where things have happened to you, where you have been a re-actor rather than an activist, where you have been wishful, rather than a planner, where you have planned, yes, projects, and school to be accomplished, and books to be written and published.

Where you must go now, (even as you anticipate New Mexico), is not a place, but a place in mind, in spirit, in wholeness. Now is the time of fulfillment. It will not look as you thought it would look in the past. During these past weeks you have been reflecting on all that, how many dreams, many hopes, while manifest in one way or another, seemed to fall short of what you had imagined, or rather dreamed of and wished for, for your Self.

The difference now, is this: we want you to see yourself as a healer, a giver of wisdom, an author, speaker, workshop giver, an encourager. Do not step back from this. The window is open, the door is open, the time is now. We will guide you, be with you, encourage you.

These are the years of not only your fulfillment, but the time for wisdom, for the healing of spirit, of mind, of life. You will not do this alone. You will not be alone. Rather, you will sense our presence, as one of refreshment, in waking and sleeping. "A blessed relief," you are laughing.

But in laughter too. Treat yourself to laughter as if it were a walk in the rain, a refreshing swim in a cool, clear pool, a ride

251

on a carousel. Laughter will refresh and strengthen you, and draw others to you.

Do you see you are not shocked nor even surprised to hear these predictions? That is because you are now in tune with us, Litheria, now one with us, now having come into your Self. Accept this, dear one, as a moment of transition, illumination, becoming.

Prepare for what is to come, and what you know you are prepared to do. You have long sensed, in yourself, and in others, this desire, hunger, thirst, for encouragement, encouragement that comes without labels, encouragement that is transferred by word, by smile, by touch. Come into the anointment of this dear one.

The time is now, yet it is timeless. Encouragement is a light, that lit, turned on, shined into the darkness of the human soul and experience is transformed into healing, ideas, movement, change, power, and love.

During the next few days, we will continue to guide you along this path of preparedness. Be faithful only to listen, and to act.

21

Experience is the name everyone gives to their mistakes.
~Oscar Wilde.

New Mexico; the trip lasted, not the two months I anticipated to get settled there, but one week. So many reasons to cut it short. My allergy-prone system could not cope with my friend's little dog, and the location of her house, far enough from public transport to make me dependent on her for rides. But finally, Santa Fe is not for me, not Taos. What was I thinking? I found that, once again, I'm so unable to live in someone else household. I am, I suppose, a hermit and need an attic, a cottage, a "room of my own" as Virginia Woolf would say, where all that I love is there, and there are windows to watch the changing of nature, and a door with no steps, to walk through and out into the changing seasons.

Taos still tugs at my heart, but when a sudden wave of illness hit me two days ago, I was frightened, and felt I needed to quickly get back "home" where I had medical coverage. Were I seriously ill, and stayed on with S., I would have been a burden to her, and to my sister. I suspect some psychic sense, unacknowledged by me, is at work here too; the "world" being too much with me, as some scriptures put it. I did not handle well the stress of travel, traffic, living in someone else's environment, being surrounded by the swirling tornado of consumerism, the frustrations of battling my way through bureaucracy for the privilege of teaching in a part of the country that needs good teachers, but does not make it easy for them to find open doors…and the sense that I would be, caught up in all this, end up abandoning my Self, she who needs contemplative time, and time to write, time to create.

I wanted to teach to be able to support my creativity in an environment I imagined to be beautiful, peaceful, and found it to be an imagined scenario. I suppose I saw myself living at Georgia O'Keefe did, in her rustic house with the windows and the view of ever changing sky and dessert. I experienced a sense of joy at the seeing the huge, golden orange, autumn moon against the dull gray screen of dawn as I prepared to leave New Mexico.

Now, I experience irritation at the moth on my bright computer screen, who eludes my grasp, and the freedom of release I would give it, through an open door. Outside my window, the wind dances with the leaves, a dancing in the dark, as the moon has hidden out behind clouds, as have I. My sense of aloneness is so deep as to overwhelm me. Where do I belong? Where is home? Where is love?

Litheria: The answer to all of these questions for you is in the immediate now. You needn't be concerned about whether you made right or wrong decisions. You followed your heart, and there were others available to help you on that path.

Daily, even though you cannot see this in your reality at times, you grow closer to belonging, being "at home," and experiencing love. You've opted, instead of a life filled with the daily challenges of teaching in large city, merely in order to be where you felt your heart and creativity would be nurtured, to return to a life-style which offers more time for contemplation, and for creativity.

254

While too often, your contemplation is at a level just beneath the surface of daily life, and rewards you with a sense of grief, and while you long for the financial rewards of your creativity and the physical manifestation of "love," in the form of another individual, a "true love" life companion, there is, in you, an equally deep need to be alone and live a contemplative life.

What you can have in the now, is a community of others like yourself. Search this out. Adopt again a sense of service to others through your art, through your writing. One thing will lead to another. We are almost complete in this phase of our communications with you, and it is nearly time for you to publish. In these recent communications, you have expressed great concern with "finding your place" in this world, on this life-plane, in this time frame.

We counsel you to once again return to the knowing that the spirit, your Self, is always "at home," always in the "right" place, always learning the right lessons, always making a contribution, in the eternal scheme of things, to the expansion of the spirit, the self, the soul; is always making a difference in the life of others, either for good, or not-so-good, or evil, depending on how close to, or how far from the individual has distanced him or her self, from God, from Spirit, from Source, from eternal aliveness, from evolving Life.

Be at peace, Litheria. Breathe. Smile. Appreciate. The life-line you live on the earth plane draws towards its conclusion, that is true, but you will, we promise you, live more fully in your remaining years, make greater contribution, and celebrate life, love, nature, people, the planet, more than ever before. Do not struggle to see rewards. Make what you think, do, create, available to others. Receive that which they have to give you.

255

While we know that you turn away from the negative, whether it is the daily barrage of bad news spewed out by television, or negative conversation by others, we wish to make you hungry, thirsty, to fill your mind and heart and soul, with the "peace which passes all understanding."

Turn away, yes, but bathe your self, clothe your self, restore your self, reward your self with all that is good and positive, all that is uplifting and encouraging, all that is beautiful and healthy and holy in the sense of "wholeness;" all that is the presence and enduring eternity of the Spirit. It is this you long for: the fullness of your own spirit, merging once again with the Spirit which creates, eternally, each of us.

There was never a promise made to any "starwalker" who chose this earth path, of peace, or love, or even the joy, however brief, of seeing the good results, the fruit, as it were, of his or her life, efforts on this life-plane. But "consciousness" requires that, of it: in other words, to be conscious of consciousness. There is, in the path you have taken, a promise to encourage. Let your Self be so encouraged, Litheria. Remember, remember, remember: life is in the now, but Life, is not just for now, but is forever.

This view, this awareness, this consciousness, will allow for the peace, the joy even, that comes from the eternal view, for yourself, for others, for that which you learn and that which you do, and for humanity, the planet, this life-plane, the cosmos, and Life that while it is beyond comprehension, can, in a dawning sunrise, in movement of a breeze dancing with the leaves, in the sound of waves breaking on the sand, in the laughter or tears of another human being, encourage. Be then, encouraged, and filling yourself moment to moment with the light that comes from returning to memory of the eternal, encourage others. This, Litheria, is love.

22

We must become the change we want to see.
~Mahatma Gandhi

I have come "home" although it is still only partially home for me, back to my apartment in San Rafael. Feeling sick the past few days, with increasing pain that has, in the past, signaled bronchitis, I concluded I might have the flu, perhaps something picked up from the crowded airports and planes, perhaps just my body reacting, as it does, since I internalize all feelings, to the stress and frustration of exploring the New Mexico possibilities.

So, my sister, as much for their own sakes (not wanting to "catch" my illness) as for mine, drove me home, slept overnight and left in the dark of the morning. Before leaving their place, on closing up my e-mail, I found a note from the director of the Canadian overseas recruitment firm that had secured my Taiwan teaching, recruiting for a position in Saudi Arabia were I ready to leave in two weeks.

Now, I am neither up to going, nor being rejected re age, so did not answer. Others at the agency had repeatedly told me that my age was a limiting factor in trying to get me a job now.

A feverish drive home, though we stopped for dinner, (asparagus and a baked sweet potato for me, a small steak and salad for my sister, celebrating a bit her amazing twenty pound

257

weight loss. Then, I was suddenly opening the screen door to my apartment and it seemed as if I had been away for months, instead of the one week, and it felt good to be there, surrounded by my own things.

Inside the screen lay a large envelope. Opening it, I laughed out loud, incredulous, despite how miserable I felt. The envelope held my New Mexico Internship Teaching License, good for the next three years, though dependent on my completing some tests that I was now not in New Mexico to complete.

They'd said to expect approval to take "four to six weeks." They must have put the license in the mail the day after I was in the Santa Fe office.

Concerned now only with the task of restoring both my own energy (what IS this sickness?) and some pleasant energy to my apartment. It's so energizing to see my weavings on the wall. I wish there were room to hang my paintings too, and do some more.

Two days of sleep despite much discomfort, and am beginning to feel better. The view from my window is autumn, with a light breeze, after rain, blowing amber leaves onto the roof-top that would be a wonderful place for a patio garden, but alas, no access, only the view beyond my window.

Above the trees, wispy clouds, some shadowed gray with pockets of unreleased rain, others, like spun sugar algae floating on a slow moving river, I beneath it.

I love autumn, when I can sit here, bundled in a sweater (and sometimes a scarf, preferring to keep the window open) and write. I sometimes look for magic, that which can occur when a word or phrase is typed in for an Internet search, and the likely, or unlikely, pops up.

Feeling better today after three weeks of sickness, and have rearranged the apartment, so that I have art work space in the bedroom, and all the weavings on branches or wood are hung. Still, the painting, paper mache so messy; ought to be done in a workshop. I'll see though if this space will work for me. It was pleasant there today, with rain-cloud filtered sunlight coming through the big window. I only need a pretty, rustic daybed to make it complete, then away with the air mattress on the floor!

Leytha: Here I am. Can I not then have some success, or at least be useful?

Litheria: You must learn to smile, to laugh, to enjoy. Why so grim? You are not the only one who seeks fulfillment and you are not the only one to find recognition of or money for your work out of reach.

Here is a key: focus with joy. Grimness, sadness, grief, regret, remorse deflect your dreams in a boomerang effect. Joy sends them flying on the wind, determination holds them aloft, discipline (exercising and increasing your knowledge and skills) helps them find their mark.

We have talked of this before. It is true that you can try to bend another's will to your own, but to try to do so is to create a rift, a tear in your universe, in the world which is personally your own.

You can, however, come to sense timing and pathways to the universe which is beyond your own personal one.

In simpler terms, this is called "luck." Convinced that you don't have it, you do not see it in operation, nor do you often conclude (thinking others luckier than you), that there is a result in your life that has neither been conjured up by you through careful planning nor intense expectation. It is the "something which just happens."

There are principles which create this activity, and these results, but plainly speaking, it is likely that in some past time in your life, a hour, day, year or years ago, you have planted the seeds of desire and knowingly or unknowingly, have nurtured them by thought, or activity, or perhaps appreciation and gratitude.

It would be well to begin to acknowledge, in detail, the results in your life that you consider to be of good fortune. Opening your heart and mind and soul to this awareness may actually set "luck" into action, but more, doing so provides a well-lit "landing" strip for good fortune to continue to find you.

Having done this (and continuing to do this), you will open your heart-space to more specific good fortune; in other words the fruition, the realization of dreams.

Here is a lesson, Litheria, which may help you eliminate anxiety. Your dreams, hopes, needs, desires, as well as there opposites, are not something you've conjured up as "Claudia," born to certain parents under certain conditions in this life-plane. They are challenges you gave your soul before experiencing this time and place in order to learn, develop, expand, become.

If you can come to understand, comprehend fully this truth, you will embrace all things past and present in your own life, and in the greater world, universes, cosmos, as one of becoming; that which you, and others perceive of as bad luck, or good luck, are the temporary manifestations of these challenges.

It is as if there were many comets flying through the sky. Some will fly past you, and you may, on looking up, think, "how beautiful;" others may flame out, and you will sense "what a shame," others may crash through into your universe and you will cry, "how terrible!"

260

But suppose these same comets were kites, or clouds or leaves, your response may still be "how beautiful," or "what a shame," but you will not likely respond with "how terrible." Many of your psychologists and teachers of soul-work have come to realize that the "catastrophe" or trauma scenarios can be tempered, and not only that, but after-the-fact, seen by many, as having blessing contained within them.

You have not been a "catastrophe" nay sayer, but rather, there is a tendency in you to verify the worst (on, say a scale of one to ten), rather than to verify the best, and you tend to hover around that gray scale just below five!

You may well ask yourself what virtue there is in continuing to do this, and even, if you wish, what purpose it has served you, and what challenge you set for yourself that you seem to experience the lesser rather than the more of life.

On the other hand, you can change all this in an instant if you will begin to focus on the "good" (as you see it) that is your life, and manifests in your life on a daily basis.

Perhaps a list will help you, a diary of "good," a diary of blessing, a journal of luck. Are you willing to try this?

Yes, of course, you are right. I will do this. Thank you Leytha. Let me begin with you! You are my wisdom, and my blessing.

Humm. Perhaps I can write a "Book of Ten Good Things," in a way that people will want to buy! Having thought this, I read, though, this morning with my coffee, from Virginia Woolf, in *A Room of One's Own*, the admonition to write what one wants to write.

261

Well and good, but re writing, or making art, without readers, or without those take your art to home or building, one is a dancer who dances alone in a darkened and empty auditorium, a musician whose composition has no listeners, a maker of songs, whose words and music have no singers, a chef even, who has no one to cook for.

A few blocks' walk to the neighborhood grocery, then, returning, I picked purple, yellow flowers and stalks of lavender from bushes extending over the sidewalk, But I am deeply tired again. Obviously, I'm not quite recovered from my illness.

I encountered fellow resident Ali, originally from Iran, at the little bridge, and he asked if I could read two of his writings. He, and Jen, who stopped me outside the office to ask if I would read two of hers, were in my writers' group here at the apartment building. I'm complimented, but today I've no energy for them, nor another workshop. Perhaps in one of my tomorrows.

I've often said I never cared for the color blue, but looking around my living, dining area, I see I have added touches of midnight blue… a found fabric swatch thrown over my table, blue glass bottles in the window; some blue glass beads hung from a branch inserted into a Gallo wine glass jug., blue yarn woven in among the rust, and olive greens, ivories and beiges of my weavings, a blue bowl container for some of the yarn.

I see too, in the photo montages on the walls of my dining nook, images taken in Paris in 2001, blue doors, blue windows, blue canopies, blue storefronts.

Leytha: Does the color blue have significance for me?

Litheria: Blue is the color, on your life-plane, of sky and sea, and indicates above and below for you, and sky and sea, changing as they do, through the filter of sun, and seasons, rain and snow, winds and tides, growing things and dying things, so blue represents for you a more whole, and wholesome attitude in your life, a time filled with color, sunlight, nature, and all life.

Blue was a mood you were in before, which has now been transformed into the blue which, like the glass beads and vases in your window, filters the sun, refracts the light, creates new images.

Blue is a place of healing for you, of transformation, of being born again of sky and sea, soaring freely in the one, swimming deeply in the other.

Where else do you see blue today?

Ah, let's see: my bank checks are a gray blue; my passport is blue; the cover of the novel I'm planning to read is blue; there is a blue plate on my dining area counter.

Of what do I make of this: Checks represent money to pay, or spend or earnings or gifts received; passport, travel of course; novel, well, my love of reading and writing; plate, my love of good food; though, this plate, being empty and decorative, perhaps suggests a fasting of sorts to regain my health. Two of my books have blue ribbons attached to them! The sky today is blue, free of the rain clouds of yesterday.

A couple of weeks later: A resident neighbor has given me some blue bottles. I've placed them on the wrap around window sill of my writing nook, along with a Gallo wine bottle with a wonderful branch, to which I've attached strings of blue glass beads. I've thrown a swatch of mauve and marine blue sari cloth over the desk lamp-shade, and am enjoying a glass vase of purple mums that have lasted over a week.

Someone has e-mailed me to request my suggestion for which of my children's books to give to the parents of his two year old grandson. *Clara Cow and the Country Fair*, is the read-to book

263

of the trio, and as I didn't have that book on hand, gave him info on how to order it on-line.

The site gave him problems, so I'll order that book, and another he wants, *Of Love and Longing*, and send them to him directly. How pleasing it is to me right now, with my tendency toward depression when ill, to have someone want to read my "rites," and especially, to give something of mine as a gift to a child

September runs to cross its finish line. Today an e-mail from the Harvard Grad School of Education, re a program, a doctorate, and so, nearly bringing closure to the New Mexico quest, I'm considering this.

I'd started to apply the first of this year, and found the deadline had passed. On reviewing the application, still on-line, I found, happily, that it was complete except for the addition of two more recommenders (one had already responded), one probably will, and I'll ask both of them if they know a third academic person I can make a request to.

It's been such a while now since my graduations that I'm lucky to still have Duncan and Mary as both friends and supporters of my wildest academic dreams. Mary hasn't replied, so busy with both her head of department duties, and her own second doctoral studies. Peter, my geologist friend has said he will give me a reference though, based on his familiarity with my writing.

The application deadline is December, and will need to be submitted with an $85 fee. But must try to recover from the expenses of this past month's pursuit of the New Mexico teaching license I finally received, and now, don't wish to use. So, I've stepped into another possibility.

I also came across the name of a literary agent that another had shared a manuscript of mine in 1995. She'd written me a lovely, detailed, "no." Now, she's apparently living in New Mexico. I'm hopeful she will consider the novel.

Meanwhile, once again updating my web sites, continuing to post 140 words several times a day on Twitter (as I explore that odd form of global communication). My niece. who has found real people and business opportunities doing this, encourages me to keep at it.

Dreadful global events, with the flooding in the Philippines, and the tsunami that hit the Samoans. Here I sit, comfortable with my "fixed income" re Virginia Woolf (social security though it is) and my "Room of One's Own," and I almost feel guilty.

I made a pot of vegetable stew, and starting with dinner, have spent the whole evening, five hours, doing some braiding for an art piece and watching PBS; tonight, amazing programs on exploring Mars, and the history of astronomy.

October is here, and how I love autumn. Even in this green-green San Rafael area, I can enjoy the turning of leaves by walking back of the apartment building to a wooded area. It is carpeted with amber leaves.

Jen, working in the apartment office, placed the following short poem of mine in the October newsletter:

life is a kite...
I launch it on the wind

watch it soar;
in a while, falls, fluttering, down;

comes the breeze,
away away and up it goes again
playing notes against the sky

seduced by autumn song and kite
I catch life by the tail
and fly!

An e-note from the literary agency I thought might give some attention to a new request, explained that agent had now retired, and none of the books I mention caught their interest. I had "broken the rules" in pitching them all., the "rule" being one book at a time, but doubt it would have made any difference.

The fact is everything is driven by the "bottom line" today, and unless a book that promises mass popularity lands on an agent's desk, there is no interest. So much for literature. Poetry, while it still gets published, is almost totally the output of university professors. Ugh! I'm chewing sour grapes and bitter herbs!

Well, I will still keep writing, what other course have I? It's an urgent call from my heart to write. But who will read? What will happen to my books, in their on-line publishing files, when I go through my "exit" door?

I have submitted my application (with the hard-to-come-by fee) to the Harvard doctoral program (to begin in fall of 2010). Duncan, my former art prof at CBU, and Peter, my Colorado geologist friend have given me refs, and I await one more.

My transcripts are packaged and ready to mail once I decide to walk over to the post office. Then, it will be a matter of waiting until April for the yea or nay.

Reflecting, I'm reminded that I first began communicating with Leytha some years ago, I was still living at the beach in Tijuana, waitressing across the border, in great despair about my life, with neither college degrees nor published books even a whisper in my mind.

This evening, watching the mind-boggling beauty displayed on a Nova documentary, I sensed Leytha dancing with others like herself, among the stars, where questions, and answers and the wonders of discovery surround us, beckon to us, and wait patiently perhaps for us to wake, reach out, and say hello.

Litheria: It is through your sense of wonder and appreciation that you will experience the voice of the cosmos, feel the dance of the clouds, inhale the breath of earth life.

It is well to remember this and take yourself, through walk or trip, or book or film, art, music, poetry, sharing a cup of coffee with someone with whom you've agreed to explore friendship.

Wonder and appreciation are not dependent on what you've achieved, or possessions accumulated, but on the intake of each breath.

You are alive, and still on this life-plane to experience, to learn, discover and share.

You worry still about whether others approve you, your decisions, your creative efforts. You do not breath their breaths, nor they yours.

You are as unique as the starlight, the windsong, the leaf, the rock. While they are interdependent with all life, they do not need the approval of other beings. Why should you?

Life is not a popularity contest, contrary to popular attitudes in your time-frame. It is, instead, an experience, an experiment even, in aliveness.

The ultimate experience for you, is merely to breathe. There, you see? You are alive! Is this not wonderful? All else follows.

Replace worry, anxiety, need for approval, boredom, shame, fear, longing with other, more joyous, more life-affirming feelings.

267

It is easier than you think. Throw them away like old, worn, used up possessions. Walk through the meadow of your mind and pick a new bouquet.

Your life has been, not as a runner in a race, but as one walking, wandering, suddenly coming to a stream and, pausing to consider, making your way across stepping stones to the other side. Looking back, you reflect on from whence you've traveled.

Wander still, if you wish. Your life is your own to live. There will always be stepping stones.

Winter would come and go, with writing accumulated, and weavings made. A few times a week to the gym next door. A meal out (eaten guiltily, needing to just be out in a social setting even if alone, but regretting the money spent).

Somehow, a transition was taking place. Whether I started doing the writing workshops because I could, or whether sensed others, older adults might enjoy and take pride in writing about some special times or people in their lives, I don't know. Perhaps I did it for me. Unable to endure my aloneness any longer I decided to share what I knew and had experienced with others.

But in April, I taught another writing class, now calling it Remembrance Writing 101, in the community room of my apartment building. In May, after nervously "presenting" myself and proposal to the local center for seniors, began a writing workshop there, attended by three people.

In July, I gave workshops in four locations, loving most the presentation at the Civic Center Library, where, to my surprise, and the delight of the librarian, forty people showed up.

23

Only a life lived for others is a life worthwhile. ~ Albert Einstein

It is the end of summer, 2010. I am less mournful, more focused, but still living more in my inner world than the outer. I continue to live in Marin County, in a building that is quiet, with my cherished view of trees from my second story apartment. Most days I have no sense of others around me at all, unless I walk downstairs to leave a book I've read or newspaper (shared with me by another resident), for yet others to read.

I have continued to develop my Remembrance Writing 101, the workshops I now give for older adults and created a lovely website for it; though most of the participants in my workshops are not Internet savvy! Meanwhile, I'm currently planning an anthology of their writings, to be published by the end of the year. I experience real joy during my workshop sessions, and plan, when some further writing projects of my own are completed, to expand the on-going workshops to other centers for seniors.

I've sketched an outline for a guidebook, *Remembrance Writing 101,* and though I teach with a good deal of improvisations, I keep hearing from both students and others, that I should create a guidebook and workshop to teach others to facilitate Remembrance Writing workshops wherever they might live. I have not crossed the "money" or "success" bridge (in terms of money), but feel satisfaction in being able to give the workshops at a fee level that those, who like myself at the moment, live within limited income.

I've met with some of my "students," doing what I call "lite-touch" editing of their work; mostly suggestions that will brighten the short writes from their yesteryears, and have assisted three of them to create personal chapbooks of their writes.

For my own books though, I am in need of "others" who will take these "over the bridge" as well as those who can help me take my workshop-facilitating to a national level, should I want this. Perhaps the group's anthology, and my guide-book will open doors for this.

I've also finished the "write," phase of my quirky fictionalized year-long search, *Becoming a Madwoman*. It is a complicated novel, and will take a couple of month to add corrections to my computer copy before publishing it via an on-line source.

I don't know if I will write, as I had planned, in 2008, the sequel to *Code of the Running Cross* this year or not. With the same characters, the one in Taos, the other in Paris, I both fear I would create a sense of longing for these places and their real-life counterparts. Because F. played such an important role, via e-mail, as encourager, listener, creative muse, I'm not sure, since he is no longer accessible, that I want to undertake this novel on my own. It is, though, part of a "triolgy dream," with the "prequel" written already. Perhaps, in one of my tomorrows...perhaps even in Taos.

I've self-published four of my children's stories, but they need illustrating. Perhaps these, one story, one agent at a time, are the ones I should be submitting to agents. My play, *Clinton and the Treehouse,* published by Kids for Saving Earth in 1994, has been updated, and KSE now offers it on-line. As of this writing, a local educational theatrical group is considering the play. The play won a "Best of Class," at our county fair. In the past, all four of my self-published children's books have won blue ribbons.

Recently too, the ESL teacher recruitment that arranged for me to go Taiwan, asked me to articles to their new web site for potential overseas teachers (younger than me of course). I suggested they go to my web sites, and either download the book, 1000 Steps, or lift a chapter. They've posted the first excerpt along with my web site URL, where readers can view my photos from Taiwan, and also, my published book storefront, in case someone wishes to order the book.

A local newsletter, the Silver Express, put out by a seniors' coordinating council, has published two of my Remembrance Writing 101 columns. A recent arrangement with a weekly county-wide tabloid, means the newsletter will now be inserted into the news mag once a month, and this for me, will mean a greater readership, and potentially more workshop participants. A woman activist in the county, who edits a lovely homeowners print and on-line magazine, has published my "October Country" article, and asked for a similar column for a future date, also publishing my poem, "Almost, Uniquely, Me, Seventy-three," written before my birthday last year.

I've never been almost 73 before
nor, has anyone else on the planet been me, almost 73, before.
I *am not* almost 73, surely, but my birth certificate says, certainly
and certifies too that I am uniquely, *only*, me
born of certain parents, certain place, certain time,
certain year of the current age,
so I must be me, almost 73.

But in some countries, some languages, they would say,
"I *have* almost 73 years"
I like this: this owning of years makes ageless "me"

271

a collector of my years.
the *I am* me, not an age, but rather
the me who has collected almost 73 years of experiences
on planet Earth, in the Universe, in the Galaxy
(all of whom *are* a bit older than almost 73 me)
in a Cosmos in which, unless a parallel world exists
there is no other human being that lives
or ever lived, or ever will live
who is so uniquely, me, almost 73.

Perhaps I'm a "national treasure!"
An antique? No, more like a one-of-a-kind mosaic
co-created by the Creator,
my Ancestors, and the life-journey of my Self?

Am I, not (and aren't we all)
a never-existed-before, first timer,
an only-one-that-will-ever-walk-the-earth
alive-and-kicking-now,
adventurer, explorer, life-learner, space-traveler,
gypsy, creative and free
experience sharer, ready to go
one for the money, two for the show
still on the planet, get ready on three
gratefully, uniquely,
soon-to-be, 73
the only me?

This month too, have corresponded with the executive editor of a USO magazine, *On Patrol,* re excerpts of some of the letters I wrote, and received during Operation Desert Storm/Desert Shield, in Kuwait. She has said the editorial staff is excited about the letters, but will need to track down the writers, for their permission to print.

That's exciting all the way around, both that I am getting a "yes," re this submission, but that they might be able to find these former military people, some twenty years now since they served in the Gulf.

My art work waits, both for more space (my walls are covered) and time (though I tend to "make art" during T.V. watching time. I'm pleased though re the "Best of Show" award for my southwestern piece, a three foot in diameter "Dreamcatcher" at the local fair.

I have put together a photo montage I created, the photos taken during a 9/11 memorial service in 2001, when living in Brookline, a suburb of Boston, just beginning Harvard. I'll ship this "remembrance" piece to the city manager or head librarian of Brookline.

This summer, I have seen my daughter after several years, so happy to see that she's studying the guitar, and singing. A friend of my son's, finding me via the Internet, connected us via e-mail. I experience both joy, that they want a relationship with me, and I can now encourage them in a way I could not before, and discomfort, that coming from unsought memories and regrets. My niece, Tambra Harck, has published her first book, *Sacred Truths.* My sister, defying age labels, continues to collect certifications to further her consulting, working when she wishes.

Leytha: Whither go I, and to what purpose? When and where will I be able to say simply, I am, and here I am, and this, that I do, and contribute is the way it is meant to be.

Litheria: In completing these writings, you have, in a sense, created a painting of your interior life, and what you've written will, though you do not see this now, be shared with others.

Do not give up on the dreams for your outer world experiences. There is a way, and you will see it soon. Let love

273

continue to lead to share what you know with others, but do not neglect your Self.

There is little more we can teach you now, Litheria. You have come to a place where your parallel worlds have merged. It is time to believe in yourself, however, and to encourage yourself, in the same way you believe in, and encourage others.

Peace, child. Peace.

It is October, 2010. A favorite type of day, with rainfall collecting on the roof beyond my second story window, creating a shallow pond, the gentle drops creating harmonics in my soul, the windows, weeping, not with sorrow, but with life-givingness.

Ending a book for me, is something like coming home from a vacation. It is bittersweet. It requires, ought to have, champagne and laughter shared with a special friend. Perhaps that, a special friend, a house in Northern New Mexico, a chance to see Paris again when they aren't on strike, the fulfillment of publishing, the showing and selling of my art, and the continuance and expansion of the workshops I am developing, will come yet in my tomorrows.

I listen to a Wayne Dyer presentation, "No Excuses," while I write, and pause to make my own list of excuses, and solutions. Hoping to see the end of my complaining "writes," I quickly create some e-mail "heads up" to potential workshop venues directors. I Longing, on one hand, for a friend, a companion, with whom I can talk about the insanities coming through the tube as news, with whom I can share a meal, or see a play, or take a trip or talk to about my art and writing, someone to with whom to share creative work-days, I e-mail my Madrid, and New Mexico friends. But there is in me a deep need to be alone, so this is likely why I am. I will though, make no excuses and imagine that both are possible.

I cry for Haiti, and Afghanistan, and those everywhere who hurt, for the continuing humiliation of women and abuse of children, the helpless. I long for a soapbox to shout-out against the ignorance re our rainbow society and thinly disguised racism of so many running for office in the U.S. this election. I forward the President and First Lady's e-mails and pray that critical thinking, wisdom and patience will prevail, and try to remember, and tell others to remember past history, even recent history, and to treasure the fact that we humans, though stumbling, know how to make wrongs right when there is a will.

Mostly, I'm grateful to have a "room of my own," and a space in time, to allow me to experience the deep satisfaction now that comes from encouraging my older adult friends to write, and to help them publish their voices.

What next then? For myself, glad to still be on the planet, I look forward to learning to live, with joy in today. For you, may your own angels in forever, guide you with love.

to be continued in forever

THANK YOU TO MY REAL TIME ANGELS

My sister Rosalie, a witness, supporter, provider, my connection to reality. My brother-in-law John, for having a computer in his house and allowing me to learn to use it, and hauling, without protest, me and my stuff from place to dream-place and back again. My sister's kids: Shawna, husband Joe, and their kids, Josh, Alyana, Alyssa, for the times they helped me move; Tambra, for encouraging my writes; for Gina, allowing me to gift her with my "If Only," poem, the only gift I could give at the time, and to Gina, Rob, their children, Megan and Sammy for driving down from Brussels to visit me in Paris.

My kids, Melody (and her artwork and singing), and Michael (his music and laughter), for a million lessons learned and still loving me after all we experienced together and apart.

My aunt Hazel, uncle Walter, and cousin Nathan, Teddy, Ernie, Helen and Loretta for adding me and my little sister to their "Ma and Pa Kettle" family when our mother died (I was six). My daddy, for being a good, quiet and patient one, a teller of stories, a grower of beautiful flowers. My stepmother Lily, for a million gifts, a million expectations and misunderstandings, a million lessons learned. My aunt Mae, uncle Paul, and cousin Paul (from my stepmother's side), for camping trips, and more lessons learned.

The librarian in small-town Fillmore, for her Saturday afternoon story hour. And my best friends over these many years, writers of books; the list would cover all the sections of the library.

276

My third grade teacher, for showing me how to walk across a room with a shallow bowl of water without spilling it. My sixth grade teacher for allowing us to paint Californiano murals on the walls. My tenth grade English teacher for encouraging me to write, and giving me a copy of Rachel Carson's "The Sea Around Us."

My husbands and other temp partners: the one, for the two children he gave me, while we were still not yet grown up; another, for the few years of "family" (his Polish immigrant grandparents, his two children, my two, and dog, Toothpaste), Venice Beach and Malibu, and all the joy and turmoil, creativity discovery and years of recovery for us all after what was Camelot. And to and for, (paraphrasing Willie Nelson) "all the boys / men and women I knew and loved" and the good, the not-so-good, lessons learned about being a girl/woman/ creative type, too trusting, too naive in a man's world. To all those I knew (and miss) in the 60ies, for their music, art, poetry, writing, marching and believing we could make a difference.

To my professor friends in the 90ies, Mack, Duncan, Mary, (and her support while I was at Harvard) the latter two still my e-correspondents today, and others who gave me references for Harvard. To Mark and Josephine for their support and friendship during the seven summers of camp arts and crafts instruction for kids-at-risk.

To Shar, my kind, supportive NM buddy; and D. Gallegos, the Taos County DA who helped me so much with local color for my novel; to Peter who read and like it, to Moby Dickens Bookshop, Taos, for first offering it for sale.

To Harvard School of Education, just accepting me, and the year of challenge, learning, discovery in Jessica's Arts in Education program; giving me the chance to be in Boston to volunteer at Ground Zero. To the Ice Cream shop businessman in Cambridge, who bought my 9/11 memorial sculpture and to all the people over the years who've placed green or silver in my palm to take home a painting or drawing of mine.

277

To F., who, an ocean away in Paris, through his enthusiasm, support, encouragement, played the role of "muse," for my novel *Code of the Running Cross;* to J. in Madrid who believes in me...to them both who, with their European fondness for older women, found me "smart, sexy and ageless!"

To all those who've published one of my writes, so that others could share my thoughts. To recent friends, in the world of older adults, who have, through invitation and participation, encouraged me to teach Remembrance Writing 101, and to help some of them publish their own writes.

WRITERS AS ANGELS

The Sea Around Us, Rachel Carson
Published: Oxford University Press, 1951

The 13 Original Clan Mothers, Jamie Sams
Published: Harper Collins 1992

Soul Retrieval, Mending the Fragmented Self, Sandra Ingerman
Published: HarperSanFrancisco 1991

Care of the Soul, Thomas Moore
Published: Harper Collins 1992

A Room of One's Own, Virginia Woolf
Published: Harcourt, Inc. 1929

Sacred Truths, Tambra Harck
http://tambraharck.com/sacredtruths/home

To other writers: Charles Bukowski, Robinson Jeffers, Anais Nin, Kerouac, Henry Miller, Hemingway, C.S. Lewis, J.D. Salinger,

Jess Lair, Henry David Thoreau, Shakespeare, the Bible, old and new, Dickens, Tolkien, Lewis Carroll, Alan Furst, Dan Brown, Mark Twain, Tolstoy, Chekhov, Dostoevsky, Freud, Jung, Austen, Jules Verne, Ray Bradbury, Oscar Wilde, Hans Christian Anderson, Bronte, Emerson, Ibsen, Richard Bach, Marshall McLuhan, Lillian Helman, Louisa May Alcott, Anne Frank, Orwell, Ayn Rand, McCullers, Koestler, Laura Huxley, William Glasser, Karen Horney, Steinbeck, Pearl S. Buck, Faulkner, Fitzgerald, Thomas Mann, Kahlil Gibran, Joyce, D.H. Lawrence, Kenneth Graham, London, H.G. Wells, Kipling, Zola, Melville; Kierkegaard, Dumas, Friedan, Sontag, Gabriel Garcia Marquez, Shaw, Wilde, O'Neil.

The list would be a book in itself, were I to continue. This one seems to indicate I almost stopped reading at the end of the 60ies! But it is true, that I have a preference for books written from that time backwards to centuries past. But to the spirit-selves of all book writers, play-wrights, song-writers, poets, letter writers: I say thank you, that through the miracle of your words, we met.

AFTERWORD
The Merging of My Selves

I've included some "me and my selves" dialogues, to encourage you to do the same. If you give writing, theater or therapy workshops, you might find these to be helpful models.

Since I am still and always will be, in the process of continuing my quest to become my Self, I have found these dialogues, some amusing, to be helpful. The following writes are not my usual impressions of angels, but the "others" who showed up were no less my teachers.

ME, SHE, and the CIRCLE

ME, LOST and THEY

ME, CHUBBY GIRL and BODY SELF

ME , NEGA-TIVITY and POSITIVELY

ME and the HOLD-OUT KID

ME, and MR. DEPRESSION

ME and MS ANXIETY

ME and MY SELF

ME, SHE, and the CIRCLE

ME

Today I'm going to walk along the seashore,
    gather shells, and write.

SHE

You can't go without me. Stay. I am sad and waiting for magic.

ME

Then stay behind and stand there in your circle drawn by others
    hands. As for me, I'm going down to the sea
    and feel the breeze, and breathe.

SHE

You can't, you know. Just leave me here and go your way, just go
away and play like that. If you're too happy, well who knows? My
circle's safe. I look out and others smile or frown and I know
    plainly where I stand.
    But look at you, how wild, how care-free.
    Just going off to see the sea.

ME

281

Don't envy me, don't shame me. There's no room for me in your
circle. Step out and skip the sand with me.
Why be so sad? You've not been bad.
They've kept you here to stifle fear.
Not for your own good! Oh no!
They fear their lives without their bird
in-circled in love-hate chains.

SHE

You'll make me mad! I'll run away. Then what! No place to go,
no place to be! No one to know. Just naive me.
Saying yes to everyone who smiles.
You want to make me feel I'm free to be wild like you.
Don't make me mad.

ME

Dear self. They've captured you, can't you see that?
You're just a lucky cricket, a rabbit's foot, a wishing star.
You're not real.
Just stuff that others in their need
have put down on the floor and walked on.

SHE

I am so real. You just don't care.

ME

I care. I just can't be bothered any more by pain.

SHE

It's not your pain. It's mine. It's all I have. Why everybody knows
me thus. That's how I know I'm real. Without my pain who would
I be? They'd not know that I was me, and I'd not be here at all.
When they come in to frown at me, to criticize, to laugh,
where would I be? Where would they be? Poor things.

ME

I'm leaving now. They need your pain more than I.
SHE

Don't leave me here alone. I didn't mean to make you sad.

ME

Then come with me. I hear the wind. The seagull cries.
The clouds are right for photographs. The fisher-boy
will row his boat around the point and bring a lobster for our lunch.

The old man who plays guitar will share our wine and sing a song.
The girl will bring us fresh tortillas hot from mama's stove.
Come with me.
I am weary of your circle.

SHE

I don't believe you'll really go.

ME

I'll go.

SHE

Then take me, too.

ME

I cannot. You must agree to leave your pain
and come of your own free will.

SHE

Take my hand. I'm afraid.

ME

Reach for me.

SHE

I don't know if I can....

ME

I know. I hear the wind, the seagull's cry.
Reach for me.

SHE

The clouds are low.

ME

Just right to photograph.

SHE

They'll miss me.

ME

They have themselves.

SHE

The fisher boy will row around the point.

ME

The old man will share our wine.

SHE

The child will bring us food.

ME

You're doing fine.
Don't look back.
Just one step more and you'll be free.

SHE

The circle. It was safe.

ME

There is no circle.
SHE

285

I hear the sea, the seagull's cry.
I feel the sun, the breeze.
I breathe.
How strange.
How new.
How wild.
To be free.

ME

You're not afraid?

SHE

I feel odd. Am I with you?

ME

Yes.

SHE

Should I not go back?

ME

No.

SHE

Today, then, I am going to walk along

ME

286

...the seashore and gather seashells

SHE

...and write. Yes, about the...

ME

...fisher boy and the old man

SHE

...and the circle drawn by other's hands.

ME

You remember!

SHE

Yes. But I am not afraid.

ME , LOST AND THEY

ME: Who are you? Why can't you see my life is miserable enough without your constant haranguing?

LOST:There's no point talking to me, you know. I'm lost, hopeless and off-track. Disaster walking. Go away. Don't touch me.

287

ME: But I must touch you. You are overwhelming me, dragging me under. You've stolen my smile, the light in my eyes, the dreams of the future, the joy of the present. Why?

LOST: I can't face it.

ME: Face what? What are you afraid of?

LOST: Afraid? Afraid to die. Afraid to turn to dust. Afraid of having lived a useless life. No, not afraid.

ME: If not afraid, then what?

LOST: Ashamed. Embarrassed. Tired of living lies, making promises, starting over. Tired of watching other people do the same. Can't do it any more. Can't face it.

ME: Must you do the same things over again? Or be concerned with what others are doing?

LOST: Have no energy left to say yes to anything.

ME: But you have a lot of energy! You're wearing me out with your energy! You are my constant companion, complaining, frowning, shuffling, hurting, doubting.

LOST: Well, you've just said it all. I'm lost. I don't know how to get out of this mess. How to fix it. So why not forget it?

ME: I can't forget it! I've got to get in touch with you. You've got to help me change things! I want to smile again, be glad, laugh! I want to create, and dream, and be healthy! But you've nearly overshadowed me in your shame. You've stolen my spirit! And I want it back!

LOST: You'll get no help from me. I'm worn out.

ME: Then go away and let me live.

LOST: Are you ready for that? For life?

ME: Yes!

LOST: Are you?

ME: Yes! Yes! Yes!

LOST: O.K., then. I think you'd better meet the others.

ME: Others? There are other voices in my head?

LOST: I'm afraid so.

ME : Like who?

LOST: Well, there's Nega Tivity....and Chubby Girl...and the Hold Out Kid, and then there's ...well, you know.

ME: No I don't know! Who else lives in my mind?

LOST: I shouldn't tell you. But *they* live in your mind. They talk to you all the time! They say...

ME: They say what? Lost? Answer me Lost! What do they say? Lost? She's gone. She's probably lost again. I suppose I should go looking for her. Lost? Where are you? What is that noise?It sounds like a mob scene! Maybe they've found Lost!

THEY: We're not lost! You are! You don't belong here! Wrong way! Wrong Way! You've made a mistake! You're stupid! You can do this! Who do you think you are?

THEY: You're not dependable you know. You're here one day, gone the next. We need someone to fill our slots, cog our wheels. Why can't you just be a number on a payroll card and be content?

ME: I've asked myself the same thing. But I was never content. Besides, who asked you?

THEY: Nobody needs to ask us. Especially you. We'll tell you who you are without asking. If you insist on coming in and out of our world and upsetting our notion of things, then who are you not to listen?

ME: There are too many of you. That's not fair. I know what you're saying is true.

ME: In fact you could probably put me in the World Book of Records for the most one-night stands, the most geographic, the most last minute change of plans, and certainly, oh most certainly, the most meaningless, deadening string of jobs. But I'm beginning to wonder if I've been listening to you, rather than to me, whoever I may be.

THEY: You're a gypsy.

ME: That may be true.

THEY: Why aren't you arguing with us? What are you up to?

ME: Up to? Why nothing really. It's just time I stopped fighting you, trying to change you.

THEY: We refuse to change. We've always been like this and we always will be!

ME: I know. And I thank you for showing me that. I can never change you, or any of the they's or them's. I'll do the changing. And the first thing I'll do is stop listening so much to you.

THEY: What fool thing do you have in mind?

ME: Well first of all, to accept that I *have* a mind, and it's mine to control, not yours. And second, to find a way to get all of *you* out of my mind. So take notice of your pending eviction.

THEY: We'll never move. Won't budge an inch. We're comfortable here. You've been a wonderful landlord. Like a puppet really. We've just pulled your strings and off you went. Very entertaining. What would we do without you?

ME: Well if you won't move, you'll just have to get used to living with the new tenants.

THEY: New tenants? Did you consult US? We're already too crowded in here!

ME: I certainly agree with that! There are definitely too many of you, and I've allowed you to live in my mind much too long. It's time for a change.

THEY: Don't get off the subject. Who are these new tenants?

ME: Oh you wouldn't recognize them. They are newcomers. I only met them recently myself.

THEY: Well, bring them round so we can check them out.

ME: Are you sure you want to meet them?

THEY: Stop stalling. Introduce us.

ME: Well, you asked for it. Remember that.

THEY: We remember everything you do. Especially the stupid things. And this will probably top the cake. New tenants indeed! Who are they?

ME: Well, O.K. Here goes. I'd like you to meet Humor. He has the oddest quality of finding something funny in everything. And this is Faith. No matter what happens she thinks, no, she knows, everything will work out. And this is Persistence, who knows that day by day, little by little, anything can be accomplished.

And this . . . hello? Are you still there?

How strange. the room is empty. Apparently "they" can't share my mind with my new tenants. But what a mess! Cobwebs everywhere! Looks like I need a little mental spring-cleaning!

ME, CHUBBY GIRL AND BODY-SELF

ME: Fat self, hurt self, self that overeats, self that eats the wrong foods, self that doesn't exercise; I want to talk to you.

CHUBBY: Did you bring me a candy bar?

ME: Why must I bring you something? I just want to talk to you. Isn't that enough?

CHUBBY: But how will I know you love me, if you don't give me something to eat?

ME: Well, the thing is, I don't love you.

CHUBBY: Oh no! Oh no! Oh I can't talk any more. I have to eat an ice cream sundae to feel better.

ME: Please! Can't you stop eating for just one minute?

CHUBBY: Mind your own business!

ME: But you are my business! And when you keep eating like this *you make me fat. And unhappy.*

CHUBBY: So-o-o-o sorry!

ME: Please! Don't put that biscuit in my mouth!

CHUBBY: Have to. Have to!

ME: Why do you *have to?* The food won't make you feel better, and it certainly won't make me look any better!

CHUBBY: Well, who cares about you anyway?

ME: I care about me. I want to be strong, healthy, beautiful.

CHUBBY: Beautiful girls get into trouble.

ME: What? Who told you that?

CHUBBY: I just know. Everybody knows. Fatty girls are safe.

ME: Chubby self! What are you saying? Safe from what?

CHUBBY: Bad mens. Jealous womens!

ME: I see. That's a very threatening idea. Especially to a child.

CHUBBY: So even if you don't love me, I protect you from *bad mens and jealous womens.*

ME: So you came to live in my mind to protect me? Did I invite you to live there?

CHUBBY: No. Came when you scared. Nobody to save you. I saved you. Fatty self safe.

ME: Well, that's certainly an amazing revelation! I apologize. I didn't mean I don't love you, really. It's just that I'm so unhappy wearing all this extra flesh you make for me, to ah, protect me.

CHUBBY: You safe now.

ME: Chubby? What would happen if I didn't need you any longer?

CHUBBY: Oh no! Don't say that! Hungry now!

ME: I mean, what if you and I became one person again. We'd be stronger that way. You could protect me in other ways couldn't you?

CHUBBY: Can't do it! Can't change things!

ME: Fatty self! We have to change! I can't bear this weight any longer! Either you give up this eating and protection game, or leave my mind!

294

CHUBBY: Going now. Not safe here any more!

ME: Chubby! Wait! Can't we become friends? Can't you just control what you eat so you won't make me so fat?

CHUBBY: No, no control. Not my nature. Can't live here any more. Uh oh. Somebody else coming. Going now.

ME: Fatty self! Who's coming? And where are going? I'm so confused! Why didn't I just leave things the way they were?

CHUBBY: Going now. Here's telegram.

ME: (Reading the note): Dear Me: You never needed fatty self to protect you, but it was the best defense you could come up with as a child, unknowing in the ways of people and emotions. But now, you have wisdom lacking in a younger self. You know about cause and effect. Fatty self was your effect. But you were the cause that created fatty self. Now you are free to create a new effect, that of health, energy, vitality and freedom. Don't look for Chubby Girl to return. Listen instead to the voice of your body self.

ME: My body self? But who is that?

BODY SELF: Let me introduce myself!

ME: Who in the world are you? And where is Chubby Girl?

BODY SELF: One thing at a time! Let me introduce myself. I'm the Voice of your Body.

ME: Nice to meet you...I think. Are you Chubby Girl?

BODY SELF: No. You see, a long time ago, you invited Chubby Girl to move in with you.

ME: I invited Chubby Girl into my life? But I never wanted to be chubby!

BODY SELF: You never really wanted to be chubby, but you decided somewhere along the way that the voices you were hearing were too frightening, too threatening. You didn't know how to listen to your own voice, to listen to your Body's voice - my voice, because all you could feel was pain.

ME: That's true! All I could feel was fear, and anger!

BODY SELF : It won't be easy. You may have to forgive yourself, and those who made you frightened and angry. But I'll be here for you.

ME: How w ill I recognize your voice?

BODY SELF: You'll know. You'll hear me tell you to breathe. To drink water. To eat food from nature's garden. To walk. To stretch. To love yourself. To love me.

ME: You make it sound so simple.

BODY: It is simple. Listen to Chubby Girl or listen to me Listen to life. Learn how to play. Try laughing a little. And listen to me!

ME: You're right BODY SELF. Where would I be without you?

BODY SELF: Now you're listening!

ME, NEGA-TIVITY AND POSITIVELY

NEGA: You're wasting your time here, nothing will happen for you. You've been through this before. Got your hopes up before.

ME: Shut up, you. You know what? I'm getting tired of listening to you! I need someone in there who'll support me. Believe in me, say yes I can, yes I will, you see?

NEGA: You've hurt my feelings. I've always been here for you.

ME: No, that isn't true. You've always been there for you.

NEGA: Well, I was just trying to save you from disappointment. It's for your own good.

ME: Well, don't do me any favors. I need to know I can do what I set out to do. If not this time, then next time.

NEGA: Yeah. And next time. Face it, you. You'll never find your place. Never amount to anything. You're a born loser.

ME: No! I'm a winner. I've survived out here in spite of you, and believe me, *that* has not been easy!

NEGA: Well that sounds like you. Easy. You always want the easy way out.

ME: You're impossible. I wish I could show you the easy way out. Out of my mind!

NEGA: You can't do that. I've always lived here!

ME: Stop whining. Besides, you haven't always lived here, have you?

NEGA: Well, almost always. since you were a child. I stopped by to visit and just never left. Your mind was dark and gloomy and suited me just fine. Why should I leave? You've always been so hospitable.

ME: Well, I suppose you're right about that. I'd just shoved a lot of fear and regret into my mind early on in my life. No wonder you felt at home there.

NEGA: Well, I've kept all that stuff in tip-top shape. even added some stuff of my own.

ME: You've added stuff to my mind? Like what?

NEGA: Well I've modernized you might say. Like with this instant response feeling feedback console.

ME: How does it work?

NEGA: Works great! You send me a picture, an image, on the monitor here, and I give you an instant response to feel – fear, doubt, tension. You know very well you can feel awkward or old or fat or not good enough in an instant, don't you? well, that's me and the console at work. Gives you everything you ask for.

ME: Everything *I* ask for?

NEGA: Sure, stupid. How long since you've demanded any positive emotions, any good feelings? Got you programmed right here on the negativity channel.

ME: See, there you go again! Calling me stupid!

NEGA: Hey look. It beats me why you want to feel bad. But I'm an expert on this stuff. Look at this room! Regret, blues, resentment, depression, procrastination, unforgiveness, the place is over-flowing with bad feelings. Cobwebs everywhere!

ME: Well, clean it out. I don't need that stuff any more.

NEGA: Clean it out? If the stuff goes, I go.

ME: Now you've got the right idea.

NEGA: But you'll miss me. You'll feel lonely, abandoned, rejected.

ME: How can I feel that way if you aren't in there to prompt me?

NEGA: Aren't you listening?

ME: Oh yes, I've been listening. Loud and clear. And I'd like to thank you.

NEGA: Thank me? What kind of nauseating positive talk is that?

ME: Well, I'd like to thank you for being so very, very negative. You've allowed me to hear you clearly for the first time in my life. I never really realized you were in my mind before. Or at least that you were such a busy-body.

NEGA: Now you're complimenting me. I'm confused. You know how that nicey-nicey stuff affects me.

ME: No, how does it affect you?

NEGA: Makes me wobbly. You know, all that thank you very much stuff.

ME: Oh really? You mean when I speak positively you get weak at the knees?

NEGA: Yeah, like *Krypton* and *Superman,* you know what I mean? Can't live in the same room with that brightness and light stuff.

ME: What an interesting thought! You mean when I accentuate the positive you . . .

NEGA: Eliminate the negative. So you can just stop that feel-good stuff right now.

ME: Well this is turning out to be a very edifying conversation. I'm glad we talked today. But then, what are friends for?

NEGA: That's it! I'm warning you. If you keep talking that drivel I'll do my disappearing act.

ME: Oh? You mean if I say things like "Every day in every way I'm getting better and better," or "I think I can, I think I can..."

NEGA: You stop that! I'm practically invisible as it is!

ME: How interesting! Well, I'm certainly grateful to you. You've made me realize I need to be more careful about who I allow to share in my head room.

NEGA: Grateful! Ugh! I detest that word!

ME: Are you alright? Your voice is becoming very weak. Maybe I'd better let you rest. You've shared so much information with me today you're probably tired.

NEGA: Considerate. That's almost more than I can take.

ME: Nega? Are you still there? I can hardly hear you. I hope you're not leaving. I just wanted to tell you one more thing..

NEGA: One more nicey-nicey from you and I'm out the door.

ME: You see, now that I know that you really exist, and how strong you've become, I know that the only thing for me to do is just to – well, to love you.

Nega? Are you there? Nega? That's odd....she's gone. And who are you? *Posi- tively?* Is that you? When did you move in?

POSI-TIVELY: Hey! I'm the one who moved Nega-Tivity out! Let's get together sometime!

ME and THE HOLD-OUT KID

ME: O.K., Kid. The question here is, why are you holding out on me, holding back, not going all the way?

H.O. KID: Not going all the way to where? What's so bad about where we are? It's familiar isn't it? How come you're never content with where you are? Always wanting something better, aren't ya? What's with you? We aren't good enough for you?

ME: It's not that you're not good enough for me! What I mean is, I just have this nagging feeling that I, well, that someone, or some *thing,* is holding back, you know, not letting me be the best that I can be in this life.

H.O. KID: Ho hum, here we go again, reaching for the stars, trying to be better than us regular folks.

ME: It's not like that at all! I'm not trying to better than anyone! It's just that I'd like to be free from whatever, or *whoever*, is holding me back from being my fittest self, my most confident self, my richest self, my free self— you know, my *Self!*

H.O. KID: Sure, kid, I understand. Look, I know when I'm not wanted. I'll just sit here alone and let you do your own thing. Don't bother about me. I'll be O.K.

But let me warn you, if you aim too high in life, it's a long way to fall when you fail!

ME: Oh my, I feel so hopeless talking *to,* you. I feel obligated to stay here with you, but if I do, how can I ever face what's out there and maybe even overcome it? Still, you've been right before, and I have made mistakes in the past, and if I'd just have settled for less I would not have been disappointed so often! Now see what you've done! Got me talking just like you!

H.O. KID: That's the spirit! See how much more comfortable you are when you talk like us? No more discontent. Just good old complaining, moaning, sighing. You know, just resign yourself to being ordinary. It's easier thataway!

ME: I am going to take a deep breath and ignore what you've just said. I am going to remind myself that the reason for this conversation was to find out, from you, why you are doing this to me. Why are you holding me back, holding back on me?

H.O. KID: Well, if you insist. Look kid, I'm just doing what comes naturally to me. You should know that! You assigned this job to me. I don't have any choice except to keep carrying out my assignment. You might say I'm just like a thermostat. You set the dial, kid. I just turn up the heat!

ME: What are you saying? I assigned you to hold me back? What nonsense! You're trying to tell me that you are keeping me from going all the way with my life, because I want you to?

H.O. KID: Surprises you, huh kid? Well look, I've been with you a long time. I'm kind of a combo deal you might say – a little doubt, a little fear, a whole lot of negativity, a kid's way of taking in whatever the world dishes out and concluding that's the truth of things. Yeah, I'm pretty complicated to have such an easy assignment. Beats me why you want me to keep you from being who you want to be and doing what you want to do...fear of losing somebody, I'll bet, or fear of losing somebody's idea of love.

Figure it this way, kid. Somewhere way back you felt like you didn't fit in and you had these dreams, talent, ideas. And you couldn't share them with anybody. So, you had to be two bodies. Maybe more. With the nobodies, you play a nobody. With the somebodies, you feel false, a phony, 'cause you can't shake off the nobody disguise.

So look kid, when you want to "go for it," like getting slim, getting successful, feeling loved, feeling good, you got no energy left. You used it up playing these nobody, somebody games.

Dangerous stuff that, kid. But don't take my opinion for it. I'm just following orders. Your orders, matter of fact.

ME: I don't know what to say! You've rather overwhelmed me just now.

H.O. KID: Yeah. Well you might say I wasn't holding out on you.

ME: But I'm holding out on me.

H.O. KID: Ah, kid. You're doing O.K. What you are doing, is running' scared. About what people will think of you. You wanna know something? Those same people are running' scared, too. Think they're stayin' up nights thinking about you? Nope. They're wondering how *they* did, what others think about how they did, and how they're going to do tomorrow. Life goes on, kid. Relax.

ME: Not so easy. You, I, we've been holding back a long time. I don't know how to change it.

H.O. KID: Reset the thermostat.

ME: Reset the thermostat? What do you mean?

H.O. KID: Look, it's smart to set the heat up in the winter when it's cold outside, right?

ME: Right.

H.O. KID: So you set the dials in another season of your life, in another climate. Now the weather's nicer, tranquil, like spring, with everything wanting to burst into bloom, and you're still living in wintertime.

ME: Living in the past, you mean?

H.O. KID: Look kid, you did what you had to do back then. You came to some conclusions, made some decisions, then set your dials. I've just kept you on course.

ME: I think I see what you're saying. I set my course, or my dials, as you say, in the winter of my life, when I didn't know how to cope. It was O.K. for then, but not for now, right?

H.O. KID: It's your life.

ME: But that's the point of this whole conversation! It's not my life, at least, it's not a no-holds-barred life.

H.O. KID: Look, kid, I've done my tour of duty. Mind you, I'll go for the long haul if that's what you really want. But if you decide to turn down the heat, kid, then I'm off for early retirement.

ME: You don't mind losing this assignment?

H.O. KID: Look kid, I only hung around here 'cause you needed my negative energy to keep the reins on you, to keep you from going for the winner's circle. Seemed dumb to me, but I only take orders.

ME: But what about me? I mean if you leave, who'll...?

H.O. KID... protect you?

ME: Yes, I suppose that's what I meant to ask.

H.O. KID: Stop leading with your chin, kid.

305

ME: Leading with my chin?

H.O. KID: Yeah, you know. A boxer sticks out his chin, he's gonna get K.O.'d. Keep your chin down, lead with your power, you know, your mind, your talents, the stuff that makes you happy.

ME: H.O., how about a change of assignment? I mean, how about staying on as my trainer?

ME :Instead of holding me back, you could teach me how to go for it. You know, with my mind, talents, and all that stuff.

H.O. KID: Aw, kid, that's the nicest thing you have ever said to me. But I got no energy left. You don't need an old worn out voice like me any more. You got your own energy now.

ME: Funny, I'll miss you.

H.O. KID: Yeah? Like a toothache!

ME: No, like a familiar friend that I just don't have time for any more.

H.O. KID: Them's the breaks, kid.

ME: Well, so long....Did you want to say something Hold Out?

H.O. KID: Uh, I was thinkin'. About that new assignment. All I have to do is teach you how to hold on, right? How to hold on for the best in yourself?

ME: That's right.

H.O. KID: O.K. I accept. You've got yourself a coach!

306

ME: That's great! Hey! You're gonna need a new name though! How about "Hold On!".

HOLD ON KID: Hey. You know what kid? This could be the start of a...

ME:... beautiful friendship!

ME and MS ANXIETY

One day, I encountered Anxiety. Anxiety makes her presence known in a different way than MMD. While he drapes a heavy cape over me, Anxiety pricks my nervous system. She is hyper. She flits from fragile branch to branch like a hummingbird, unable to lite, to stay. She sees a fox in every movement of leaf. She has no nest. Something calls her but she does not know its voice, foe or friend, and concludes foe, as she has no friend.

ME: I wish to talk to you, Anxiety. Do you hear my voice?

MS ANXIETY: Oh I hear. But I fear you'll do me harm. Go away. You are too close to me. You will catch me if I lite, and I am tired of flitting so

ME: But I mean you no harm. I only want to know what purpose you serve in my life! You visit me so often? Why do you come? What do you wish to say?

MS ANXIETY: Oh please. I need a place to Be. I need to shut out the noise and fear and bad news. I need to know that who I am is fine with me. I need to be able to be quiet and at peace and not be afraid to answer when a voice calls.

ME: A voice? What voice?

MS ANXIETY: A teacher. A mother. A boss. A creditor. An impulse. An addiction. An obsession. The voices of anger and threat. The voices of memory filled with fear   and pain and panic and regret.

ME: I understand. But you can stop being afraid. Now you know that you can listen to other voices. You can hear the voice of the Holy Spirit. You can hear an angel. You can hear a wise and loving guide.

You can hear the voice of nature in the wind and rain of winter, and the breeze and birdsong of spring. You can hear thank you in the voice of someone you've befriended. You can hear laughter. And music. And you can hear your own voice now.

MS ANXIETY: But I have no voice. I am only the voices of all those others.

ME: Then listen to my voice.

MS ANXIETY: But that is why I have come to you. To fill you with my voices. When my mission is accomplished, I am emptied out and set free.

ME: You know only half the truth. If you fill me with your voices, you are emptied, but you live still in me. You are not free.

MS ANXIETY: But how then shall I be set free?

ME: I have told you. Listen to my voice.

MS ANXIETY: How then shall I know your voice?

308

ME: It is the voice of love. The voice of forgiveness. The voice of mercy. The still small voice that calms, and heals, and restores.

MS ANXIETY: But how will I hear this still small voice? How will it be heard amidst the the cacophony of futility which bangs and clangs about my world?

ME: Breathe.   Be   Still.   Become.

MS ANXIETY: Become? Become what?

ME: The Voice of Love.

MS ANXIETY: The Voice. Become the Voice of Love? May I - may I try that now?

ME: Please.

VOICE OF LOVE: I am...

ME: That's right. Continue. You're doing fine.

VOICE OF LOVE: I am love. I am light. I am music. I am laughter. I am the voice of the trees.

I am prayer. I am encouragement. I am inspiration. I am healing. I am the voice of the seas. I am peace. I am joy.

I am gifts of the earth. I am creation. I am becoming. I am beingness. I am you, and I, and they. We are one. And we are one with the One.

When I hear the voice of the One, I hear my own Voice. I hear, then, because I listen.

309

And because I hear, I speak, and it is the Voice I hear coming from my own soul, the Voice you hear spoken from my lips.

Love spoken. Love heard. The Voice of Love heals, inspires, creates becomes. I *am* the Voice of Love.

ME: Anxiety? thank you for being willing to change.

VOICE OF LOVE: Anxiety?   Who is that? I'm sorry. There's no one here by that name.

ME and REAL SELF

ME

Real self, I'd like to talk to you. Can you tell me about you?

SELF

Oh certainly! I thought you'd never ask. You've heard from me before, you know. I'm the thinker, the observer, the caring sharing person, the healthy whole person, the witty, the funny, the sensitive, the growing "I know who I am becoming" person.

ME

That's a lot of selves to have inside of my mind!

SELF

I'm not really inside you, in your mind. I'm really truly you.

310

ME

But why do you hide from me? Why don't you come out of hiding, manifest yourself, and let me become me, and get on with living?

SELF

Well, we are in the process, aren't we? We're pulling off the layers of crud and callous that the world has grown over us, like barnacles on pier pilings, you know. And you, as you still see yourself as apart from me, or not comfortably aware of me, are still searching your inner rooms to see who's there, isn't that so?

ME

Yes, that is the process going on right now.

I seem to become aware of you, like a tide coming in, and just when I'm getting comfortable with you, you're out to sea again.

Can't you stay?

SELF

Yes, I'd like to stay. But your receiving and acceptance abilities are not yet strong enough to keep me *tuned in.* I fade in and out like a weak radio signal.

ME

Well then, how do I tune you in, and stay tuned in?

SELF

Well, silence first. Quiet time in which you just come to be with
me, talk with me. Each time you do that, I, we, become stronger.
Just say to yourself
I am the person I was born to be;
I do the things I was born to do;
I encounter, love, and interact with those with whom I was born to
meet, teach, and will always be.
Act as I act, speak as I speak, think as I think,
feel as I feel, do as I do.
Listen, sense, for the voice you know is your real voice,
your real thought.
You know your own voice, don't you?

ME

I'm afraid. I'm so used to being separate from my Real self. It's
painful. It has been terribly confusing.
Still, it is comfortably familiar.

SELF

Yes, I can understand that. But this is what you want isn't it?
To merge with your real self?

ME

Yes.

SELF

To become me?

ME

To become *me?* Yes.

SELF

I am . . .

ME

The person I was born to be

SELF

Have always been

ME

And am becoming.

SELF

I am

ME

My Self.

To be continued for lifetimes to come

BOOKS BY CLAUDIA CARROLL (aka: cj carroll)

The following books by Claudia Carroll (or, pen name, cj carroll) are or will be published by the not-for-profit DREAMCATCHER Books, available on Amazon.com and the following sources:

On-line: http://lulu.com/cjcarrollbooks

From the author: cjcarrollbooks@yahoo.com

ANGELS IN FOREVER

CODE OF THE RUNNING CROSS
(a prequel & sequel in progress)

1000 STEPS, An ESL Teaching Adventure in Taiwan

SHARED UNEVENLY: POEMS

RIVER POEM, A Winter in Northern New Mexico

REMEMBRANCE WRITING 101, The Easy Way to Write and Share the Stories of Your Life; a Guidebook

Imagine That: A Collection of Stories for Children

SHMADIGGLE & THE IMAGINATION ASTEROID

OLD DUMPLING & THE RAINY DAY

MISSY MOUSE & THE ROCKET SHIP

CLARA COW & THE COUNTY FAIR

VARIED WRITING

Newsletters:

Silver Express: 2010: *Tasty Memories; Skeletons & Souls*
Terra Linda Wind: 2010: *October Country*

On-Line:

Engnow (on-line): 2010: Excerpt from *1000 Steps, an ESL Teaching Adventure in Taiwan*

Newspapers:

Taos News: 2007 *Arts in Education;* Press Enterprise:senior supplement magazine: feature articles; Banning Gazette: some 300 articles and photos, column; La Prensa San Diego, articles and column.

Not-for-profits:

Wildlife Refuge Center (article); Share International (video script), Fresh Start Farms (slides and script). Copy writing & marketing.

Poetry:

Many small journals, including *Ode to Bukowski,* Wormwood Review; independently published collections: *Dare to Dream, Of Love and Longing, River Poem, A winter in Northern New Mexico; Shared Unevenly.*

Plays: *Clinton and the Treehouse*, published by Kids for Saving Earth, 1994. Musical: *Scrooge.*

ANTHOLOGY FACILITATING and PUBLISHING

Selected writings of older adults: *Voices of Sea Turtles, 2009; Lost, Then Found,* 2010 ; Individual chapbooks: *Who Was She Really,* Carole Colucci; *A Few Stories for My Children,* Ali Rostambiek; *Reflections on My Life,* Fran Cohen, 2010,

WEB SITES:

http://lulu.com/cjcarrollbooks

http://claudiacarroll.biz

http://claudiacarroll.biz/dreamcatcher

http://claudiacarroll.biz/remembrance_writing_101

http://claudiacarroll.biz/code_of_the_running_cross

http://claudiacarroll.biz/teaching_esl_taiwan

For workshops, speaking engagements, contact Claudia Carroll

cjcarrollbooks@yahoo.com